RALPH BUNCHE

RALPH BUNCHE
The Man and His Times

EDITED BY
BENJAMIN RIVLIN

Foreword by Donald F. McHenry

HM

HOLMES & MEIER   New York / London

Published in the United States of America 1990 by
Holmes & Meier Publishers, Inc.
30 Irving Place
New York, NY 10003

This book has been printed on acid-free paper.

Library of Congress Cataloging-in-Publication Data

Ralph Bunche, the man and his times / edited by Benjamin Rivlin.
    p.   cm.
  Includes bibliographical references.
  ISBN 0-8419-1145-2 (alk. paper)
  1. Bunche, Ralph J. (Ralph Johnson), 1904–1971. 2. Statesmen—
United States—Biography. 3. United Nations—History. I. Rivlin,
Benjamin.
E748.B885R35 1990
341.23'3'092—dc20
[B]   89-24666
                                               CIP

MANUFACTURED IN THE UNITED STATES OF AMERICA

In Memory of
Ruth Harris Bunche

CONTENTS

Foreword by Donald F. McHenry   xi

Preface   xiii

Chronological Biography   xix

Benjamin Rivlin   Introduction   xxv

PART I SCHOLAR ACTIVIST

· 1 ·
Benjamin Rivlin   The Legacy of Ralph Bunche   3

· 2 ·
John B. Kirby   Race, Class, and Politics: Ralph
                           Bunche and Black Protest   28

· 3 ·
Charles P. Henry   Civil Rights and National Security:
                           The Case of Ralph Bunche   50

PART II AFRICANIST AND DECOLONIZER

· 4 ·

Nathan Irvin Huggins　　Ralph Bunche the Africanist　　69

· 5 ·

Martin Kilson　　Ralph Bunche's Analytical
Perspective on African Development　　83

· 6 ·

W. Ofuatey-Kodjoe　　Ralph Bunche: An African
Perspective　　96

· 7 ·

Lawrence S. Finkelstein　　Bunche and the Colonial World:
From Trusteeship to Decolonization　　109

· 8 ·

Herschelle S. Challenor　　The Contribution of Ralph Bunche
to Trusteeship and Decolonization　　132

PART III WORLD STATESMAN

· 9 ·

J. C. Hurewitz　　Ralph Bunche as UN Acting
Mediator:
The Opening Phase　　157

· 10 ·

Shabtai Rosenne　　Bunche at Rhodes: Diplomatic
Negotiator　　177

· 11 ·

Brian Urquhart　　Ralph Bunche and the Development
of UN Peacekeeping　　186

Kenneth B. Clark　　Postscript:
Ralph Bunche, the Human Being
and the International Statesman　　211

APPENDIXES:
SELECTED SPEECHES AND WRITINGS OF RALPH BUNCHE

APPENDIX A
Letter to Dr. William E. B. Du Bois   217

APPENDIX B
UCLA Valedictory Address: The Fourth Dimension of
Personality   220

APPENDIX C
Nobel Peace Prize Lecture: Some Reflections on Peace in
Our Time   225

APPENDIX D
Lincoln's Day Address: The International Significance
of Human Relations   236

APPENDIX E
The Attack on the UN   246

APPENDIX F
On Race: The Alienation of Modern Man   252

Bibliography   265
Contributors   268
Index   271

Photographs appear on pages 146 to 153

FOREWORD

Donald F. McHenry

Ralph J. Bunche was a man of many facets. He was known around the world as a distinguished diplomat. As an official of the United Nations, he was a principal and pioneering architect of the world's collective efforts to keep the peace, and early in his diplomatic career he won the Nobel Peace Prize for his successful mediation in the Middle East. Bunche was also a distinguished scholar and educator whose pioneering studies of colonialism prepared him superbly to play an important role in the drafting of those portions of the United Nations Charter that in less than twenty-five years contributed to the largely peaceful attainment of independence by almost half of the world's population. These two accomplishments alone are enough to merit admiration and to justify continuing exploration of Bunche's life and work.

But for Americans, Ralph Bunche is of special importance. He was an American black who, with some inner determination, catapulted himself above many, but by no means all, of the racial limitations imposed upon his race by fellow Americans during his lifetime. Bunche could have taken refuge in his international work—and, indeed, he once refused to be considered for a high-level post in the United States government lest his family be subjected to the widespread racial discrimination then prevailing in Washington—but he remained deeply committed to American ideals and interests. He believed strongly that he could serve mankind, and thereby his country, by putting nationalism aside and becoming an exemplary international civil servant. However, his dedication to American ideals and his own experiences in America caused him to never lose sight of the unfinished struggle for racial equality in the United States. Ralph Bunche, citizen of the world, was also an active participant in the civil rights movement in the United States.

The essays that follow cover the many facets of the life of Ralph Bunche. They are based on presentations first made at a two-day conference on the life and works of Bunche, held at the Ralph Bunche Institute on the United Nations of the Graduate Center of the City University of New York. The writers were in many instances Bunche's close personal friends and colleagues from his days as a scholar and later as a diplomat. What emerges is the picture of the scholar who had the good fortune to put theory into practice. It is the picture of a man of superior accomplishment, a man who nevertheless was, in the words of his long-time associate and successor, Brian Urquhart, "the kindest, most compassionate of men, the indefatigable friend and champion of the weak and oppressed."*

These essays, which provide insight into Bunche's life and work, are of particular interest to those interested in conflict resolution and the development of multilateral diplomacy and institutions. But the essays also serve a wider social purpose. In an age when yesterday too quickly fades into ancient history it is important for young Americans of different races and backgrounds to know of Bunche's remarkable achievements, for they stand as an inspiration for generations to come.

---

*Brian Urquhart, *A Life in Peace and War* (New York: Harper and Row, 1987), p. 127.

PREFACE

When Ralph Bunche died on 9 December 1971, several thousand people filled Riverside Church in New York City to pay tribute to this first black man to be awarded the Nobel Peace Prize. Extensive obituaries were carried in newspapers and magazines throughout the world. Panegyrical editorials extolled his singular and outstanding contributions to the furtherance of international peace, human rights, and brotherhood among all peoples. United Nations Secretary-General U Thant, in the *New York Times* of 10 December 1971 acclaimed Bunche as "an international institution in his own right, transcending both nationality and race in a way that is achieved by so few." *The New Yorker*, devoting "The Talk of the Town" section of its 1 January 1972 issue entirely to Bunche, noted that he "was one of the greatest Americans of our clouded and mind-numbing times." Bunche was not only an outstanding personality of his times, but he left an important legacy for the future, particularly for our times. Yet today, just a bit over a decade and a half since his passing, it is a sad fact that he is little remembered by most Americans, although the memory of his forceful personality and extraordinary achievements is deeply embedded in the consciousness of the many former students, friends, and colleagues who survived him.

The generation that has grown up since Bunche's death seems to be, by and large, ignorant of the importance of his pioneering work. As a professor of international affairs, talking with college students—black and white—including those purportedly interested in pursuing careers in international affairs, I have been chagrined to discover that they had only the vaguest notions, if any, as to who Ralph Bunche was. I have had similar experiences talking with people in all walks of life, even younger diplomats and Secretariat members at the United Nations. On being introduced as the director of the Ralph Bunche Institute on the United Nations, not infrequently have I been met by the query, "Who was Ralph Bunche?" And as one who, as a young man, had the privilege of working for Ralph Bunche, and one who was greatly influenced by him, I felt a strong need to try to rectify this situation. That is what prompted me, as director of the institute at the Graduate School of the City University of New York that bears Bunche's name, to organize in May 1986 a conference—"Ralph Bunche: The Man and His Times"—to examine the unique significance of his career and to help convey that rich legacy to the new generation that has grown up since his death. Publication of this volume is one important step toward this end.

The remarkable nature of Bunche's career was recognized during his lifetime throughout the world. Among the numerous medals, accolades, citations, and honors, in addition to the Nobel Peace Prize, he received sixty-nine honorary degrees, the Spingarn Medal of the National Association for the Advancement of Colored People, the First Annual Distinguished Public Service Award of the Yale Political Union, The American Brotherhood Award of the National Conference of Christians and Jews, and the Medal of Freedom, the nation's highest recognition. He was featured in magazines like the *Saturday Evening Post, Ebony, Time, Newsweek,* and similar foreign publications. He was among the most sought after of public speakers. At the time of his successful mediation efforts in the Middle East in 1949, a *Reader's Digest* article noted: "In the short space of a year Ralph Bunche has become a legend in the land. His countrymen . . . have warmed to him with a fervor usually reserved for ball players and movie stars." Clearly, Ralph Bunche was among the best-known figures in America and at the same time among the best-known Americans in the world during the last two decades of his life.

Ralph Bunche's path and mine crossed for the first time in 1943. I was then a soldier assigned to the Army Specialized Training Program (ASTP) on North Africa at the University of Pennsylvania, and Bunche was one of the guest lecturers brought in by the head of the program, Dr. Heinrich (Heinz) Wieschhoff. (Wieschhoff, an Africanist who worked with Bunche during the war and later at the United Nations, was killed in the 1961 plane crash in the Congo along with Secretary-General Dag Hammarskjöld.) I recall the occasion in the auditorium of the

University Museum vividly. Although I had recently graduated from Brooklyn College in New York City, one of the citadels of progressive liberalism, this was the first time I was in a class addressed by a black professor. The uniqueness of the experience was punctuated by the subject of the lecture—the impact of the war on Africa and its peoples. The prewar colonial regimes were severely shaken, and how to deal with the consequence of this development was emerging as a challenge to the postwar world. This was a topic most remote from the world I and my fellow soldier-students knew. Bunche opened up new vistas that have remained with me throughout my life. Less than six months after this lecture, through the mysterious workings of the United States Army I found myself assigned to the Africa Section in the Research and Analysis Branch of the Office of Strategic Services (OSS), which was headed by Ralph Bunche. Properly deferential to my chief, I addressed him as Dr. Bunche. After a day of "doctoring" him, Bunche told me to "cut out this doctor business" and to please call him "Ralph." This was characteristic of Bunche's innate tendency to put people at ease, his aversion to pomposity, and the lack of affectation that was evident throughout his life. Basically, Bunche was an unpretentious person who never sought the limelight. Sir Brian Urquhart, who was one of Bunche's closest colleagues at the United Nations, told the conference that "if Ralph were here, he would ask us to change the subject."

Bunche's life and career merit careful study, despite his reluctance to draw attention to himself, because the substantive areas that engaged him as civil rights activist, as scholar of Africa and race relations, as international civil servant and world statesman, are of considerable historical importance. This became patently clear during the conference, which represented the first scholarly attempt to examine the many facets of Bunche's career. Although much information about Bunche was brought together for the first time at the conference, it was apparent that much research remains to be done. Commenting on papers presented at the panel on "Bunche and the American Civil Rights Movement," Princeton historian Nancy Weiss noted that "Professors Kirby and Henry have very effectively begun to suggest the shape of a more accurate, detailed understanding of Ralph Bunche's relationship to the civil rights movement. Their papers are full of good information, but also full of some tantalizing *whys*, so tantalizing we would like to know more." Much the same applies to the scope and treatment of Bunche's involvement with important issues discussed by the other panels. The conference discussions revealed a compelling story about one black American of modest origins who not only was affected by the times in which he lived but who, by his deeds and personality, influenced some of the most momentous developments in his own country and in the world: the civil rights revolution in the United States, the emergence of the Third World from colonialism to independence, the 1949 armistice agreements between Israel and the Arab states, and the role of the United Nations peacekeeping activities. The conference focused on many of the forces and factors that impelled Bunche to his remarkable achievements as he confronted the many obstacles facing a black man in a society that relegated members of his race to unequal treatment and inferior status; and that confronted an international civil servant in a state-centered world hostile to internationalism. The material in this volume represents the mature reflections of many former students, colleagues, and friends, as well as of a group of younger scholars who also felt the impact of Ralph Bunche's career and acknowledge the importance of his legacy. What emerges is the picture of a man of principle with an indomitable will and spirit in the face of adversity, determined to contribute to making the world—near and far—a better place in which to live for all peoples.

This volume can be considered only a beginning of serious inquiry into the life and work of Ralph Bunche. It is gratifying to note that several of the contributors are at work on full-scale studies of various phases of Bunche's life. In addition, I am pleased to note that a doctoral dissertation on Bunche by Souad Halila was completed in 1988 at the University of Southern California.

It has been possible to bring out this appraisal of Ralph Bunche's life work only because of the willing cooperation of many people. First and foremost, special thanks is due to the authors of the essays and articles that examine different aspects of Bunche's life and work. Without their dedication, neither this volume nor the preceding conference would have been possible. Secondly, I want to acknowledge with thanks the important contribution made by all the other conference participants—Vincent J. Browne, Hylan Lewis, John A. Davis, Robert C. Weaver, William Mashler, Nabil Elaraby, Mabel Smythe-Haith, Jean Herskovits, Nancy J. Weiss, Inez Reid, William B. Bryant, Franklin Williams, George L-P Weaver, Oscar Schachter, Richard N. Gardner, Clifton Wharton II, Irving L. Markovitz, Henry F. Jackson, Seymour M. Finger, Marguerite Ross Barnett, Gwendolen M. Carter, James Jonah, and the late Thomas F. Power, Jr.—who in sharing their views and experiences enriched the discussions and helped shape the contents of this book.

I owe a special debt of personal gratitude, and that of the Institute's, to Ruth Harris Bunche, the widow of Ralph Bunche, who has passed away since the conference was held. Without her gracious support and encouragement of the Institute's overall program and of the conference, this book would not be possible. It is no exaggeration to note that Ruth and her daughter, Joan Bunche, took more than a casual interest in the

Institute's efforts by personally extending themselves to make available important biographical material, photographs, and other pertinent information.

Special thanks are also due to Chancellor Joseph S. Murphy of the City University of New York and Dr. Harold M. Proshansky, president of its Graduate School and University Center. Both have been very supportive of the Institute's program and particularly of the Ralph Bunche Fellowship Program, which was established at the time of the conference. To the international program officers of the Ford Foundation who saw some merit in our plans for the conference and this volume and who provided the Institute with the support necessary to carry out this project, a very special thanks. I am particularly grateful to Barbara H. Nelson of the Ford Foundation for her help in locating a number of Bunche photographs and speeches. Thanks also to my editors at Holmes & Meier, Sheila Friedling and Katharine Turok. Finally, no words can express the gratitude I owe to my colleagues in the Ralph Bunche Institute, Nancy Okada and Michael Speer, and to the other members of the staff, Johncy Itty, Annette Phillips, and Alanda Jordan, who provided most able and affable assistance.

In bringing out this book as in holding the conference, the Institute did not aim for a nostalgic reminiscence but rather a serious undertaking designed to help inform a new generation that has grown up since Bunche's passing. We hope that this volume contributes meaningfully toward this end, although much remains to be done.

Benjamin Rivlin
May 1989

RALPH JOHNSON BUNCHE

A Chronological Biography

1904   Born on 7 August in Detroit, Michigan; son of Fred Bunch, a barber, and Olive Agnes Johnson.

1910–
1914   Started elementary school in Detroit. When family moved to Toledo (Ohio) and Knoxville (Tennessee), continued schooling in nonsegregated schools, except for short period in 1910 when family lived in segregated section of Knoxville.

1914   Family moved to Albuquerque, New Mexico.

1917   Orphaned in Albuquerque; moved to Los Angeles to live with his maternal grandmother, Mrs. Lucy Taylor Johnson, and mother's sisters and brother; changed spelling of his name to Bunche.

1918   Graduated with honors from 30th Street Intermediate School in Los Angeles where he was first shunted into "practical" courses for Negro children until his grandmother insisted that he be given academic courses to prepare him for college.

1922   Graduated first in his class and valedictorian from Jefferson High School in Los Angeles; denied election to citywide scholarship honor society because of his race; while in high school worked as newsboy for the *Los Angeles Times* and in his last year as a carpet layer.

Entered southern branch of the University of California (later to become UCLA) on a scholarship, which he augmented by working at a wide variety of jobs, including summers on a coastwise merchant ship; excelled in football, basketball, and baseball; president of debating society; student council leader; college newspaper reporter; majored in political science and philosophy.

1927   Graduated summa cum laude from UCLA and class valedictorian.

Wrote to William E. B. Du Bois, requesting help in finding an opportunity to perform social service for his people before going on to graduate school.

Received a tuition fellowship for graduate study in political science at Harvard; received additional support from a black ladies' organization, The Iroquois Friday Morning Civic and Social Club, which established The Ralph Bunche Scholarship Fund to help cover transportation and other expenses; worked in Philips second-hand bookstore at Harvard Square.

1928   Upon completion of M.A. in political science at Harvard, was appointed instructor at Howard University in Washington.

1929   Organized and chaired Howard's first political science department; promoted to assistant professor.

Awarded Osias Goodwin fellowship at Harvard to complete course work for doctorate.

1930   Married in June to Ruth Ethel Harris; spent summer at Harvard working on his doctoral dissertation.

1931   Returned to teaching at Howard; appointed as Assistant to President Mordecai Johnson.

Organized protest against presentation of *Porgy and Bess* at the segregated National Theater in Washington, D.C.; succeeded in having theater integrated during run of play.

1932   Awarded Julius Rosenwald Fellowship to do field work in Africa on his doctoral dissertation comparing rule of a mandated area, French Togoland, with that of a colony, Dahomey.

1933   Promoted to associate professor at Howard University.

1934   Completed Ph.D. in government and international relations, the first black man to earn this degree at Harvard; awarded the Toppan Prize for the year's best dissertation in political science at Harvard.

        Resumed teaching duties at Howard.

        Was co-director of the Institute of Race Relations at Swarthmore College during the summer.

1935   Helped organize conference at Howard University assessing the role of the New Deal on the economic crisis facing Negroes in the United States; presented critique of New Deal social planning.

1936   Undertook postdoctoral study in anthropology at Northwestern University.

        Awarded a Social Science Research Council Fellowship to pursue postdoctoral studies in anthropology and colonial policy at the London School of Economics and at the University of Cape Town in South Africa, and for field research in South, East, and West Africa.

        Helped found the National Negro Congress, which Bunche described as the first sincere effort to bring together, on an equal plane, Negro leaders, professional, and white-collar workers with Negro manual workers and their leaders and organizers.

        Published monograph, *A World View of Race.*

1937   Joined NAACP picket line in Washington.

1939   Participated in historic and memorable Carnegie study directed by Swedish sociologist Gunnar Myrdal on the status and life of blacks in the United States, which resulted in the publication, *An American Dilemma: The Negro Problem and Modern Democracy.* A manuscript prepared for this study, *The Political Status of the Negro in the Age of FDR,* was published posthumously by the University of Chicago Press in 1973.

Prepared a report at the invitation of the Republican party's Program Committee on why blacks had deserted the party of Lincoln.

1941   Called upon to work as senior social science analyst in the Africa and Far East Section of the Office of the Coordinator of Information (OCI), which later became the Office of Strategic Services (OSS).

1942   Appointed as head of the Africa Section of OSS's Research and Analysis Branch.

Collaborated in the drafting and publication of *The Atlantic Charter and Africa from an American Standpoint* as member of the Committee on Africa, the War and Peace Aims.

1944   Joined the State Department's postwar planning unit; worked on future of colonial territories.

Served as specialist on colonial matters with the U.S. delegation at the Dumbarton Oaks conference on the future of a world organization.

1945   Appointed to the Division of Dependent Area Affairs in the Office of Special Political Affairs of the State Department.

Served as adviser to the U.S. delegation at the San Francisco conference that drafted the UN Charter.

Served as adviser to the U.S. delegation to the 27th and 28th sessions of the International Labor Organization Conference.

Appointed U.S. Commissioner on the Caribbean Commission.

Served as member of the U.S. delegation to the preparatory committee of the United Nations that met in London.

1946   Served as member of U.S. delegation to the first session of the
            United Nations General Assembly in London in January.

            Joined the newly formed UN Secretariat as head of the Trust-
            eeship Department.

1947   Assigned to the United Nations Special Committee on Pal-
            estine (UNSCOP) as Special Assistant to Dr. Victor Hoo, the
            representative of the UN Secretary-General on this body.
            Drafted both majority and minority reports on Palestine par-
            tition.

1948   Appointed Principal Secretary, United Nations Palestine
            Commission, and later Personal Representative of the Secre-
            tary-General with the United Nations Mediator on Palestine,
            Count Folke Bernadotte.

            Succeeded Bernadotte as Acting Mediator on the latter's as-
            sassination in September.

1949   Chaired UN mediation efforts at Rhodes, successfully nego-
            tiating an armistice agreement between Egypt and Israel.
            This agreement set the pattern for additional armistice agree-
            ments reached between Lebanon, Syria, and Jordan, respec-
            tively, and Israel.

            Awarded the Spingarn Medal of the NAACP; became a direc-
            tor of the NAACP, serving until his death.

            Received an honorary Doctor of Laws degree from Harvard
            University. (In all, Bunche received 69 honorary degrees.)

1950   Awarded Nobel Peace Prize; Bunche was the first black per-
            son to be accorded this recognition.

1953   Elected president of the American Political Science Associa-
            tion.

            Turned down offer of post as Assistant Secretary of State by
            President Truman because of Jim Crow conditions in Wash-
            ington, D.C.

            Appointed full professor of political science with tenure at

Harvard; deferred assuming position and eventually re-signed; opted to continue his service in the United Nations.

1954 Appointed Under Secretary-General (without portfolio) of the United Nations.

1955 Appointed trustee of the Rockefeller Foundation, serving until his death.

1956 Helped organize and then directed UN peacekeeping operations in the Middle East after the Suez Crisis.

1957 Became Under Secretary-General for Special Political Affairs with prime responsibility for UN peacekeeping activities.

1960 Organized and headed UN peacekeeping operations in Congo.

1962 Organized and directed UN peacekeeping force in Cyprus.

1963 Designated by President John F. Kennedy to receive the Medal of Freedom, which was presented to him by President Lyndon Johnson.

Set up the UN Observation Mission that operated in Yemen following the war between Yemen and South Yemen.

1965 Participated in Selma, Alabama, civil rights march.

Supervised the cease-fire following the Indo-Pakistan War.

1971 Retired from the United Nations due to ill health.

Died on 9 December.

INTRODUCTION

Benjamin Rivlin

The essays brought together in this book analyze and assess major aspects of the career of the scholar and statesman Ralph Johnson Bunche. The essence of Bunche as scholar and statesman is epitomized in the observation made by one of the essayists that Ralph Bunche "will be remembered . . . as a major contributor to the development of black political and social thought in the twentieth century" and that "in the 1930s and early 1940s, [he] had anticipated many of the later campaigns and conflicts of the black struggle." This evaluation applies to Bunche both on the American and international scenes.

Bunche started out early in his life laying the foundation for his later significant contributions to efforts to better the conditions of life for people in America and throughout the world. In June 1927, Ralph Bunche, the only black graduate in the class, delivered the valedictory address at the commencement exercises of the University of California at Los Angeles, in which he said, "Man *learns* and *knows* but he does not *do* as well as he *knows*." Clearly, the young Bunche was concerned that knowledge be put to useful purposes. Bunche's life and career, as it evolved after he left UCLA, bore out this self-admonition.

Bunche's bent towards interrelating scholarship and activism emerges as one of the principal themes recurring in this collection of essays.

Regardless of which aspect of Bunche's work is considered, the interplay between the committed scholar and the man of action is striking. He was by no means unique in this respect. The image of the scholar as an ivory tower recluse is a myth. Academicians, perhaps to a larger extent than other citizens, are often active politically and socially on matters closely related to their discipline, or, in many instances, far afield from their scholarly specialization. Throughout his career, Bunche's form of activism was closely related to his scholarly discipline, in a sense being a case of applied political science and international relations.

From the outset, Bunche's activism involved both scholarly work in applied research, as in connection with the Carnegie-Myrdal study on the condition of the Negro in the South, and active participation with respect to public issues, pressuring in favor of particular causes, and providing leadership to public advocacy organizations. In this role, Bunche was not unlike the prominent senior black scholar/activist, Dr. William E. B. Du Bois, the distinguished black sociologist who earned his Ph.D. from Harvard several years before Bunche's birth, and who was recognized as the outstanding American black intellectual for most of his life. Bunche's activism, however, took a unique turn when he entered government service during World War II, becoming a practitioner in his area of academic specialization. The uniqueness of Bunche's experience derives from the fact that until his recruitment into the United States government and his eventual rise to prominence internationally, black scholars in the United States, as a rule, had not been enlisted in public service as practitioners of statesmanship and the governmental arts.

Ralph Bunche started his career as a scholar—a student of government and the relations between peoples and nations, focusing on American democracy, Africa, and race relations. He concluded his career as one of the world's premier practitioners of international diplomacy, concerned with the reconciliation of conflicts and tensions throughout the world. Although scholarly interests and pragmatic activism were inexorably intertwined during Bunche's career, it may be convenient to divide that career into two parts, the first phase lasting from 1923 to 1941, in which he was primarily a scholar, and the second lasting from 1941 to his death in 1971, in which he was primarily a practitioner. But it also would be a mistake to compartmentalize his professional life in this manner since its two phases constitute a single continuum. The collection of essays that follow bear this out. The opening essay "The Legacy of Ralph Bunche," and the concluding postscript, "Ralph Bunche, The Human Being and International Statesman," present assessments of the continuity of Bunche's entire career, while each of the other essays focuses on a specific period in his life. Separately and collectively, the following chapters portray Bunche as a driven, but level-headed, combatant in the struggle for the achievement of the American dream—

political equality, social justice, and equal economic opportunity—for all people of the world regardless of race, color, or creed.

Although the diverse essays present Bunche from varying perspectives, it is clear that Bunche's professional preoccupations, whether as scholar, activist, or practitioner, reflected his situation as an American black, growing up and functioning in the stifling environment of segregation and discrimination that permeated the social and political atmosphere of the United States. During the first phase of his career, the areas of his activity were all intimately connected with the world view of a bright and concerned black American living in the United States in the period between the first and second world wars: the causes with which he chose to be identified were racial equality, civil rights, and decolonization; the subjects in which he specialized were political science, anthropology, and race relations; the field research he undertook was in Africa and the American South; his major publications were *A World View of Race* and *The Political Status of the Negro in the Age of F D R;* and his initial government service was as specialist in African and colonial affairs.

Bunche's thinking on the condition of the American black population during the thirties and early forties, and his efforts to do something about it, is analyzed in the essay by John B. Kirby entitled "Race, Class and Politics: Ralph J. Bunche and Black Protest," in which the interplay between Bunche's scholar and activist roles is explored. Kirby indicates that as Bunche the scholar thought about the situation of black Americans, Bunche the activist was engaged in trying to implement his ideas. Bunche's core beliefs—against black separatism and for total integration—are at the heart of much of the tactics, centered on coalition building, that he advocated. This is reflected in the central role he played in founding the National Negro Congress, in challenging his old hero Du Bois, in reassessing his views on the New Deal, and in adopting a critical attitude toward the American Communist movement. Kirby notes a "consistency" between Bunche's total involvement with racial issues in the United States in the thirties and forties and his several post-World War II roles in the international arena. As Kirby observes, Bunche had a "comprehensive view of society and the world and the manner in which people, excluded from their natural rights as citizens or as nationalities, justly sought to become equal participants in their respective communities," a viewpoint that clearly links the struggle of blacks in the United States to a worldwide quest for racial equality and justice.

In the following essay, "National Security and Civil Rights: The Case of Ralph Bunche," Charles P. Henry discusses Bunche's "radical" activities and "Marxist" writings as a scholar/activist involved in the civil rights struggle in the 1930s and early 1940s. It was this activity that provided the pretext for Bunche's ensnarement in the McCarthy period's obsession with Communists in government, including American employees of the United Nations. This proved to be a most distressing episode that jeopardized Bunche's career after he had attained international renown. In his essay, Henry analyzes Bunche's prominent role in the civil rights movement of the 1930s and concludes that "for Ralph Bunche there could be no national security without civil rights, and there could be no international peace without human rights."

The essays in Part II focus on Ralph Bunche's work as an Africanist and as an authority on colonialism, both as scholar and activist. Bunche's concern with the condition and experience of indigenous peoples and cultures subject to colonialism paralleled and was linked to his interest in the condition and experience of black people in his own American society. To Bunche, racism and economic deprivation were pervasive among people of color throughout the world.

Nathan Huggins's essay traces Bunche's development as an Africanist, from his youth through his fieldwork in Africa in the thirties. While Huggins is unable to find evidence of a particular early interest in Africa on Bunche's part, he alerts us to the importance of race in shaping Bunche's life. Bunche seemed intent on writing his doctoral dissertation on a topic concerning race outside the United States. His first choice was Brazil, but he settled on an African subject once it became clear that he could get funding for field research in Africa. Huggins's analysis of Bunche's work on Africa and the colonial system suggest that Bunche developed a profound understanding of the African people, and the colonial dilemmas they were caught up in, which was rare for its time. It also suggests that Bunche's work on Africa was incomplete. He hoped to transform his extensive notes on his postdoctoral fieldwork into a book, had he remained in academia. Instead, Bunche became what might be called an "applied Africanist"—in the United States government and in the United Nations—where he put his knowledge of Africa to work.

Bunche's basic approach to Africa, as it was to race issues in the United States, was a blend of idealism and pragmatism. Martin Kilson, in the next chapter, analyzes Bunche's ideological framework. Kilson finds that Bunche's approach was "sophisticated and essentially accurate," particularly in anticipating the problems besetting newly independent African regimes. A third view of Bunche's work as an Africanist is provided by W. Ofuatey-Kodjoe, who suggests that Bunche's perspective on Africa was less concerned with Africa per se than with the global context provided by imperialism and race, that is, the impact of colonialism and imperialism on indigenous Africa, and the consequences for African development. From Kodjoe's vantage point as an African, Bunche's analysis had one important weakness: it accepted the then prevalent premise concerning the "backwardness of African society." To Kodjoe, the "principle of 'trusteeship,' 'guardianship' or 'wardship' to which Bunche subscribed in fact represents an affirmation of the [imperialist's] civilizing mission."

Bunche's involvement in the formulation and application of the trusteeship provisions of the United Nations Charter is the subject of the final two chapters in this section. Lawrence S. Finkelstein contributes an analysis, presented against the background of Bunche's views of colonialism, of Bunche's relationship to the development and implementation of the trusteeship provisions of the UN Charter. Finkelstein's essay is based in part on his personal recollections of events and on discussions with Bunche, with whom he worked in the State Department and at the United Nations San Francisco Conference in 1945. His analysis raises several critical questions concerning the Trusteeship System, for which Bunche held high expectations but which in itself did not prove to be the vehicle for decolonization. Nevertheless, according to the essay by Herschelle Challenor, Bunche's influence on decolonization was profound because of the key role he played in negotiating and drafting the provisions of the UN Charter dealing with colonialism, not only the chapters on the trusteeship system but also the important Declaration Regarding Non-Self-Governing Territories. The essays dealing with Bunche as Africanist and decolonizer elucidate his involvement with these issues, both as scholar and activist, and underscore his understanding that the condition of American blacks and that of Africans, as well as other colonial peoples, was part and parcel of the same complex set of problems derived from racism and economic deprivation.

Bunche's emergence and role as a world statesman is the focus of the essays in the last section, or Part III, of this book. There is no doubt that Bunche's varied experience as scholar and activist in the 1930s and early 1940s, as well as his governmental service especially in connection with the establishment of the United Nations, contributed significantly to his ability to confidently assume the responsibilities that were suddenly thrust upon him when he became Acting Mediator of the first Arab-Israeli War in 1948. His academic background prepared him well to deal with the complex issues entwined in the Palestine dispute. At the same time, by virtue of his involvement in the multifaceted, sensitive strategizing and bargaining that was part of both his active participation in the black struggle for equality and his governmental activities, Bunche had already mastered the skills of an accomplished mediator-negotiator. The essays in this section make it evident that Bunche brought to the negotiating table not only a rich and pertinent background, but also a personality unusually suited to the task and an ability to gain the trust of even the most trenchant enemies. Background, experience, and personality were, no doubt, important components of Bunche's success. But, in the informative chapter by J.C. Hurewitz we learn how Bunche's role was almost aborted. According to Hurewitz's research based on hitherto unavailable sources, Bunche was able to maneuver through the diplomatic minefields because of the combination of skill, luck, and timing. The procrastination of others (the British Foreign Office and the U.S. Department of State) in establishing the Palestine Conciliation Commission that was to replace the role of Mediator, combined with Bunche's astute receptivity to signals emanating from the Arab and Israeli sides, enabled him to play the effective mediating role that lead to the armistice agreements that were signed in February 1949.

Bunche's skillfulness in the actual armistice negotiations is the subject of the next selection by Shabtai Rosenne, who was a member of the Israeli negotiating team at Rhodes. Rosenne provides a firsthand account of Bunche's extraordinary personal efforts in forging an agreement that implacable adversaries were able to accept.

Bunche's role as Acting Mediator in the successful negotiation of the armistice agreements propelled him into the international limelight, culminating in the awarding of the Nobel Peace Prize in 1950. However, it would be a serious error to see that role as his only, or most important, contribution to the United Nations and the world community. Indeed, as previously noted, Bunche had already contributed significantly to the world community by the role he played in negotiating and drafting the sections of the United Nations Charter on colonialism. Following his success in Palestine, Bunche's career increasingly focused on building the UN's mediation and peacekeeping capabilities and on troubleshooting for the Secretary-General in one difficult conflict situation after the other. Thus, in the twenty years between the armistice agreement of 1949 and his retirement, Bunche became the key United Nations figure in the organization's handling of numerous crises, such as Cyprus, Sinai, Yemen, Congo, and Bahrain, working closely with the first three secretaries-general, Trygve Lie, Dag Hammarskjöld, and U Thant.

Bunche's resourceful manner in dealing with the United Nations' operations in the foregoing crises is the subject of the final selection, "Ralph Bunche and Peacekeeping," by Sir Brian Urquhart. Urquhart, who was a close associate of Bunche's at the United Nations for many years and who succeeded him as Under Secretary-General for Special Political Affairs, provides significant and thoughtful insights into Bunche, the man and statesman. He describes Bunche's personality traits of integrity, perseverance, humor and sensitivity in some detail, seeing in them a basis for his success in international institution building. Bunche "had the most highly developed sense of personal responsibility I have ever encountered," writes Urquhart, noting that "the immense confidence he inspired, derived from these qualities, but also from his personality." According to Urquhart, Bunche played a "dominating role" in the development of the United Nations peacekeeping activities and, through his unique combination of skill and personality, set "an unmatched example of international service."

Although the full impact of his work at the United Nations and as a world statesman is yet to be fully researched and analyzed, it is clear that in the two decades following the Nobel Peace Prize, Bunche went on to build a truly remarkable record of achievements in the United Nations. To many, throughout the world, both inside and outside the organization, Bunche was the embodiment of the United Nations, actively, but pragmatically, pursuing its high ideals.

RALPH BUNCHE

PART I

SCHOLAR ACTIVIST

· 1 ·

THE LEGACY OF RALPH BUNCHE

Benjamin Rivlin

I believe in the United Nations. I believe in the rightness and vision of its purposes, as I believe in the rightness and vision of the American Constitution. Just as there were long years of disputation, travail, and cynical doubt before our federated Republic became firmly established under our Constitution, it is neither surprising nor discouraging that the young United Nations has experienced difficulties in the implementation of the Charter. These difficulties will be overcome. We will see realized the peaceful and just world which the United Nations strives incessantly to achieve, just as at home we will see realized the fully democratic America which our Constitution envisaged.
—Ralph Bunche, July 1949[1]

I

Ralph Johnson Bunche was suddenly thrust onto the center stage of international diplomacy when the United Nations Mediator of the first Arab-Israeli War, Count Folke Bernadotte, was assassinated in September 1948. Named Acting United Nations Mediator, Bunche reached the pinnacle of world recognition when he was awarded the Nobel Peace Prize in 1950 for having successfully brought about an armistice between Israel and four neighboring Arab states, Egypt, Jor-

3

dan, Syria, and Lebanon. The armistice represented the United Nations'
first tangible success in containing a war, and it was recognized that
achieving it was in no small way due to the personal efforts of Ralph
Bunche.

Although prior to 1949 Bunche was a relatively obscure figure in the
select world of diplomacy, he had by then already made his mark as a
pioneer in a number of critical areas. He was in the forefront of the
struggle for civil rights in the United States in the thirties and forties and
an early leader in developing an American understanding of Africa.
Furthermore, he was involved in the creation of the United Nations and
played a central role in the evolving process of decolonization. Bunche
was not a fleeting phenomenon. Indeed, from 1950 and until his death
in 1971, he was a principal adviser to three successive secretaries-general
of the United Nations and the architect of its international peacekeeping
activities, an area in which the United Nations has proven effective.

In the last decades of his life, Bunche was one of the most widely
known figures on the international scene for his reputation as a *diplomat
extraordinaire*. However, few were cognizant of his prior achievements or
of how they provided him with a reservoir of knowledge and experience
that helped prepare him for an unprecedented role. If one were to have
speculated on a likely American candidate for a successful international
diplomatic career in the two decades immediately after World War II,
Ralph Johnson Bunche, a black, son of a barber, orphaned at an early
age and raised by a maternal grandmother, might seem least likely to fit
this role. Yet Bunche did succeed, leaving an enduring legacy for both
his country and the world. Even when he was put into situations by
circumstances not of his own making, he was able to seize the moment
and shape events by virtue of his personal impact.

Ralph Bunche's success derived from the complex interrelations of his
subtle mind, intellectual brilliance, rigorous scholarship, sensitivity to
human relations, determination, and sheer hard work. As a member of
the black minority subject to discrimination and humiliation because of
his race, Ralph Bunche's life epitomizes the triumph of merit over
prejudice. Yet, the challenge of being a black person in the United States
was doubtless a critical element in shaping Bunche's perspective. "We
Negroes must be great realists," he wrote in 1949:

> The road over which we must travel is clear, though the prospect may not be
> pleasant. We suffer crippling disadvantages because of our origin. But we are
> Americans in a basically democratic society. . . . To make his way, the Negro
> must have firm resolve, persistence, tenacity. He must gear himself to hard
> work all the way. He can never let up. He can never have too much prepara-
> tion and training. He must be a strong competitor. He must adhere staunchly
> to the basic principle that anything less than full equality is not enough. If he
> ever compromises on this principle, his soul is dead. . . . There is no substitute

for hard work as the key to success in American life. This is true of white Americans. It is even more true for black Americans."[2]

Long before he achieved international fame, Bunche had already made his mark on the American scene as a scholar and activist, concerned with the condition of subjugated peoples at home and abroad. Vernon E. Jordan, Jr., of the Urban League noted, "Bunche's name has been an inspirational beacon to young black people for decades. As an educator, scholar and activist, he was in the forefront of those building a great, new black consciousness in the thirties and forties."[3] Bunche, of course, shared this role with a number of notable peers, but he was unique because, in the words of Roy Wilkins: "Of all the capable men which Negro Americans have produced he was the only one to have achieved success in the general world of diplomacy in endeavors not strictly in behalf of his race."[4]

Bunche's life and career may seem, in retrospect, almost to have been carefully planned, moving so orderly and logically from one stage to another. First, his experience as an American Negro, subject to racial discrimination and humiliation, prepared him for his role as a civil rights militant in the struggle for racial justice. And it was his role in this struggle that stimulated his great interest in the people and culture of Africa and in colonialism. His studies at the University of Southern California and Harvard prepared him for his role as scholar and teacher. Field trips in Africa and his doctoral dissertation prepared him for his function as adviser to the American government on African and colonial affairs and eventually as head of the United Nations Trusteeship Department.

These situations set the stage for Bunche's central role in the UN's involvement in the Palestinian problems to which he brought all his previous experience in dealing with human conflict and the modalities of international diplomacy. Finally, his success as United Nations Mediator designated him as the troubleshooter par excellence for the world body and thrust upon him the task of shaping the United Nations' innovative peacekeeping operations.

By the time Bunche became the first black person to be awarded the Nobel Peace Prize, he had already experienced a number of significant firsts. From the time of his youth, he attained many successes. When he graduated from high school, he was the first of his race to be valedictorian. He repeated this achievement upon graduating from the University of California in Los Angeles and he was the first black to receive the degree of Doctor of Philosophy in Political Science from Harvard University and, indeed, the first in the entire United States. Furthermore, he was the highest-ranking black to work on the famous 1938–1940 Carnegie-Myrdal study of the conditions of black life in the South that resulted in the publication, *An American Dilemma: The Negro Problem and Modern Democracy.* Then, during World War II, he was the only black to head a section of the prestigious Research and Analysis Branch of the Office of Strategic Services, serving as peer with some of the country's outstanding scholars.

When he moved to the State Department, he was the first black professional officer in the department. With the cooperation of then Major Dean Rusk, during the war, he broke the color bar in the officers' dining rooms. He was the only black in the American delegation to the Dumbarton Oaks Conference, which laid the foundation for the creation of the United Nations Organization at San Francisco, where again he was the only black among the American delegation. Several years after receiving the Nobel Prize, Bunche attained the highest rank for an American in the United Nations Secretariat, that of Under Secretary-General, ranking just below the Secretary-General. (It should be noted that Bunche attained a unique status in his professional life. After he had been awarded the Nobel Peace Prize, he became the first, to this date the only, black to be chosen president of the American Political Science Association.)

II

Robert C. Weaver provides a clue to Bunche's later success in his insightful observation of Bunche as a graduate student at Harvard. Weaver, who himself attained distinction as the first black presidential cabinet member, during the administration of President Lyndon Johnson, noted:

When in 1927, Bill Hastie returned to his second year at Harvard Law School, John P. Davis entered that law school, and I began my junior year at Harvard College, we heard of a new black graduate student from Los Angeles who was due to arrive shortly. His advance notices were rave and he lived up to them. We lived in close proximity and had almost daily contact, both in playing cards with a strict time schedule, discussing what university students talk about, and reserving the weekends for serious bull sessions, where race relations and strategies for attacking the color line were the dominant themes. . . . Bunche was extremely attractive, quite vocal, articulate and approachable. He made male and female friends with ease and charm, and he had a well-developed sense of humor, which embraced the capacity to laugh at himself. What impressed me most about Ralph in those days was his optimism. I soon realized that it was not rooted in wishful thinking, as was often the case, but rather based on a long history of overcoming obstacles and an uncanny ability to produce stupendous amounts of work over long sustained periods of application. I watched this capacity grow in proportion to the critical nature of the issues. It maximized the impact of his knowledge, the brilliance of his personality, and was in my opinion the chief factor in his spectacular career.[5]

Bunche came to Harvard University on a tuition fellowship and, following the pattern of many graduate students of modest financial resources, completed his studies at Harvard in several stages. After earning a Master's degree in 1928, he left to join the faculty of Howard University in Washington, D.C. A year later, he returned to Harvard as the recipient of the Ozias Goodwin Fellowship to complete his course work for the doctorate. He resumed his teaching at Howard in 1931, only to leave again in 1932 to go to West Africa on a Julius Rosenwald Fellowship to pursue field research for his doctoral dissertation comparing French administration in the mandated territory of Togoland and the neighboring colony of Dahomey. In 1934, he received the Ph.D. in government and international relations and was awarded the Toppan Prize for the year's best dissertation in political science at Harvard.

The years that followed at Howard University were pivotal in Bunche's career. At Howard he established the Political Science Department and also became one of a group of gifted young black intellectual activists, seeking a way out of the gnawing problems, compounded by the Depression, confronting the black American population—racism, poverty, second-class citizenship, segregation in education and the workplace, and powerlessness.

In their search, Bunche and his cohorts explored various radical ideas, including socialism and Marxism, engaged in organized protest, and sought to relate their learning to the struggle for racial equality. As Dr. Hylan Lewis, a former student and colleague of Bunche, points out, Howard University at this time provided "the setting and staging ground for the attack on *Plessy v. Ferguson*."[6] Part of the ongoing debate at Howard was over the tactics for breaking the segregated and confining mold into which American blacks had been cast, particularly in the labor market. Nevertheless, at this time, when most American unions were bastions of segregation, a number of Bunche's colleagues at Howard were involved in organizing the New Negro Alliance, an effort to mobilize black workers. Bunche opposed this move.

According to Dr. John A. Davis, who helped found the alliance, Bunche viewed it as a reinforcement of segregation that ran counter to his goal of "trying to get black people to think in a more cosmopolitan fashion, to think in terms of bigger alliances . . . and the unity [of black and white workers] within the labor movement." Bunche, Davis maintains, was anxious "to pull blacks into a larger framework of social action that was related not only with regard to imperialism and race, or colonialism and race, and a caste system in America, but also with regard to what he felt was soon going to be a struggle for the very existence of democracy."[7]

In the 1930s Bunche was very active in the struggle for civil rights and racial equality and emerged, in the words of Dr. Charles Henry, as "a true model of a scholar activist."[8] He was a co-founder of the National Negro Congress and a member of the Board of the National Association for the Advancement of Colored People for twenty-two years. In 1937, he was on an NAACP picket line in Washington, and his presence and influence contributed to the relentless pressure organized by the black community of Washington, in the thirties, to desegregate the nation's capital. For example, he organized a protest against the presentation of *Porgy and Bess* at the segregated National Theater in Washington and succeeded in having the theater integrated during the run of the play.

Activism implies involvement in the affairs of one's times. For the black American of the thirties and forties activism meant relating, at every turn, to the struggle against racial discrimination—in employment, education, and the civic polity; to the Depression and the New Deal; to Marxism and the American Communist party in particular; and to the Second World War. Bunche was involved in some way in each of these areas, both as a participant and a scholar.

Ralph Bunche's leaning toward a career as a scholar-activist was manifested early in his life. A basic theme of the valedictory address he delivered at UCLA in June 1927 evokes the need to combine knowledge with action:

> One need not be indicted for pessimism in declaring that "all is not well" with the world. . . . There are, in short, vital conditions in human associations which bode only ill for man's future. . . . Prejudices—antipathies—hatreds still disrupt with their sinister influences the equilibrium of the world. . . . Man *learns* and *knows* but he does not *do* as well as he *knows*. The future of peace and harmony of the world are contingent upon the ability—yours and mine—to effect a remedy. [Emphasis in the original][9]

Bunche's concern for the socially valuable individual, which he expressed in this commencement address, was not simply rhetoric. That he was intent on practicing what he preached was evident in a letter he sent to Dr. William E. B. Du Bois on 11 May 1927, before he graduated from UCLA. He wrote that his "plans for the future," which were "rather definitely formed," included not only taking advantage of the opportunity to go on to graduate study at Harvard but to be of "service to my group," which has been "the goal of my ambition . . . since I have been sufficiently old to think rationally and to appreciate that there was a 'race problem' in America, in which I was necessarily involved."[10]

Toward the end of the decade of the thirties, Bunche achieved a reputation as one of the keenest students of race relations in the United States. In the summer of 1936, he was co-director of a race relations institute at Swarthmore College. Meanwhile, in February 1939, the program committee of the Republican party commissioned Bunche to prepare a study as to why blacks had defected from the party in the last two national elections. As reported in the press at the time, this affiliation between the conservative Republican party and the "ultra-liberal" scholar-activist was somewhat discomforting for both sides. Bunche justified undertaking the project in a letter to Dr. Glenn Frank, former president of the University of Wisconsin, who was then chairman of the Republican program committee. Bunche wrote:

> As a Negro, and therefore as a member of a disadvantaged minority group in this country, I am actively interested in any measures or policies leading toward amelioration of the problems of my group. Moreover, as a member of a faculty of a university which receives considerable support from public revenues, I feel obligated to perform whatever service of a public nature it is within the range of my ability and training to do. For these reasons, and because the procedure you have followed is sound, constructive, and honestly designed to be of aid to the Negro people, I am willing to assume responsibility for the drafting of a report setting forth . . . the needs of the Negro.[11]

Vouching for Bunche to the Republicans was his unnamed Republican classmate at Harvard, who while regarding Bunche as an ultra-liberal, felt that "any survey he made would be scholarly and objective and uninfluenced by his own political views." Bunche's report pulled no punches. "Despite the extended periods of power enjoyed by the GOP and the long-standing loyalty of the Race, the party has made no significant progress toward the realization of the fundamental political objectives of the Race; namely, enfranchisement in the South, protection of civil liberties, anti-lynching legislation, and appointment of members of the Race to policy-forming and other responsible positions." Furthermore, black voters defected from the Republican party, overcoming their long-standing suspicion of the Democratic party, because of basic "bread-and-butter" considerations. Since the black population had learned the shrewdness of political bargaining, Bunche noted that the party that could respond to black needs would get the black vote.[12]

Bunche's preoccupation with the conditions of the American black was further evident in his close association, between 1938 and 1940, with Gunnar Myrdal, the Swedish sociologist, in collecting data throughout the South for the seminal study of the black in American society, *An American Dilemma: The Negro Problem and Modern Democracy*.[13] Bunche prepared four unpublished manuscripts ("Conceptions and Ideologies of the Negro Problem," "The Programs, Ideologies, Tactics, and Achievements of Negro Betterment and Interracial Organizations," "A Brief and Tentative Analysis of Negro Leadership," and "The Political Status of the Negro") that were used extensively throughout the study, particularly the chapters on politics. In 1973, the last of these manuscripts was published by the University of Chicago Press as *The Political Status of the Negro in the Age of FDR*.[14]

III

During the thirties, Bunche's major lines of thought achieved their distinctive quality. Although concerned with the plight of the American black, his vision extended beyond the United States. His was a more universalistic view. A consistent theme was emerging in Bunche's thought and action, which George L.-P. Weaver, a distinguished black labor authority, described as "the struggle to secure racial change in America and throughout the world."[15] Thus, while he wrestled with the plight of his fellow American blacks and sought to improve their condition, he extended his horizons to Africa and the entire colonial world.

As mentioned earlier, he carried out fieldwork both in the American South in connection with the Carnegie-Myrdal study and in Africa for his doctoral dissertation. When he took a leave of absence from Howard University to go to Africa for research, President Mordecai Johnson scoffed, "Bunche is going all the way to Africa to find a problem."[16] But, to Bunche the black problem in America was very much related to the colonial problem in Africa. The denial of basic human rights and the exclusions of people anywhere in the world from participation as citizens were part and parcel of the same problem. Bunche's publication *A World View of Race* (1936) presents this comprehensive perspective.[17] Ever disdainful of racism, he argued, however, that the fundamental issue for "the great masses of the black and yellow races was not skin color" but "the status of economic and political inferiority which they have been compelled to accept." Although Bunche wrote that "their [the black and yellow masses'] organized and direct support of the working class of the dominant populations of the world will bring an unchallengeable power to this class" and though he predicted a future "gigantic class war" rather than a "race war," he became a sharp critic of American Communists who, for their own sectarian interests, penetrated and exploited black organizations, such as the National Negro Congress which he had helped found. Clearly, the core of Bunche's thinking on race was his commitment to total integration.

As the plight of his fellow black Americans and that of the people of Africa, their ancestral continent, were of primary concern to Bunche, his attention moved from the domestic scene to Africa and then back again. His work with Gunnar Myrdal on the Carnegie study of the American black, published in 1944, was matched by his collaboration in the preparation of a 1943 study by the Committee on Africa, "The War and Peace Aims," published as *The Atlantic Charter and Africa from an American Standpoint*.[18]

Bunche's focus on the experience of indigenous peoples and cultures subject to colonialism was linked to his interest in the experience of black people in his own American society. To Bunche, the condition of the

American Negro and that of blacks in Africa, as well as that of colonial peoples throughout the world, was part and parcel of the same problem of racism and economic deprivation. As noted in relationship to both sets of problems, Bunche functioned both as scholar and activist.

The issues and questions that engaged Bunche as he wrestled with colonialism concerned the relationship between racism and class and the relationship between native culture and the modernization-westernization process. As a scholar, Bunche began grappling with these questions intellectually in his doctoral dissertation (1934) and continued the argument in his monograph *A World View of Race*. Bunche's awareness of the inherent complexity of the issues led him to seek training outside his own academic discipline. Therefore, after completing his doctoral degree in political science, Bunche broadened his experience by undertaking postdoctoral work in anthropology at Northwestern University with the leading American Africanist Melville Herskovits; at the London School of Economics with the world renowned scholar Bronislaw Malinowski; and at the University of Cape Town in South Africa with the eminent anthropologist Isaac Schapera. He also did additional fieldwork in Africa, this time in South and East Africa. It was during this trip, in 1936, that Bunche began to confront the issues of racism and class as an activist. Although he was in Africa as an anthropological researcher with a grant from the Social Science Research Council, his attention to research did not deter him from stepping out of the scholar's role into that of an activist. For example, during this time in South Africa, Bunche often gave what he called pep talks to the groups of wretched and forlorn natives he was observing.[19]

IV

In 1941, Bunche's career assumed a new focus. He left academia for government service, temporarily he thought, for the duration of the war. Although he continued to be on leave from his position at Howard University for nearly a decade, he never again returned to college teaching—despite having written to President Mordecai Johnson when he requested leave from Howard upon his appointment to the United Nations Secretariat in 1946: "I have never intended to divorce myself from academic pursuits. My prime interest has always been and remains in scholarship and teaching."[20] With his move into the United States government as an expert on colonial problems, his work now centered on the international scene, in particular the colonial world and Africa.

On joining the government, one of his first assignments gave Bunche the unique opportunity to introduce Africa literally to thousands upon thousands of Americans. Every G.I. sent to North or West Africa was given two small handbooks, *A Guide to North Africa* and *A Guide to West*

Africa, which Bunche had authored. Both provided, for an average American audience, a model of sensitive interpretations of a strange and unfamiliar culture and way of life. Bunche, as the only black of professional rank concerned with colonial affairs in the United States government, became an important point of contact for many of the emerging local African and Caribbean leaders. Inevitably when any one of these leaders came to the United States their primary, and in most cases their only, access to the United States government was through Ralph Bunche, in his office as chief of the Africa Section of the Research and Analysis Branch of the Office of Strategic Services (OSS), and later in the office of Dependent Area Affairs at the State Department.

In the State Department, Bunche worked in the postwar planning division, headed by Dr. Leo Pasvolsky. Bunche's assignment was to help develop postwar plans for the colonial world. This was an exhilarating experience for Bunche. He was working at the nerve center of the government on a subject he felt strongly about, professionally and personally, contributing, he hoped, to a progressive American position on colonialism in preparation for the Dumbarton Oaks and San Francisco conferences on the structure and principles of the United Nations.

Bunche served as an adviser on colonial matters with the United States delegation to San Francisco and to the subsequent Preparatory Commission in London. In January 1946, he was on the staff of the American delegation to the first General Assembly session in London. By chance, he found himself sitting as a delegate the United States at a plenary session. In a letter to his wife he described the unusual circumstances:

> Last night your husband sat as a delegate in a plenary session of the General Assembly! There was a night session beginning at 9 and all of our delegates, including Mrs. F.D.R., who has been most conscientious of the lot, had engagements or were ill. So Alger Hiss told Dorothy Fosdick and me to sit for the U.S. in order that we should be represented. Ben Cohen joined us later, so I told Dorothy, it was "minorities night" on the U.S. bench, with a woman, a Negro and a Jew representing the country. All we needed to complete the picture was an American Indian. Gromyko sat just two seats to my left, Jan Masaryk of Czechoslovakia was directly behind me, and Noel-Baker, British Minister of State, and Paul Gare-Booth were directly in front of me. I wish you and the children might have been there to see me. I would certainly like a chance to address a plenary session of the Assembly some day![21]

Little did Bunche know at the time that, within less than three years, he would be addressing the Security Council and, not too long afterward, the General Assembly.

Ralph Bunche became one of the foremost individuals participating in one of the great historic phenomena of the twentieth century: the process of decolonization, the dissolution of the great European empires, and the reassertion of independence by people of color throughout the world in the aftermath of World War II. As a leading scholar of Africa and colonialism, Bunche was in a singular position in the United States to draw attention to conditions in the colonial world and to point to the need for basic changes in the institutions and practices of colonialism in the postwar era. Both in government (in OSS and in the State Department) and outside it (in various public policy organizations, such as the Committee to Study the Organization of Peace and the Committee on Africa, the War, and Peace Aims), Bunche developed the theme that a major catalyst for change in the colonial order after the war had to be an organized world community. He had concluded from his doctoral dissertation (on the administration of the League of Nations mandate in Togoland as compared to French rule in the neighboring colony of Dahomey) as well as from his fieldwork in other parts of Africa, that a system of international responsibility, accountability, and supervision would be necessary to ensure that colonial peoples might freely exercise the right of self-determination. Bunche was very influential in the drafting of the parts of the United Nations Charter dealing with the colonial world: Chapter XI, "The Declaration Regarding Non-Self-Governing Territories" and Chapters XII and XIII, "Trusteeship System."

Bunche's role in the decolonization process constitutes an important chapter in his life and career. Even had he not been catapulted into the Palestine issue as Acting Mediator, for which he was awarded the Nobel Peace Prize, his involvement in the decolonization process in itself would have ensured his place in the pantheon of colonial liberation.

V

When Bunche joined the United Nations Secretariat in 1946 as director of its Trusteeship Department, one could hardly have foreseen the weighty responsibilities that lay ahead of him. He was not unlike many of the other individuals of considerable achievement in their specialized fields as scholars and practitioners who were drawn from throughout the world to staff the United Nations Secretariat. As an international civil servant, he was not likely to be chosen to head a delicate mission for the international body. The fact that he was a national of one of the world's major powers also militated against such a selection. A head of a mission, in the early days of the United Nations, was either a delegate of an appropriate member state or a distinguished personality from a more or less neutral power. Leading officials of the Secretariat were assigned to missions as staff advisers, working quietly behind the scenes, primarily as rapporteurs.

It was in such a capacity as a member of the Secretariat staff assigned to the United Nations Special Commission on Palestine (UNSCOP) that Bunche first became involved with the Palestinian problem in 1947. Representatives of eleven states (Australia, Canada, Czechoslovakia, Guatemala, India, Iran, Netherlands, Peru, Sweden, Uruguay, and Yugoslavia) constituted the commission. This configuration of UNSCOP's membership was an attempt to balance various points of view: pro-Arab, pro-Jewish, and some states considered uncommitted to either side as well as states considered pro-West or pro-East. The head of UNSCOP was its member from Guatemala, José Garcia Granados, and the top Secretariat official was not Bunche but his superior in the UN hierarchy, Dr. Victor Hoo, Assistant Secretary-General for Trusteeship and Non–Self-Governing Territories. Dr. Hoo was the Secretary-General's personal representative to UNSCOP and when in 1949 Count Folke Bernadotte of Sweden was chosen by the Security Council as Mediator of the Arab-Israeli War, Secretary-General Trygve Lie designated Ralph Bunche as "Chief Representative of the Secretary-General in Palestine," a subordinate staff role, certainly not one likely to lead to a Nobel Peace Prize.

A number of circumstances beyond Bunche's control altered the situation in the Middle East and projected him into the limelight. The first was the assassination of Bernadotte. By a quirk of fate, Bunche's life was saved. Several border control mixups as well as language barriers made Bunche an hour late for his meeting with Bernadotte in Jerusalem. Had he reached the Mediator at the appointed hour, he would have been in the car sitting next to Bernadotte when the assassination took place. Instead, in Bunche's own words, "when finally Bernadotte decided to leave without me, he invited Colonel Andre Serot [head of the U.N. military observers in Jerusalem] to take my seat in the rear of the car."[22] Bunche felt that Serot took the bullet that was meant for him. As the second in command of the Bernadotte Mission, the role of Acting Mediator fell to Ralph Bunche.

During the months that followed Bunche's appointment as Acting Mediator, he was almost denied the opportunity to effectuate an armistice between the belligerents. It is important to note that Bunche's assumption of the role of Acting Mediator, as the title clearly implied, was merely transitory; for at United Nations headquarters, plans were being made to replace the Acting Mediator by a tripartite Palestine Conciliation Commission. Yet, there was another circumstance contributing to Bunche's ascendancy that was due to the diplomatic jockeying, within the British Foreign Office and the U.S. State Department, to alter the terms of the original Palestine Partition Resolution. This led to procrastination in establishing the commission and also left the door open to Bunche to act astutely on signals coming from the belligerents and to position himself to play an effective mediating role between the Arab states and Israel.[23]

It has been suggested that Bunche's success in the Middle East in 1949 was an accidental quirk; he happened to be in the right place at the right time. Thus, he became Acting Mediator when his chief, Bernadotte, was assassinated. He was able to pull off the cease-fires and the ensuing armistices because Israel and each Arab state had good political and military reasons for entering these agreements. By implication, such critics conclude that Bunche's role was merely incidental. An analyst of the effects of all the mediators of the Arab-Israeli conflict from 1948 to 1979, asked: "Did he [Bunche] really deserve credit for the armistice agreement?" After reviewing the record in great detail, he concludes, "Bunche's successes can be explained by the fortuitous coincidence of circumstances, his own astute political judgment and flexibility, and bargaining power. The absence of any of these ingredients would have spelled failure." In the words of this analyst, Bunche was "a skillful chairman," whose "contribution was both procedural and substantive." The combination of Bunche's "intelligence, expert knowledge of the problems, and skill in draftsmanship" and his uncanny ability to formulate "compromise solutions to issues on which the parties disagreed" proved to be of crucial importance in drafting the armistice agreements to which all parties could agree.[24] According to Dr. Shabtai Rosenne, the distinguished international legal scholar who was a member of the Israeli armistice negotiating team, Bunche's extraordinary personal efforts were instrumental in forging an agreement that implacable adversaries were able to accept.[25]

There was no precedent for Bunche working out the armistice agreements. He had to start from scratch. The Security Council, to which he was responsible, did not give him much guidance in calling for "agreements being worked out forthwith." One of his close collaborators in the Middle East, William Mashler, reported that Bunche was confronted by a most unique situation: the challenge to bring about "an armistice within a political situation."[26] This was quite unlike the usual armistice that is determined primarily by the military situation at hand. Bunche judged that to succeed he would have to control the negotiating situation. Hence he made the decision to have the armistice talks take place on the island of Rhodes, as Mashler put it, "away from the area of conflict but close enough to it if it were necessary to visit it; and far away from New York." Another of Bunche's procedural innovations was to carry on separate and distinct mediation efforts—one-on-one between Israel and each of its Arab adversaries. He thus avoided what had and has proven to be one of the great obstacles in dealing with the Arab-Israeli conflict, attempting to negotiate with the Arabs as a unified group.

Assembling the various Arab states in one negotiating setting has placed each state in competition with the others in asserting its purity in defending the goals of Arab unity by not compromising with the enemy. Bunche saw to it that no such situation arose. Instead, relying on the moral authority of the United Nations, which still commanded attention at the time, he provided the Arab states with an acceptable way to enter into armistice agreements with the very state they had vowed to destroy.

All who participated in the Middle East negotiations—Arabs, Israelis and Secretariat members—attribute a large part of the success of the negotiations to the force of Bunche's personality, his good humor and charm, his patience, his physical resilience, his calm (he never seemed to lose his temper), his stubbornness as well as flexibility, and his shrewdness in dealing with people. But, in no small part he succeeded because he was perceived as even-handed and empathetic to the needs of the rival parties. In short, he was trusted.

It would be a serious error to consider Bunche's success of 1949 in the Palestinian dispute, for which he was universally acclaimed, as his only or most important contribution to the United Nations and world community. Indeed, in many ways it was only the beginning of a distinguished career of creative and dedicated service at the United Nations in the cause of international peace. Upon conclusion of the Arab-Israeli armistice agreements, Bunche returned to his position as director of the Trusteeship Department in the Secretariat.

VI

Undoubtedly, Bunche did happen to be in the right place at the right time, enabling him to be catapulted onto the center of the world arena as Acting Mediator in the Middle East. Similarly, he just happened to be in the Congo attending its independence ceremonies when the newly independent government called upon the United Nations for help in ridding the country of Belgian troops and he was instantaneously put in charge of the United Nations peacekeeping operation. In both instances, he proved to be not only in the right place at the right time but the right person in the right place at the right time.

In the Congo situation, similarly, no precedent existed for the full-scale peacekeeping operation that Bunche had to design and organize. There were no established rules for managing an international crisis through the United Nations. It fell to Bunche to create such rules in the field. Responding to the complex and shifting immediate situation with his skill and indefatigable energy, Bunche evolved, on the spot, a set of rules for crisis management that eventually became the model for United Nations peacekeeping operations in other parts of the world, in Cyprus, Kashmir, and Lebanon.

It was not long before he was called upon, once again, to deal with a thorny problem in the Middle East. In 1954, a dispute between Israel and Syria over the uses of the Jordan River came before the United Nations, and Secretary-General Dag Hammarskjöld established an interdepartmental Secretariat committee, under the leadership of Bunche, to make a study of all parties' plans for utilizing the waters of the Jordan. Known as the Bunche Committee, this body's main purpose was to provide the Secretary-General with the background he needed to be able to "take a position with conviction." The Jordan River issue was one of the earliest instances in which Hammarskjöld called upon Bunche for counsel.

In 1954, Hammarskjöld, as part of his reorganization of the Secretariat, appointed Bunche and Mr. Ilya S. Tchernychev of the Soviet Union to two newly created Under Secretary-General positions. These new posts were outside the regular Secretariat departments and, in Hammarskjöld's words, "their work load will be based on *ad hoc* assignments, mostly of an interdepartmental character."[27] The new posts were established primarily to enable the Secretary-General to utilize Bunche's talents and expertise more readily. There is little indication that the Soviet Under Secretary-General was given any significant *ad hoc* assignments, but it is evident that the Secretary-General increasingly called upon Bunche. Thus, in 1954 Hammarskjöld entrusted Bunche with the responsibility of heading the Secretariat committee that conducted the preparatory studies on the organization of the International Scientific Conference on Peaceful Uses of Atomic Energy and of a proposed new agency to deal with this important subject. When the General Conference International Atomic Energy Agency met in Vienna in 1957, it was Bunche who delivered the Secretary-General's message at its opening session.

Meanwhile, after the Sinai War in 1956, Bunche was pressed into service once again as "personal representative of the Secretary General" in a Middle East conflict. Bunche worked closely with Hammarskjöld in developing the United Nations Emergency Force (UNEF), an international military contingent made up of personnel from ten member states, which was placed on the Egyptian-Israeli armistice demarcation line. The UNEF force represented a first of its kind, for which there was no previous experience. Arrangements had to be improvised, with the responsibility falling heavily on the Secretary-General and his close associates, with Bunche foremost among them.

This was the beginning of what has come to be called United Nations *peacekeeping* operations, one of the rare areas of positive accomplishments by the United Nations in the realm of international peace and security. A concept not originally envisaged in the charter, it presents the anomalous situation of military personnel, without enforcement powers, helping to maintain or restore peace in areas of conflict. Bunche played a key role in all phases of these innovative efforts—initial planning, implementation in the field, and control from headquarters. In fact, United Nations peacekeeping operations were introduced in many troubled areas in the years that followed, and Bunche played a major role in most of them—in the Congo, Kashmir, Yemen, Cyprus—improvising and innovating as each *sui generis* situation required. Directing the United Nations' operations in each of the foregoing crises fell primarily into the hands of Ralph Bunche. According to Brian Urquhart, who succeeded Bunche as Under Secretary-General, Bunche played a "dominating role" in the development of the United Nations' peacekeeping activities and through his unique combination of skill and personality he set "an unmatched example of international service."[28]

The Congo Crisis of 1960–1961 brought Bunche once again into the limelight of world diplomacy. In Leopoldville to attend the independence day ceremonies when the crisis erupted, Bunche soon found himself orchestrating the United Nations' peacekeeping operation there, working in tandem with Secretary-General Hammarskjöld in New York. But this is only part of the story of Bunche's Congo involvement. As the conflict in the Congo erupted, there loomed the dreaded possibility of an East-West confrontation, spilling out of central Africa to other parts of the world. Bunche was determined that the cold war be kept out of the Congo. Professor Jean Herskovits has noted that at a time when "[President John F.] Kennedy . . . and others within his administration had been flirting with the idea of unilateralism there" it was "because of Bunche's personal persuasion [that] President Kennedy got behind the UN in the Congo in that pivotal month of September 1961."[29]

Bunche continued his most influential role in the United Nations under Secretary-General U Thant, who succeeded Hammarskjöld after the latter's tragic death in the Congo. Now, as Under Secretary-General for Special Political Affairs, Bunche directed all UN peacekeeping operations. Although Dag Hammarskjöld and U Thant were of totally different backgrounds, personality, and temperament, Bunche succeeded, in his service with both of them as adviser and confidant, in contradicting the notion that no one is indispensable. When U Thant was completing his first term of office he made it known that he would not accept a second term if Bunche would not stay on with him. Bunche yielded to Thant's insistence, although he had many attractive and less strenuous options open to him at the time. Why did Bunche not leave? Perhaps, the answer is in the observation made by Professor Richard Gardner that "Ralph understood more than any other single man that I ever knew what it is to be an international civil servant, to have one's loyalty to the organization and the purposes and principles of the Charter."[30]

Dedicated to the ideals of the United Nations, which he personified in the minds of so many people throughout the world, Bunche nevertheless projected a very realistic understanding of the United Nations and international organization in human history. In 1966, he represented Secretary-General U Thant at the general conference commemorating the tenth anniversary of the International Atomic Energy Agency. Bunche chose this occasion to ruminate over the nature of the United Nations System. "It is precisely because of the threatening chaos in international relations and the appalling dangers involved," Bunche noted, "that the whole United Nations concept of international order had been formulated and given tangible expression by the creation of a number of interrelated international organizations." Placing the United Nations in perspective, Bunche pointed out that "it is obvious that the problems of thousands of years could not be solved in a decade or two by the enunciation of a series of principles . . . and by the setting up of new organizations to give effect to them. International organizations are only at the beginning of a monumental task; their main work lay ahead and they should not be discouraged if the difficulties appeared at times to be insurmountable." Because he saw "no acceptable alternative" to "the efforts being made to develop a system of international order" due to "the arsenal of destructive weapons, not to mention the problems of famine, disease, pollution, overpopulation and economic anarchy," he felt that "international civil servants should never lose sight of the ultimate goal—an effective system of international order" and that "the necessity of achieving that goal must serve as a stimulus and an inspiration."[31]

In the original design of the top echelon of the United Nations administration, the leading Secretariat posts were allocated to the major powers. Ralph Bunche did not hold one of these posts when he joined the Secretariat. Actually, Bunche attained the highest position below that of Secretary-General on his own merits. Largely through his own accomplishments, Bunche advanced from directorship of the Trusteeship Department. Although Bunche never could become Secretary-General, because he was a national of one of the superpowers, his international prestige equaled or surpassed that achieved by any of the secretaries-general, other than perhaps Dag Hammarskjöld.

Bunche retired as Under Secretary-General for Special Political Affairs shortly before his death in 1971, but his legacy remains at the United Nations. Marrack Goulding, the current occupant of Bunche's previous office, remarked that Bunche's influence is ever present in his department. Richard N. Gardner has identified three qualities that characterize Bunche's international legacy. First, he was committed to "practical internationalism," or the use of the international agencies by political leaders to achieve compromises that they could otherwise not attain through a process of international legitimization by third parties. Second, he personified the "moral authority" of the international civil servant, projecting the positive image of independence, sensitivity, balanced judgement, expertise, and competence as he embodied the ideals and principles of the United Nations Charter. Third, he conceived the United Nations as an "impartial place" for quiet diplomacy, not as a place where adversaries shout at each other, but where differences are peacefully resolved.[32]

VII

Men and women are usually products of their times, but only a few can be said to have influenced their times. Bunche was such a person. The little more than five decades between Bunche's student days and his death were marked by many momentous developments in the world. None was more telling than the emergence of the resolute movement of "people of color," in the United States and throughout the world, for freedom and equality, and the establishment of new international institutions dedicated to the achievement of peace and justice among all peoples. Bunche was engaged with all these developments, often at the center—thinking, arguing, prodding, cajoling, demonstrating by example, and leading. Throughout his life, he believed that the world could be made a better place in which to live and in which justice and right would prevail. Toward the end of the 1930s, when Nazism, Fascism and racism were rampant, Bunche noted, "I temporarily lost my faith in the essential good sense and decency of people and I became intensely cynical, fortunately only for a short period."[33] Fundamentally he felt that "despite so much wickedness and evil design in the world, man is essentially good." But despite this optimistic outlook, Bunche was no pie-in-the-sky idealist. His was a realistic idealism. If anything, he was a down-to-earth realist, very much aware of the human condition and concerned about its future. This is clearly evident in the introduction he wrote to the proceedings of a Harvard conference on the "Near East and the Great Powers" held shortly after he received the Nobel Peace Prize.

> It seems self-evident that our [i.e., American] policy should always be such as to find us squarely on the side of the people. If we are to discharge our present immensely heavy and unparalleled responsibilities effectively and with dignity, we have first of all a vast job of self-education to undertake. Cultural understanding is something which properly must begin at home. We need to realign our human relations' sights in the most basic way, in order that we may come to think of the peoples in the Near East, the Far East, the Caribbean and Africa—with regard to their abilities and potentialities—as equals, really as equals, and to be able to treat them as such in our policies and actions in a convincing way. That, I think, is one of the most imperative jobs

that we in this country have to do in meeting the new responsibilities which have come to us as a result of the role of leadership assumed by this country since the end of the last war.[34]

Bunche's realistic idealism is also clearly evident in his remarks on "brotherhood."

> May I say a word or two about brotherhood? I used to make speeches about brotherhood but I never mention it any more. Brotherhood is a misused, misleading term. What we need in this world is not brotherhood but coexistence. We need acceptance of the right of every person to his own dignity. We need mutual respect. Mankind will be much better off when there is less reliance on lip service to brotherhood and brotherly love and much more practice of the sounder and more realistic principle of mutual respect governing the relations among all people. There are a hell of a lot of people in the world, black and white, that I wouldn't want as distant cousins, much less as brothers.[35]

Bunche, however, rejected the cynicism that often masquerades as realism. In his acceptance speech, "The Alternatives: Peace or Ruin; Justice or Demagoguery," for the NAACP Spingarn Medal in 1949, he said, "cynicism and hysteria are too prevalent today. Too many people are talking about war and accepting it as inevitable. Too few people are actively working for peace, although virtually everyone wishes peace."

Because of his reputation as an international figure, in his later years Bunche was perceived by some as detached from the struggle for civil rights in the United States and somehow above racial issues. This is a mistaken perception. When Bunche moved on to the center stage of world politics, he did not suddenly cut himself off from his life experiences, shedding his background as an American black. As one black journalist noted, the "[light] pigment of his skin did not insulate him from the same realities faced by less special blacks—not even in the midst of a well-educated and presumably open-minded class of men known as diplomats."[36] He never forgot a childhood encounter with racism in Albuquerque when he, his mother, and sister were told to move to the rear of the nickelodeon because they were Negroes. Nor did he forget his travels through the South with Gunnar Myrdal on the Carnegie project. Each evening, after dropping Myrdal off at the leading local hotel, Bunche would search out accommodations for himself, usually at the home of the local black clergyman or some other black professional. On one occasion, a night that "the Klan was riding and no Negro would dare open his shutters," Bunche finally found a place to sleep, on a slab in a black mortuary, separated from a cadaver by a screen.

Nor could he forget being restricted to only one restaurant in wartime Washington—the Gateway at Union Station—where he could dine with white colleagues and friends, at the very time that he was a member of the American delegation planning the United Nations organization at Dumbarton Oaks. As Roy Wilkins, then head of the NAACP noted, "Never in his soaring career was Ralph Bunche apart from or indifferent to the treatment visited upon his people in his native land."[37] Moreover, when he rejected President Truman's offer to appoint him Assistant Secretary of State, which would have made him the occupant of the highest U.S. government position to be held by a black, he tersely said: "It is well known that there is Jim Crow in Washington. It is equally well known that no Negro finds Jim Crow congenial. I am a Negro." Peggy Mann noted, in her very informative popular biography of Bunche, that "when Ralph Bunche turned down the job . . . he [uncharacteristically] did *seek* publicity on the subject. He had a message he wanted to get across to as wide a public as possible—the reason he was turning down the job."[38]

As a leading member of the United Nations Secretariat, however, Bunche was restricted in what he could say and do. One of the cardinal rules of the international civil service is that its members are not permitted to become actively involved in domestic problems and politics, but Bunche would not be silenced. He had an understanding with the secretaries-general under whom he served, Trygve Lie, Dag Hammarskjöld, and U Thant, that he would be able to speak his mind on racism. Indeed, many of his speeches and articles skillfully examined the practices of racism as violations of the United Nations Charter, as in his Lincoln's Day address of 1951, "The International Significance of Human Relations," which is included in this volume.[39] Nor did he permit his international position to deter him from participating in the 1965 Selma march alongside Martin Luther King, even though his legs suffered from the pain of phlebitis and his body was weakened by diabetes.

After receiving the Nobel Prize, Bunche became a renowned figure in American popular culture, for he was an affirmation of the success of the American way. Even before this award, Bunche had already been recognized within sectors of American academia, and also official Washington, as an unusually talented and pragmatic intellectual, with whom they felt perfectly at ease, albeit he was a black. Now, the broader white elite welcomed him in their midst. Earlier, however, when Bunche sought a university teaching position after completing his graduate studies at Harvard University in the thirties, the only positions open to him (as it was for all blacks having doctoral degrees) were in the Negro colleges of the South, of which Howard in Washington, D.C. was considered one of the best. Later, Bunche received numerous offers from prestigious universities throughout the land, including a chair at Harvard, which he accepted but never assumed. Bunche became a board member and trustee of some of the country's leading universities, foundations, and civic organizations, including Harvard University, the City University of New York, Oberlin College, the Rockefeller and Ford Foundations, the Institute of International Education, the American Red Cross, and the National Advisory Council of the Girl Scouts of America. Blacks particularly took great pride in his accomplishments—he was featured on the cover of *Ebony* magazine—for he was an American black who had become an international hero.

Black leaders—the Roy Wilkinses, the Walter Whites, the Thurgood Marshalls, the Whitney Youngs, and the A. Philip Randolphs, with whom Bunche had labored in the struggle for black civil rights in the earlier years—welcomed his success. But among the emerging new generation of black militants of the sixties, a sense of resentment of Bunche and his prominence was sometimes manifested. Stokeley Carmichael's pithy comment "You can't have Bunche for lunch!" epitomizes the new militants' resentment of having Bunche's success story thrown up to them, as it was by many whites, in an effort to negate the movement's condemnation of the American civil rights record. Bunche was aware of their feelings, but this did not deter him from continuing to identify with and fight for racial justice as he perceived it, even if as a recent study indicates, his United Nations responsibilities "were so intricate, time- and mind-consuming that his involvement in domestic affairs—when time allowed—could only be peripheral, rhetorical, and symbolic."[40] When he came under attack from Adam Clayton Powell, the black congressman from Harlem, and from Malcolm X for allegedly being an "international Uncle Tom" Bunche made his views well known:

> I deplore Negroes embracing, as the Black Muslims and Adam Powell have done, a black form of the racist virus. I take my stand firmly and unflinchingly as an American. This is my country. My ancestors and I helped to build it. I say my color has nothing to do with it. I have a stake in this country and I am determined that I and my children will cash in on it. I am determined to fight therefore for what is mine. I want no one—Malcolm X or anyone else—to tell me to give up the fight because equality is unattainable and to look elsewhere in some mythical, fanciful state of black men for my salvation. I say that is surrender and escapism and I want none of it.[41]

Bunche understood well his symbolic stature for the civil rights struggle in the United States. Attending Martin Luther King's funeral in Atlanta in 1968, he deliberately chose to stay at a black-owned hotel, Pascal's, because "I wanted to be with other Negroes . . . with those boys in Mau-Mau jackets," and he noted that "all those boys couldn't have been nicer to me. Even Stokeley Carmichael was nice."[42]

VIII

Bunche's earlier career as scholar, as civil rights activist, and as middle-level government official in wartime Washington, working on the structure of the postwar world, helped prepare him for his brilliant achievements in the United Nations. As we have seen, none of these earlier activities was carried on in tranquil backwaters of the American scene. On the contrary, they were replete with constant debate, attempts to understand and explain complex human behavior and yearnings, devising strategy and tactics, and negotiating with groups and individuals in conflict situations.

These experiences did not preordain Bunche's achievements as an architect of international mediation and peacekeeping; but they did contribute in a very real way. Once given responsibilities in these areas, he was able to draw on his rich earlier background in human relations. Throughout his earlier life Bunche was a pioneer and innovator. This he continued to be during his United Nations career. In his work as head of the Trusteeship Department, as Acting Mediator in the Middle East and as the Secretary-General's special representative in the Congo and elsewhere, Bunche was forced to innovate and travel uncharted courses.

Bunche was not prone to overly dramatic or foreboding pronouncements. His style was generally cool and analytical. But in July 1969, in what turned out to be his last major address, his words took on a prophetic quality. His topic was "racism," which he called "the foremost obstacle to harmonization of people." Noting the "growing alienation of the black American" was becoming "ever more severe and dangerous," and that "there were no more abrasive issues in the United Nations than those involving racial injustice," Bunche concluded: "White men, whether in the majority in the United States and the United Kingdom, or in the minority, as in South Africa, Southern Rhodesia and the world at large, must find a way . . . to purge themselves completely of racism or face the ultimate fateful confrontation of the races, which will shake the very foundations of civilization and, indeed, threaten its continued existence and that of most of mankind as well."[43]

Ralph Johnson Bunche was not only a man of his times, but he, obviously, was very much a man for our times as well. Bunche's legacy was aptly summarized by his former student and colleague at Howard University, Dr. Robert E. Martin. In a paper presented at the 1986 meetings of the American Political Science Association, he wrote that "Ralph Bunche left an enduring heritage, an invaluable set of social values and precepts. He taught us:

—that fundamentally there is one race—the human race . . .

—that nationalism had served constructive purposes historically but was presenting dangerous problems in the contemporary world . . .

—that a declaration of independence was essential in the course of overthrowing colonialism and engaging in nation-building but that equally there was a need for a declaration of interdependence among the nations of the world . . .

—that mediation and arbitration were preferable to confrontation in international relations . . .

—that national security was more dependent upon international understanding, organization, and stability than upon armaments and competition in arms races . . .

—that respect for international law and courts of justice was indispensable in the modern world . . . and

—that hard work and untiring search for excellence are necessary for success."

While the entire impact of his work at the United Nations and as a world statesman is yet to be fully researched and analyzed, it is clear that in the two decades following his receipt of the Nobel Peace Prize Bunche went on to build a truly remarkable record of achievement in the United Nations, at a time when the United Nations was a more important force in world affairs than it has been in the seventies and eighties. To many, he was the embodiment of an effective United Nations.

Throughout Bunche's many notable achievements, one is impressed with the application of theory to practice and the tempering of idealism with pragmatism without the sacrifice of principles. In describing Bunche as "modest but tough, brilliant but unassuming, and strong but understanding," Secretary-General U Thant captured the essence of what made Bunche "the most effective and best known of international civil servants."[44]

Noting Bunche's great achievement as an international mediator, *The Times* of London in its obituary tribute suggested that "his whole career, both in the United States and in world affairs, was spent in the attempt *to reconcile extremes* and to build up the basis of understanding upon which alone peaceful settlements of long-standing conflicts can be worked out."[45] However, giving the impression that Bunche was essentially a "great conciliator" is a misreading of Bunche, for it only partially conveys the essence of the man. True, he was interested in achieving peaceful settlements, and this involved compromises. But Bunche was no compromiser when it came to the basic principles of human equality and in fighting racism.

Bunche fought hard for his beliefs, and this brought him into conflict with the New Deal for shortchanging American blacks, the American

Communist Party for trying to subvert the National Negro Congress, which he had helped found, as well as some of his fellow black activists, including William E. B. DuBois, the NAACP, Martin Luther King, and Malcolm X, at one time or another over principles or tactics. Although the influences of Marxism are evident in his thinking and writing in the early thirties, he was no ideological dogmatist; but in one area, Bunche was unyielding. According to the Afro-American scholar Dr. W. Ofuatey-Kodjoe, "Bunche's commitment to human equality and natural rights was uncompromising; it was not mediated by any pragmatism since it was the only thing Ralph Bunche believed in unconditionally."[46] Bunche himself summed up his guiding philosophy in these words:

> I have a deep-seated bias against hate and intolerance. I have a bias against racial and religious bigotry. I have a bias against war; a bias for peace. I have a bias which leads me to believe that no problem of human relations is insoluble.[47]

Notes

1. From "The Alternatives: Peace or Ruin; Justice or Degeneracy," address accepting the 34th Spingarn Medal at NAACP 40th Annual Convention, Los Angeles, California, 17 July 1949.
2. "Nothing is Impossible for the Negro," *The Negro Digest* 7, no. 10 (August 1849): pp. 4–5.
3. *New York Times*, 10 December 1971.
4. Ibid.
5. From comments made at the conference, "Ralph Bunche: The Man and His Times," Panel I: "Bunche's Intellectual Interests and Academic Career." The conference, referred to in this essay as the Bunche Conference, was held at the City University of New York's Graduate Center on 5 and 6 May 1986. This volume contains revised versions of a number of papers given at this conference. A total of 35 scholars, former colleagues of Bunche from various periods in his career as well as former students, participated in it. For a newspaper account of the conference see the *New York Times*, 7 May 1986, p. 2.
6. Bunche Conference, Panel I.
7. Ibid., Panel II: "Bunche and the American Civil Rights Movement."
8. Ibid.
9. See Appendix B for the full text of Bunche's valedictory address.
10. See Appendix A for text of letter to Du Bois.
11. *Washington Tribune*, 18 February 1939.
12. *Chicago Defender*, 5 August 1939.
13. Gunnar Myrdal, *An American Dilemma: The Negro Problem and Modern Democracy*, 2 vols (New York: Harper and Brothers, 1944).
14. The volume was edited by Professor Dewey Grantham.
15. Bunche Conference, Panel II.
16. *The New Yorker*, 1 January 1972, p. 16.

17. *A World View of Race,* Washington: Associates in Negro Folk Education, 1936.
18. Bunche was a leading member of the editorial committee that prepared the 1943 report under the auspices of the Phelps-Stokes Fund.
19. Bunche's notes on trip to South Africa. Copy in the files of the Ralph Bunche Institute on the United Nations.
20. Letter from Bunche to Mordecai Johnson, 17 September 1946, quoted in Souad Halila, *The Intellectual Development and Diplomatic Career of Ralph J. Bunche: The Afro-American, Africanist, and Internationalist* (Ph.D. Diss., University of Southern California, 1988), p. 136.
21. Letter dated 19 January 1946, Bunche Institute files.
22. From transcribed Bunche notes in the Bunche Institute files.
23. This subject is explored in detail by J. C. Hurewitz in his essay in this volume.
24. Saadia Touval, *The Peace Brokers: Mediation in the Arab-Israeli Conflict 1948-1979* (Princeton, N. J.: Princeton University Press, 1982), pp. 55, 65–66, 75.
25. Further details on the negotiations at Rhodes are given by Shabtai Rosenne in his contribution to this volume.
26. Comments made at the Bunche Conference, Panel V: "Bunche as United Nations Mediator."
27. *Public Papers of the Secretaries-General of the United Nations, vol. 3: 1956–1957,* ed. Andrew Cordier and Wilder Foote (New York: Columbia University Press, 1973), p. 346.
28. See Brian Urquhart's essay in this volume.
29. Bunche Conference, Panel III: "Bunche's Impact on the American Perception of Africa."
30. Bunche Conference, Panel V: "Bunche as United Nations Mediator."
31. IAEA, GC (X) OR.101, 27 January 1967, p. 3.
32. Bunche Conference, Panel V.
33. This statement is listed as the "Greatest Error Committed" in a handbook of Bunche's statements prepared for use by his secretary at the United Nations.
34. In Richard Frye, ed., *The Near East and the Great Powers* (Cambridge, Mass.: Harvard University Press, 1951), p. 5.
35. Quoted by Brian Urquhart, "Remembrances of Ralph Bunche," *Los Angeles Times,* 15 May 1975.
36. Ernest B. Furgurson, "The Barber's Son in History," *Baltimore Sun,* 14 December 1971.
37. *New York Post,* 18 December 1971.
38. Peggy Mann, *Ralph Bunche: U.N. Peacemaker* (New York: Coward, McCann & Geoghegan, 1975), p. 270.
39. Appendix D.
40. Halila, *The Intellectual and Diplomatic Career* p. 101.
41. Quoted in Halila, p. 92.
42. *The New Yorker,* 1 January 1972, p. 17.
43. See Appendix F.
44. *New York Times,* 10 December 1971.
45. 10 December 1971.
46. Bunche Conference, Panel III.
47. This much quoted statement was first made by Bunche at a dinner meeting in his honor offered by the American Association for the United Nations on 9 May 1949.

· 2 ·

RACE, CLASS, AND POLITICS:
Ralph Bunche and Black Protest

John B. Kirby

During the momentous struggles of the late 1950s and 1960s, Ralph Bunche was best known, when he was known at all, as America's first black recipient of the coveted Nobel Peace Prize and as a United Nations dignitary engaged in peacemaking activities in such far-away places as the Congo and Cyprus. In those years, Bunche seemed not only physically but politically thousands of miles away from the intense, often violent engagements for racial change in Alabama, Mississippi, and other parts of the Deep South. Although at times he lent his name or, in the case of the 1965 Selma march, his presence, to the nonviolent activities led by Martin Luther King, Jr. and others, few of the younger civil rights activists, black or white, knew much about the man. It is ironic that Bunche, so critical of mythologizing people and ideas, had himself by the 1960s become somewhat of a mythic figure.

But perhaps the most significant irony is that even before he entered government service and assumed his role in the United Nations, Ralph Bunche, in the 1930s and early 1940s, had anticipated many of the later campaigns and conflicts of the black struggle. In fact, during the Depression, his thinking reflected much of the black experience, both prior to the 1930s and after World War II, including especially the debates of the

1960s and 1970s. Long after some sixties personalities have faded from memory, Ralph Bunche, I think, will be remembered, along with W. E. B. Du Bois and a handful of others, as a major contributor to the development of black political and social thought in the twentieth century. There was a certain consistency in Bunche's primary emphasis upon racial issues during the 1930s and his more international concerns of the 1940s and the post–World War II days. It was a consistency shaped by a comprehensive view of society and the world and the manner in which people, excluded from their natural rights as citizens or as nationalities, justly sought to become equal participants in their respective communities. By education, background, and disposition, Bunche considered the struggles of black people in America within the context of those large forces that shape the total society. In 1939 he warned: "Unless the Negro can develop, and quickly, organization and leadership endowed with broad social perspective and foresighted, analytical intelligence, the black citizen of America may soon face the dismal prospect of reflecting upon the tactical errors of the past from the gutters of the black ghettoes and concentration camps of the future."[1]

It is clear that much of Bunche's activities during the 1930s and his many writings, especially those for Gunnar Myrdal's *An American Dilemma,* set out to provide such a "broad social perspective."[2] And it is to the historical circumstances of the thirties that one must turn, first of all, in examining Bunche's perceptions and his prescriptions for political and racial reform in American life. His strengths and limitations as a commentator on, and as an activist for, black progress derived from his response to the distinctive conditions of the 1930s. Like his friends and sometime allies, among whom were Abram Harris, John P. Davis, Robert Weaver, William Houston, and William Hastie, Bunche came to political and intellectual maturity during the economic crisis of the Depression and Franklin D. Roosevelt's New Deal "welfare state."[3] This essay has two objectives. First, it looks at Bunche's thought within the context of the 1930s and on the eve of World War II, as he was about to reduce his direct involvement in essentially black concerns—that is, his critique of New Deal liberalism, black organizations and civil rights groups, black leaders, and white progressives. Second, and more briefly, it assesses the relevance of Bunche's thinking on race, class, and political protest to the struggles that took place after 1945 and during what many have called the "Second Reconstruction."

The economic collapse that came in 1929 and persevered for the next decade constituted a critical turning point in the American and black experience. Despite earlier efforts at reform, in 1929 laissez faire capitalism, with its notions that individual liberty was best guaranteed by limiting the authority of the state and that economic and political opportunity existed for all who had the ability and courage to take advantage of it, remained the accepted wisdom of the day. Under the Republican leadership of Harding, Coolidge, and Hoover, those beliefs were given renewed affirmation. Still, although many Americans prospered during the 1920s, many others did not. That was especially true for blacks, who found their conditions in the rural South as well as in northern cities increasingly difficult, at a time when racial hostility and social and political repression were on the rise. From these unhealthy circumstances, Marcus Garvey's multifaceted black nationalism emerged, and the cultural renaissance associated with Harlem and other black centers of art and literature assumed prominence. But in spite of Garvey and the achievements of the renaissance, the majority of black Americans were as segregated and as isolated from the mainstream of American economic, political, and social life in the 1920s as at any time in their history.

When the Great Depression came in 1929, two years after Ralph Bunche earned his degree from UCLA as a Phi Beta Kappa and one year after receiving a Master's degree at Harvard, an already desperate situation for blacks worsened. In 1933, the National Urban League noted that over 17 percent of the entire black population was on relief, including over half the population in the major cities. By the time of Franklin Roosevelt's election in 1932, the jobless rate for black males was between 40 and 60 percent in industrial areas like New York, Chicago, and Detroit. Throughout the South, discrimination with respect to relief was widespread. Perhaps two-thirds of the blacks, who earned their meager income from cotton production, derived little or no profits by the early 1930s. In 1931, T. Arnold Hill of the Urban League summed it up, stating that "at no time in the history of the Negro since slavery has his economic and social outlook seemed so discouraging."[4]

What made it especially harsh for blacks was that they seemed to have few political options in combating their situation. Most blacks did not have the franchise, and where they did, they saw little reason to use it. Decades ago, the Republican party had given up its supposed role as benefactor of the black race, except for an occasional appeal to the memory of Lincoln during election time. Democrats, prior to the New Deal, made little attempt to recruit black voters, and an appeal to blacks had little attraction for the dominant Democratic southern constituency because of the legacy of the Civil War and Reconstruction years. By the early thirties, some radical parties like the Socialists and Communists were endeavoring to attract blacks by taking more forceful positions on race issues. But few Afro-Americans, except in places like New York City, understood much about the radicals' programs, and when they did, they did not find them especially viable alternatives.[5] Among black protest organizations, the NAACP in particular had undergone significant changes during the 1920s that would bear fruit in the later years. But the NAACP, like the National Urban League, had lost membership during the "New Era" years; and both organizations were on the brink of financial collapse by 1930.[6] Although aspects of Garvey's nationalism survived during the 1930s, neither his movement nor his ideology of black self-help capitalism offered much hope to a people who after 1929 were confronted with threats to their very economic survival. In the early years of the Depression, black as well as some interracial organizations met to assess the circumstances confronting black Americans. Few, if any, however, had solutions to the problems they articulated. In many local communities, people did not wait for the black leadership or the nation's leaders to give them direction. In Chicago in 1929, for example, campaigns began to force business establishments located in black neighborhoods to hire black personnel or, at the least, not to replace black employees with whites. However, despite their pickets and threats of boycotts, despite occasional support from both the Communist party and local NAACP groups, what became known as the "Don't-Buy-Where-You-Can't-Work" campaigns had little success as business in general was in a downward tailspin.[7]

Yet, in a short time, the environment changed. Four years after Roosevelt assumed the presidency and New Deal economic, social, and political reforms and recovery programs were in place, the relationships of black Americans to the national government had been fundamentally altered. Led by a handful of white racial liberals like Harold Ickes, Will Alexander, Aubrey Williams, Clark Foreman, and Eleanor Roosevelt, the New Deal made strides toward including blacks within many of its public works—relief, housing, education, and agricultural policies. Discrimination, though, still occurred on many levels; housing remained segregated, as did educational funds. And planning programs like the National Recovery Association (NRA) probably did more harm than good for black workers, especially in the South. Moreover, despite his wife and the presence of other race liberals within his administration, Franklin Roosevelt and most other New Dealers showed only scant concern or understanding of black problems, refusing even to back the NAACP's efforts to abolish lynching.[8]

Nevertheless, as evidenced by the strong political support he received from black voters in 1936 and 1940, Roosevelt and the New Deal won the admiration and gratitude of millions of black people, who had a clear sense of how bad things were by 1933. And many were acutely aware that some of their race had been drawn directly into the administration itself. Bunche's friends Robert Weaver and William Hastie were only two of hundreds of prominent blacks who became race relations advisers to the New Deal. The Urban League's Eugene Kinckle Jones was another and NAACP head Walter White served as the unofficial guru on racial affairs to white liberals like Mrs. Roosevelt and Aubrey Williams.[9] Perhaps even more important was the change that occurred during the

Depression-New Deal period with respect to social values and public philosophy. The old values of individualism, competition, self-reliance, and limited government gave way for a time, in the 1930s, to an emphasis upon shared interests, mutuality of needs and sacrifices, and the belief that government had responsibility to assure equal opportunity and provide minimal security to all citizens. Henry Wallace, no friend of black people in the 1930s, argued in his book *New Frontiers* that the Depression had taught Americans "not to learn how to compete with each other for enough of this world's goods, but to learn how to live with each other in abundance." It would be government's duty, Wallace argued, to emphasize justice for all people and to assure that "individual and group interest coincide."[10] Applying the thesis more directly to blacks, Harold Ickes told the NAACP convention in 1936 that the Roosevelt administration was "seeking the greatest good for the greatest number," and under the New Deal's "new conception of democracy, the Negro will be given the chance to which he is entitled—not because he will be singled out for special consideration but because he preeminently belongs to the class that the new democracy is designed especially to aid."[11]

Ralph Bunche was in agreement with liberals like Ickes and Wallace when they affirmed the notion of class interdependency. Like most left-liberal thinkers of the period, Bunche gave primary focus to class and economic considerations. That was not surprising since, after all, the Depression was an economic crisis and during most of the 1930s, political ideas, whether of a left, liberal, or conservative perspective, tended to emphasize economic matters. But there were additional reasons why white race liberals in the New Deal stressed the theme of common class interests. For these reformers, it not only coincided with their faith in the purpose and viability of New Deal measures but provided them with a basic rationale for including blacks in government programs while not having to confront directly the ugly and persistent conflicts associated with civil rights activities. The fundamental assumption of most New Deal racial liberals was that racial change would come as economic and political change occurred, through what Ickes called the "new democracy" of the Roosevelt welfare state.[12]

For those like Bunche, concerned with the New Deal's direct benefits to black people, that thesis constituted their most basic challenge. It was made even more crucial for a black radical like Bunche who, unlike W. E. B. Du Bois during the 1930s, shared the liberal belief that class and economic interest ought to take precedence over racial interest. Du Bois left the NAACP in 1934 because his arguments for race solidarity and black economic and social cooperation ran counter both to the association's interracial views and the efforts of people like Walter White to secure legislation from the national government to ban lynching and other forms of racial discrimination. Du Bois was especially skeptical of the black and white class-solidarity theme, which he believed denied the importance of race as a central factor in the black American's oppression.[13]

Along with other young black intellectuals like Abram Harris and E. Franklin Frazier, Bunche strongly dissented from Du Bois's ideas of a "nation within a nation" during the 1930s. But his opposition to Du Bois did not make him an unqualified supporter of either the NAACP or the New Deal.[14] In fact, for most of the 1930s, Bunche remained critical of the majority of black and interracial organizations and New Deal reforms. The NAACP and the National Urban League, he argued, were hopelessly middle-class in their "thinking and living." That middle-class bias left them alienated from the mainstream of black America, pursuing goals that were "sensational" and that "evoked admiration from the Negro elite" but left the "masses of Negroes and their problem of daily bread untouched." Nor did he have much faith in grass-roots groups such as the New Negro Alliance, which supported economic boycotts as a means to force additional black employment. The "Don't-Buy-Where-You-Can't Work" movement functioned, he argued, within a "black groove," offering "only racialism with no significant hope for the mass Negro population."[15] Although Bunche conceded that boycotts of white businesses did offer the black an "inkling of his latent economic power and an acquaintance with the recognized weapons of labor," they could not create new jobs and therefore were likely to produce a "vicious cycle of job displacement." And for Bunche, the most distressing feature of this approach, which he associated with other black nationalist schemes, including those of Du Bois, was that they further widened "the already deplorable gap between the white and black working classes . . . by boldly placing the competition for jobs on a strictly racial basis." It was "absurd," he reflected, "to assume that the Negro, deprived of the advantages of full participation in American life today, will be able to gain . . . advantages or acceptable substitutes for them by setting himself up in a black political and economic outhouse."[16]

Bunche never denied the importance of race or racism in the so-called "Negro problem" of the 1930s. But he maintained that the black struggle was interwoven with the total fabric of American life, and any solution to it had to include a "comprehension of the history and the political, economic and social forces at work" in America.[17] Black and white were both victims of racial stereotypes. White racism had reinforced the black man's minority status, a status first prescribed by slavery and later confirmed by white economic and political domination. Yet Bunche believed that in responding to white racism, blacks falsely assume that all the Negro's problems were racial in nature. In contrast, he maintained that "only in the narrowly racial sense" was it possible to comprehend black people's minority status; "in every other respect," outside of race, the black American population was "subject to the same divisive influences impinging upon the life of every other group in the nation." The "only hope for improvement in the conditions of the masses of any American minority group," he constantly affirmed, was the "hope that can be held out for the betterment of the masses of the dominant group. . . . Their basic interests are identical and so must be their program and tactics."[18]

Bunche's opposition to the "narrowly racial" approach carried over in his views of black ideologies and black leadership. "Accommodationism" and "escape" were, he felt, the categories which in a broad sense "all Negro ideologies on the Negro question fall into." Various forms of black nationalism fit the escapist conception, with emphases on racial unity, internal solidarity, cultural pride, and race distinctiveness. Whatever form it took, such ideologies derived essentially from the black person's need to construct "a conceptual defense against the malevolent conception of the Negro as developed by the white man." Similarly, the accommodationist model was built out of a need to adjust black thought and behavior "in such a way as to occasion least shock to the dominant group mores and traditions and at the same time suffer least inconvenience" to blacks.[19]

Based on his appraisal of the past and on conditions in the 1930s, Bunche concluded that most black racial ideologies were simply reactions to the racist assumptions and practices of whites. The result was that few ideologies met the primary needs of the black masses; they were fashioned, whether accommodationist or nationalist, from the biases of the dominant white culture rather than from the economic, social, and political aspirations of black people. Since for Bunche the "white man's conception of the 'Negro problem'" was "less a conception of a 'problem' than a conception of the 'Negro'" formed during slavery and since the "ideologies of the white world on the Negro have all been directed at reserving participation in the major blessings of the society exclusively for the white man," it was self-defeating for blacks to shape their own beliefs in response to such mythical nonsense.[20]

Yet, that is what he felt most black intellectuals and leaders tended to do and why he considered so few of their organizational efforts adequate to what he perceived as the real needs of black people. Middle-class black leaders, those associated with the NAACP and Urban League, almost always pushed ideas that had more relevance to "disabilities" that were of "importance to the limited number of middle-class than to the vast majority of working-class Negroes. Lynching, equalization of teacher's salaries, admittance to white universities, court cases, etc." were issues that won applause from the black elites but had limited relevance to black masses.[21] Those who did have direct ties to the people were often local leaders—ministers, lodge presidents, a few labor organizers, certain politicians. But even in local communities, black leadership "influ-ence seldom filters down to the masses of black people."[22] In short, as he wrote in 1939, for any black ideology, organization, or leaders to be viable, they had to "develop an extra-racial perspective, to be able to relate the interest of the Negro to the broad currents of American life; and to exert efforts to integrate the Negro in the mainstream of that life."[23]

Mainstream America did not mean for Bunche either the pre-Depres-sion, laissez-faire capitalism of Coolidge and Hoover or what he saw as the limited welfare state of the New Deal. At the Howard University Conference of 1935, which he helped organize and which offered an ideologically diverse, black assessment of Roosevelt's policies, Bunche directed his most far-reaching attack against New Deal liberal ideology. "For the Negro population," he stated, "the New Deal means the same thing but more of it. Striking at no fundamental social conditions, the New Deal at best can only fix the disadvantages, the differentials, the discriminations, under which the Negro population has labored all along." The Roosevelt administration's economic and social planning was designed to create an unstable balance between the interests of big business and the laboring masses. The New Deal was dominated by a white, middle-class perspective that sought to maintain private enter-prise while it weakly attempted to curb some of the more blatant abuses of capitalism. Bunche saw only two real alternatives to planning in the 1930s—either the government must take over the means of production or it must allow private industry to run things. But like all middle-class thinkers, New Deal reformers sought to do both and ended up doing very little. Caught in an "intermediate position between the working masses and the finance capitalists," he argued, the New Deal failed to achieve any equilibrium between the two.[24]

For Bunche, the effect of such an intermediate position was that the Roosevelt administration fostered an expanded central government that weakened the independence of the laboring masses while it helped to increase the power of the capitalists. Fearing government ownership more than private enterprise, the middle position assumed by the New Deal amounted to utilizing the "power of the state to keep the masses in check while handling the industrialists with velvet gloves." In effect, black and white working classes had "become even more dependent upon the intervention of the state in their struggle to obtain social justice from the owners and directors of industry."[25] Worse yet, black economic oppression was legitimized through the shortsightedness of the New Deal's planning and the dependent nature of its welfare policies. If the government were truly concerned about the black man, Bunche main-tained, it would have used the National Recovery Administration to assure "blacks living wages." But this it refused to do; instead, it perpetuated the "inferior economic status of the Negro" by legalizing occupational and geographical wage differentials. In agriculture, where the majority of blacks were employed, the New Deal had even more disastrous effects. The Agricultural Adjustment Administration (AAA) left the black sharecropper and tenant farmer at the mercy of large-scale white farmers; and the subsistence homestead scheme was based on the assumption that the marginal farmer should not be allowed to join the other unemployed masses in urban, industrial centers. The effect of all these policies on black Americans was to ensure future economic and racial isolation.[26]

At the Howard conference, Bunche concluded that the New Deal constituted primarily a "great relief program" that guaranteed at "level best only a precarious livelihood of the most meager essentials for the millions of distressed workers and farmers who are on the outside of our economic life looking in." The Roosevelt administration's approach failed to change any of the traditional racial stereotypes held by white people; and it represented "no significant shift of ideas, traditions or loyalties." "In the nature of the case, [it] could at best do but little for the Negro within the existing social structure"; since blacks could not boast a meaningful middle class, they did not stand to benefit from even "some of the gains made for that class by the New Deal." In the long run, administration planning served only to "crystallize those abuses and oppressions which the exploited Negro citizenry of America have long suffered under laissez-faire capitalism, and for the same reasons as in the past."[27]

At the end of the Howard conference, Bunche joined both John P. Davis, who had served for over three years as gadfly-critic of the New Deal while heading the Joint Committee on National Recovery, and A. Philip Randolph, the black labor leader, as well as a handful of other intellectuals and activists, in creating the National Negro Congress (NNC). His role in forming the congress was one of the few times during the thirties that Bunche ventured into the world of active politics. Yet even here he remained for the most part on the sidelines. Two years after the congress was officially launched, Bunche assumed his research position with Gunnar Myrdal's projected study on black life. From the start, Davis was the major force behind the congress, its chief organizer, and major promoter. By 1940, when Randolph broke with the congress over the issue of communism, Bunche had also become a critic.[28]

Yet, initially, the NNC combined Bunche's dissatisfaction with the New Deal and with traditional black organizations and leadership. He saw the congress as a chance to forge a broad coalition based on the "extra-racial perspective," which he believed was absent in groups like the NAACP. The congress offered a means to join black and white progressive interests, "Negro and white trade unions, religious, civic, and fraternal bodies" that could formulate a comprehensive movement for social, political, and economic change. Such a movement would build on existing black and interracial organizations, reaching into the grass roots of the black community and awakening a "response from the Negro masses."[29] At a time when mass organizations had become "increasingly vital to the preservation of those meager advantages already won for the Negro," he noted in 1936 in a rare public statement on the congress, it was crucial that an intense effort, like that of the NNC, be made to "unite the masses of Negroes behind a definite program."[30]

As Davis and the congress seemed headed in the direction Bunche favored, Bunche remained optimistic about its future. After its first convention in 1936, he commented that the congress was the "first sincere effort to bring together on an equal plane Negro leaders, professional and white collar workers with the Negro manual workers and their leaders and organizers." Even more hopeful, despite what he felt was the NNC's unwise "blanket endorsement" of interracial groups and its inclusion of the "traditional reactionary philosophy of Negro business" in its platform, the convention "held to the incontrovertible truth that the salvation of the American Negro and the solution of all his vital problems is to be found in working-class unity and mass pressure."[31]

The National Negro Congress continued to operate under John P. Davis's leadership until the end of World War II. But before America entered the war, the congress had already ceased to embody the earlier hopes and ambitions that Bunche had held for it. This is not the place for an extended analysis of the rise and fall of the NNC; but understanding Bunche's rapid disillusionment with the congress, as a vehicle for his political and ideological views in the mid 1930s, is important.[32] By the end of the thirties, Bunche had not only broken with the congress but had moderated some of his harsher criticisms of the Roosevelt administration. These two developments are linked and perhaps help explain Bunche's new direction in his career in government and in the United Nations and the significance of his thinking to the struggles of the post-World War II era.

Writing for Swedish sociologist Gunnar Myrdal between 1939 and 1940, Bunche noted certain positive features of the New Deal's impact on black Americans. He praised the participation of black farmers in the Tenant Purchase program and in the cotton referendum elections sponsored by the AAA; he acknowledged benefits blacks received from Social Security, low-income housing, and wage-and-hour legislation. And he viewed the U.S. Supreme Court's upholding of the Wagner Labor Relations Act, Social Security, and the Fair Labor Standards law as doing "more to better the conditions of the Negro than the broadest conceivable decision of his equal rights."[33] He was also more willing than he had been earlier to view black New Deal advisers as a positive force, stating in

1941 that they symbolized a recognition by the Roosevelt administration of black Americans' participation in the national government.[34]

While he moderated some of his views on welfare-state liberalism, Buche stepped up his criticism of the Negro Congress movement. Believing that by 1940 the congress had become dominated by the Communist party and a few industrial unions, he commented, following the congress' third convention, that it had "dug its own grave" and would "now be reduced to a Communist cell."[35] But beyond communism, Bunche's unhappiness with the NNC came from its failure to produce either the organizational structure or the ideological perspective he considered essential to its viability. As early as its first convention, Bunche expressed concern about the "heterogeneous" composition of the congress and its tendency to rally around narrow racial issues. He especially disliked the "race leaders," whom he called "false prophets" and "rabble-rousers," black politicians, preachers, lawyers, and businessmen, who headed many of the NNC's early committees. He warned that the congress might be better served in the future if only labor and working-class organizations were represented. Yet he also acknowledged that if that happened, it was possible that the NNC would lose much of its organizational leadership and other means necessary to reach the black masses.[36]

Likewise, he remained uncomfortable with the racial emphasis that appeared to be the single value that held together the diverse groups that constituted the NNC, criticizing the "assumption that the common denominator of race is enough to weld together, in thought and action, the divergent segments of black America."[37] Yet, when the NNC made attempts to deemphasize race and concentrate primarily on class interests and specific economic programs, divisions quickly surfaced. Bunche appreciated this, as well as the historic and contemporary sources that fed black racial discontent and the consequent need to affirm a common racial integrity; but he remained convinced that purely racial appeals would distort—as it had for him in the past—blacks' awareness of their common economic plight with whites, their need to build grass-roots alliances, and a leadership and philosophy that could force changes in national social and economic policies.

Other factors influenced his political thought in the late 1930s, both his view of the NNC and the New Deal. Unlike more recent converts to the organized labor movement such as Walter White, one reason he was skeptical of the CIO's role in the congress was that he doubted the AFL or the CIO's ability to transcend their historic antipathy toward black workers. Both national organizations, he wrote in 1940, failed to serve the needs of black people. "They are both weak, ridden with factional strife and disputes, controlled by a narrow-minded bureaucracy of professional labor leaders, and more often than not, socially unintelligent."

Of course, he continued to press blacks to join the union struggle, but given what he felt was the structural and ideological weakness of organized labor and the "intensive racial prejudice" that continued to dominate its leadership, he was pessimistic that much would come from their support.[38] "There is no strong labor movement now," he concluded for Myrdal, "and there seems to be little possibility that one will occur in the near future. Nor is there any assurance that either white or black masses would give it sufficient support to build into a real people's movement."[39] Nor, despite his increased praise for the New Deal, did he believe its approach to reform would be enough to overcome the oppressive conditions faced by blacks. In direct challenge to the ideology of white race liberals, he argued: "It is not enough to say that we will solve the pressing economic and political problems of the South and that then the solution of the Negro problem will take care of itself. That simplifies the problem too greatly and affords an easy escape from the embarrassment of the racial problem for a good many glib liberals."[40]

By 1940, Bunche had set forth, for black leaders and organizations, a thirteen-point program in what he referred to as the "People's Movement." But there was little new in his ideas, as the "movement" represented most of the thoughts he had been articulating for some time: grass-roots blacks allied with white working classes; racial myth and prejudice attacked through the common struggle for economic justice; and a mass movement of black and white, constructing a new political base, challenging existing black and white institutions and the shortcomings of liberal national planning. By the end of the thirties, Bunche seemed doubtful that his arguments would gain much support. "The dice which are determining the world's future," he wrote, "and therefore the Negro's as well- -are not in the hands of black men. The Negro alone can do little or nothing to control world events." Blacks could play a "part in shaping the course of events" but only when "allied with other and stronger groups."[41]

As he completed his work for Gunnar Myrdal in 1940, World War II had begun and America was on its way, preparing for its own defense. Bunche supported the efforts of A. Philip Randolph and the March on Washington Movement (MOWM) to secure for blacks a place in the United States' defense system. After attending a meeting with Randolph and others in 1941, he wrote to Walter White that he was "much impressed by the outline of the project [MOWM]. Something of this kind is sorely needed . . . and it will constitute a crucial test for the Negro."[42] With Randolph's ties to the labor movement, the grass-roots focus of MOWM, and the March's goals of economic and military integration, it is not surprising that Bunche was supportive. Yet, unlike some black leaders, he was fearful of the war's impact on black people, especially its potential for spreading fascism in the United States. "As bad as things now are," he warned in 1940, "they can conceivably become far worse. . . . The American Negro will do very well indeed if he is able to hold for the time being the gains he has thus far made under American democracy." If fascism gained ground in America, he had little doubt that "the position of the Negro would be frozen permanently as an inferior racial caste."[43] The future of black Americans, he therefore concluded, rested "with the future of democracy. Negroes, in great numbers, despite the disillusioning imperfections of American democracy and its racial contradictions, now must know that every blow struck on behalf of democracy is a blow for the black man's future."[44] Shortly thereafter, Bunche entered government service, from where he consequently made his way to the United Nations. The rest is a different history.

In 1971, when Dewey W. Grantham published his valuable edition of Bunche's memorandum on the "Political Status of the Negro" (prepared for the Myrdal project), he stated that both the Myrdal project and Bunche's writings were essentially "historical documents" and that Myrdal's study, An American Dilemma, had "become outdated as an approach to the 'Negro problem' ". Still, Grantham went on to note that Bunche's work, as well as Myrdal's Dilemma, were important not simply because of their historical relevance to the 1930s, but because they offered a "perspective" on the "Negro revolution of our own time."[45] A brief comment on that perspective is in order.

It is fair to say that when he left the world of black politics for the arena of international affairs, Bunche was not very optimistic about the opportunities of black Americans in realizing their goals as first-class citizens. By the late thirties, his less qualified praise of the New Deal derived as much from the belief that neither black organizations nor progressive white groups had been successful in shaping an alternative to liberalism as from the belief that the New Deal constituted any salvation for black Americans. Given Bunche's fears about the war's impact at home and abroad, fears consistent with the wide perspective and context of interdependency (in which he always viewed the black struggle), he was understandably cautious and remained concerned about blacks' ability to pursue any separate course of action. Always the tough-minded realist, Bunche concluded in 1940 that one had to work with what was available. Black people "could scarcely think on the basis of what is bad and what is good; we are virtually compelled to make our choice in terms of what is less bad against something much worse." With all its limitations and imperfections for blacks, the New Deal was "less bad" than what had existed before it and without it, things indeed could be "much worse."[46]

What future hope Bunche held seemed based on a similar premise to that of white New Deal liberals: what had begun in the 1930s would be expanded and extended in the years ahead. That assumption was fundamental to the thought of white race liberals like Eleanor Roosevelt and Will Alexander and the advice they gave blacks, especially during the war years. Yet, despite President Harry Truman's greater commitment to civil rights issues than his predecessor, despite his endeavor to maintain the liberalism of the 1930s through his Fair Deal, and despite certain gains blacks achieved from the war—at home and abroad, the years between 1945 and the Eisenhower era of the early 1950s did not augur well for either an extension of reform liberalism or black progress.[47] The Cold War froze not only international relations but much of the impetus for social and political change. Domestic anticommunism produced some of the very effects—on labor, liberal and radical politics, and public tolerance for minorities—that Bunche had feared in 1940 would develop from the spread of a European-style fascism. Unlike the 1930s, the fifties and early sixties witnessed enormous economic and technological growth, expansion of consumer goods, and the centralization of corporate and public institutions. In many respects, the United States had become a much more interdependent society, culturally and economically. Even the South, due primarily to the extension of technology to its agricultural system, began to lose much of its regional economic distinctiveness.[47] But not until the U.S. Supreme Court's momentous *Brown* v. *the Board of Education of Topeka, Kansas* decision of 1954, and after, did this nationalizing trend produce any direct benefits to offset the racial and class oppression of blacks. In fact, despite advantages some blacks secured through entering labor unions during and after the war, despite the continued migration north after 1945, and despite increased participation in the political system, the changes in economic institutions, a growing political conservatism, and social and cultural conformity served to further black isolation, especially for those in the South. The year 1954 altered these circumstances: Joseph McCarthy was censured in the U.S. Senate, the Supreme Court invalidated "separate but equal," and Martin Luther King, Jr. decided to return South to Montgomery, Alabama.

From the Montgomery struggle of 1955–56 (and before) through the advent of the Black Power Movement, blacks and their allies were able to extend greatly gains begun during the 1930s. That was true both for the concrete legislation passed and the easing of the most overt forms of legal and social racism, as it was for change that took place in black and civil rights organizations and liberal politics. Thus, some of the hopes Bunche articulated during an earlier time seemed fulfilled, and certain of his fears did not appear to be realized. And yet, many of the concerns he raised during the New Deal years were just as relevant as they had been earlier.

With Martin Luther King, Jr., and the southern rights struggle he helped lead and certainly came to personify, I would guess that Bunche was much pleased. King was able to give rise to a national movement for social change that, although focused on the racial conditions of black America, was supported by a broad philosophical perspective that viewed the black struggle within the larger context of American life, including international relations. Moreover, King's ability to function as a vital link between black and white communities, incorporating others outside of the black minority into the quest for justice and freedom, was clearly consistent with Bunche's perceptions of leadership and ideology during the 1930s. Also consistent with Bunche's vision was the fact that the civil rights movement was able to energize the masses of black people and that such a movement evolved from and was supported by grass-roots black leaders and organizations.[48] That a black Baptist minister from the Deep South would achieve much of this would not have surprised Bunche, and he would have applauded King's sense that his ministry extended beyond his own regional and racial roots and encompassed all of humankind.

By the mid-1960s, there were in America a variety of forces that Bunche might have seen as a partial extension of his own activities and those of others in the 1930s. The famous March on Washington of 1963 symbolized the link between jobs and racial freedom. Black civil rights organizations, old and new, national and local, formed a solid, unified front for racial change; major legislation affecting the special circumstances of black people had been passed, most notably in the 1964 Civil Rights and 1965 Voting Rights Acts. The Democratic party coalition, formed in the Roosevelt years, seemingly had come to embrace blacks as partners in their politics; and liberal national leaders, in particular Lyndon Baines Johnson, extended the welfare-state policies through an ambitious antipoverty program and other social and economic legislation that owed its support in large measure to the black struggle. Formation of a broad-based coalition of interest groups, extension of liberal reforms that sought to rectify racial inequalities and other forms of economic and social injustice, and an activist local and national black community seemed to embody many of Bunche's prescriptions for change, articulated thirty years before.

Yet, almost as quickly as these forces for change appeared on the American scene, they disappeared. Three years after the famous Selma march in which Bunche participated, the political and social climate had been altered. In 1968, deep divisions existed among the various black and civil rights groups. Black power advocates attacked former white liberal allies and some black leaders with the same intensity with which they denounced their traditional conservative and white racist enemies. Hubert Humphrey's defeat by Richard M. Nixon in the presidential election signified the disaffection and ultimate decline of liberal politics in the late 1960s, from which it has yet to recover. Instead of class and racial coalitions aimed at securing the "beloved community," the United States became a society of deeply divided, competing groups organized around economic, social, and cultural loyalties.[49] The only apparent coalition to emerge by the late 1960s and early 1970s was that which helped send Richard Nixon to the White House in 1968 and reelected him in 1972. Nixon's "new majority" became Ronald Reagan's "moral majority" in the 1980s, and both derived considerable support from a disaffection with New Deal-Great Society policies and an ill-disguised antipathy toward organized labor, blacks, youth, the left, and especially, liberalism.

How might a Ralph Bunche of the 1930s have used his enormous intellectual and political talents to understand these events of the 1960s and 1970s? The presumption is that although he would have clearly dissented from the "racial grove" politics of black nationalism and bemoaned the separatist tendencies of various leaders and groups, he would have understood, as he had earlier, the sources that fostered those attitudes, the anguish and pain that came from the urban black ghettoes. Certainly he would have applauded King's later efforts to create a new coalition of the dispossessed, symbolized by the Poor People's Movement. And he would have given support to the continued efforts of individuals like Bayard Rustin, many of whose ideas were similar to his own, to keep alive the old black rights and progressive white coalition within the Democratic party and to focus on the need for economic change.[50]

Yet, it is probable that Bunche would have not been entirely surprised by the direction in which events of the late 1960s, and thereafter, have taken us. And had he been the Bunche of the New Deal years, his sharpest criticisms would probably have been directed at the rapid departure of white liberals not only from the cause of racial justice but from the broader cause of social, economic, and political equality in American life. What lay at the heart of Bunche's dissent from the New Deal is his sense that Roosevelt had failed to achieve fundamental change in the institutional and structural basis of the United States' political economy. He questioned whether either civil rights laws or limited extension of the social welfare state could achieve real equal opportunity for blacks and other dispossessed peoples in America. Bunche understood that for blacks to join the "mainstream" there needed to be more than simply their inclusion within government programs that offered subsistence but limited possibilities for self-determination. Liberalism, from the New Deal through the Great Society, was constructed on the premise that a mixture of extended social and economic government programs and continued expansion of the economy could eliminate poverty and racial injustice and there would be few, if any, sacrifices other Americans would be required to make. Recall the optimistic predictions by Sargent Shriver and those involved with the War Against Poverty in 1964 and 1965.

But when the black struggle shifted from *de jure* discrimination and segregation to the more difficult areas of economic, political, and institutional inequalities that combined historical patterns of racial and class injustice, the liberal formula—and its support—fell apart. The belief of the thirties—in interdependency and collective self-sacrifice—held limited meaning for the 1960s, when liberals and others celebrated the marriage between economic prosperity and individual opportunity and Lyndon Johnson affirmed, in the midst of the Vietnam War, that Americans could have both guns and butter. But that was not to be the case, and the political and social conservative renaissance that has shown so little concern for the plight of the poor, minorities, and equal rights drew much of its influence from the internal contradictions of the liberal politics of the 1960s.

Like other thinkers of the left, Bunche would have been tough in his criticism of the Great Society's internal flaws. But, unlike so many, he would not have dismissed the Kennedy-Johnson policies as being irrelevant to the cause of black freedom and economic justice. Nor would he have been very patient, however he might have understood it, with the tendency of various groups to withdraw to their own communities and denounce the value of political coalitions. Race was never insignificant to the life or thought of Ralph Bunche, but he argued constantly that preoccupation with it would lead black and white to pursuing the politics of self-deception. Race and class had to be combined, because their history was inextricably linked, in any effort by a minority people to secure the benefits enjoyed by the majority.

Throughout his career, Bunche held consistently to the belief in democratic pluralism, to the notion that all peoples, black and white, Western and non-Western, had the right to participate fully in the society that determined their individual destinies. His emphasis on class and economic forces during the 1930s derived less from dependency on Marxist ideology than on the commitment to a democratic integrationism that was economic and political as well as racial in nature. What shaped that commitment was not so much religion or morals but an abiding faith in reason and in the dignity of the common person. Bunche's personal background, the enormous impact of the Depression and New Deal reform, and his historical sense of the limits of traditional black protest each structured his early political perspective. Yet his ideas were always tempered by the insights derived from social science research and a realistic assessment of black people's circumstances. Bunche believed that black Americans needed alliances and coalitions with others because their special interests demanded, tactically and philosophically, that they join in a common cause with people who stood also to benefit from the struggle to force the United States to be a more just, equal, and open society. His ability to critically analyze the historic and contemporary conditions that challenged that endeavor and to formulate the tactical and organizational means to achieve lasting change characterized his activities as a black radical in the 1930s and his later role as political mediator and UN negotiator after World War II.

Above all, Bunche's politics and social values were shaped by compassion and concern for the little person in society. In many respects, he never lost that perspective. In 1959, he and his son were turned down by the prestigious West Side Tennis Club in New York for membership and then suddenly offered entrance when the club realized who Bunche was. But Bunche refused the offer, commenting that "No Negro American can be free from the disabilities of race in this country until the lowliest Negro in Mississippi is no longer disadvantaged because of his race."[51] It seems likely that he would have extended that to say that no person is free, regardless of their race or class, until all are free. It also seems likely that whatever it would take to get us there, Ralph Bunche would have offered his support—along with his criticism. That we are still caught up in many of the same debates indicates that we can continue to profit from what he had to tell us in the age of the Great Depression and the New Deal.

Notes

1. Ralph J. Bunche, "The Programs of Organizations Devoted to the Improvement of the Status of the American Negro," *Journal of Negro Education* 8 (July 1939): 550.

2. Bunche's major writings during the 1930s and early 1940s include: "Black and White Education," *Journal of Negro Education* 5 (July 1936): 351–58; "A Critical Analysis of the Tactics and Programs of Minority Groups," *Journal of Negro Education* 4 (July 1935): 308–20; "Critique of New Deal Social Planning as it Affects Negroes," *Journal of Negro Education* (January 1936): 59–65; "The Negro in the Political Life of the United States," *Journal of Negro Education* 10 (July 1941): 567–84; "Triumph–or Fiasco?" *Race*, I (Summer 1936): 93–96; and "Programs of Organizations," 539–50. See also Bunche, *A World View of Race* (Washington, D.C., 1936). For the Myrdal project, Bunche's memorandums are: "A Brief and Tentative Analysis of Negro Leadership," "Conceptions and Ideologies of the Negro Problem," "Extended Memorandum on the Programs, Ideologies, Tactics, and Achievements of Negro Betterment and Interracial Organization," and "The Political Status of the Negro with Emphasis on the South and Comparative Treatment of the 'Poor White'" (Unpublished memorandums for the Car-

negie-Myrdal Study: New York, 1940). Parts of these works, with emphasis on the South, are published in Bunche, *The Political Status of the Negro in the Age of F.D.R.*, ed. Dewey W. Grantham (Chicago: Univ. of Chicago Press, 1973).

3. For a general discussion of Harris, Davis, et al, see John B. Kirby, *Black Americans in the Roosevelt Era: Liberalism and Race* (Knoxville: University of Tennessee, 1980), especially, Chaps. 6–8. Also, Nancy J. Weiss, *Farewell to the Party of Lincoln* (Princeton: Princeton University Press, 1983), Harvard Sitkoff, *A New Deal for Blacks: The Emergence of Civil Rights as a National Issue* (New York: Oxford University Press, 1978), and Raymond Wolters, *Negroes and the Great Depression* (Westport, Conn.: Greenwood, 1970). Robert Weaver reflects on Bunche's ties to some of the members of the Black Cabinet and his Harvard friendship with William Hastie in Robert Weaver Interview by Joe B. Frantz, 19 November 1968, 7, Lyndon B. Johnson Library Oral History Collection.

4. Hill in *New York Times*, 5 April 1931. Gunnar Myrdal, *An American Dilemma: The Negro Problem and Modern Democracy*, 2nd ed., 2 vols. (New York: Harper & Row, 1962), I, Part 4, has some good data and description on black economic conditions prior to and during the Depression. See especially chaps. 11–13. Charles S. Johnson, *Shadow of the Plantation* (Chicago: Univ. of Chicago Press, 1934) is solid on rural conditions for blacks in the South. See also the National Urban League, *The Forgotten Tenth: An Analysis of Unemployment Among Negroes and its Social Costs, 1932–1933* (New York, 1933).

5. For discussion of the Communist and Socialist parties and their relationship to civil rights issues and black people in the 1930s, see Sitkoff, *New Deal for Blacks*, especially chapter 6; Kirby, *Black Americans in the Roosevelt Era*, pp. 87–90, 152–54; Charles H. Martin, *The Angelo Herndon Case and Southern Justice* (Baton Rouge: Louisiana State Univ. Press, 1976): Mark Naison, *Communists in Harlem during the Depression* (Urbana: Univ. of Illinois Press, 1983). Still helpful but less balanced accounts are William A. Nolan, *Communism Versus the Negro* (Chicago: H. Regnery Co., 1951); Wilson Record, *The Negro and the Communist Party* (Ithaca: Cornell University Press, 1964).

6. For background and analysis of the NAACP and NUL prior to and during the 1930s, see Nancy J. Weiss, *The National Urban League, 1910–1940* (New York: Oxford Univ. Press, 1974); Guichard Parris and Lester Brooks, *Blacks in the City: A History of the National Urban League* (Boston: Little, Brown, 1971); B. Joyce Ross, *J. E. Spingarn and the Rise of the NAACP, 1911–1939* (New York: Atheneum, 1972); August Meier and Elliott Rudwick, eds., *Along the Color Line: Explorations in the Black Experience* (Urbana: Univ. of Illinois Press, 1976); and Robert L. Zangrando, *The NAACP Crusade Against Lynching, 1909–1950* (Philadelphia: 1980).

7. August Meier and Elliott Rudwick, "The Origins of Nonviolent Direct Action in Afro-American Protest: A Note on Historical Discontinuities," in Meier and Rudwick, *Along the Color Line*, pp. 314–32; Bunche, "Critical Analysis of the Tactics and Programs," pp. 313–14. For a recent discussion of Chicago, see Christopher Robert Reed, "A Study of Black Politics and Protest in Depression-Decade Chicago, 1930–1939" (Unpublished Ph.D. diss., Kent State University, 1982).

8. General discussion of the New Deal and black Americans can be found in sources noted in note 3 above.

9. Kirby, *Black Americans in the Roosevelt Era,* passim.
10. Henry Agard Wallace, *New Frontiers* (New York: Reynal & Hitchcock, 1934), p. 254.
11. Harold L. Ickes, "The Negro as Citizen," *Crisis* 18 (August 1936): 231.
12. For discussion of racial liberalism and the ideas summarized here, see Kirby, *Black Americans in the Roosevelt Era,* chaps. 2–4, 9.
13. Ibid., pp. 189–97; Wolters, *Negroes and the Great Depression,* pp. 248–58; W. E. B. Du Bois, "Social Planning for the Negro: Past and Present," *Journal of Negro Education* 5 (January 1936): 110–25 and, "The Position of the Negro in the American Social Order: Where Do We Go From Here?," *Journal of Negro Education* 8 (July 1939): 351–70.
14. For black criticisms of Du Bois, see E. Franklin Frazier, "The Du Bois Program in the Present Crisis," *Race* 1 (Winter 1935–1936): 11–12; Abram Harris, *The Negro as Capitalist: A Study of Banking and Business Among American Negroes* (Philadelphia: American Academy of Political & Social Science, 1936), p. 180; Wolters, *Negroes and the Great Depression,* pp. 244–258; James O. Young, *Black Writers of the Thirties* (Baton Rouge: Louisiana State University Press, 1973), Chap. 2.
15. Bunche, "Brief and Tentative Analysis of Negro Leadership," pp. 25, 195; "Programs, Ideologies, Tactics," pp. 23–203, 391–92; "Critical Analysis of Tactics and Programs," p. 314.
16. Bunche, "Programs, Ideologies, Tactics," pp. 8, 393–424, 440, 783.
17. Ibid., p. 773.
18. Ibid., p. 777.
19. Ibid., pp. 103, 112–39; Also see Bunche, "Critical Analysis of Tactics and Programs" and "Critique of New Deal Social Planning."
20. Bunche, "Programs, Ideologies, Tactics," pp. 78, 159; "Critical Analysis of Tactics and Programs," p. 310.
21. Bunche, "Tentative Analysis of Negro Leadership," p. 195.
22. Ibid., pp. 25, 195.
23. Bunche, "Programs, Ideologies, Tactics," p. 778; "Programs of Organizations Devoted to the Improvement."
24. Bunche, "Critique of New Deal Social Planning," p. 62.
25. Ibid., pp. 61–63.
26. Ibid., pp. 61–64.
27. Ibid., pp. 65, 60, 65.
28. For general discussion of the Negro Congress and issues noted here, see Kirby, *Black Americans in the Roosevelt Era,* Chap. 8.
29. Bunche, "Programs, Ideologies, Tactics," pp. 319–20.
30. Bunche, "Triumph—or Fiasco?," p. 93.
31. Ibid., pp. 93–95.
32. The most comprehensive analysis of the congress is John Baxter Streater, "The National Negro Congress, 1936–1947" (Ph.D. diss., University of Cincinnati, 1981). Other discussions of the congress can be found in Kirby, *Black Americans in the Roosevelt Era,* Chap. 7: Wolters, *Negroes and the Great Depression,* pp. 353–82; Sitkoff, *New Deal for Blacks,* Chapter 10; Lawrence S. Wittner, "The National Negro Congress: A Reassessment," *American Quarterly* 22 (Winter 1970): 883–901; and Naison, *Communists in Harlem,* Chap. 7.
33. Bunche, "Negro in the Political Life," p. 577; "Political Status of the Negro," pp. 1052, 1530–31.

34. Bunche, "Negro in the Political Life," p. 580; "Political Status of the Negro," pp. 1455–59.
35. Bunche, "Programs, Ideologies, Tactics," p. 369.
36. Bunche, "Triumph—or Fiasco?," pp. 95–96, and "Programs, Ideologies, Tactics," p. 354.
37. Bunche, "Programs, Ideologies, Tactics," pp. 354–55.
38. Ibid., pp. 787, 780.
39. Ibid., p. 135.
40. Ibid., p. 777. On his general view of whites in interracial struggles, see Ibid., 559–60.
41. Bunche, "Tentative Analysis of Negro Leadership," p. 197.
42. Bunche to Walter White, May 1, 1941, NAACP Papers, unprocessed, File B-220.
43. Bunche, "Programs, Ideologies, Tactics," 788–90.
44. Bunche, "Negro in the Political Life," 582.
45. Grantham, ed., *Political Status of the Negro in the Age of FDR*, xxix–xxx.
46. Quoted in Charles Radford Lawrence, "Negro Organizations in Crisis: Depression, New Deal, World War II," (Ph.D. diss., Columbia University, 1953), p. 317.
47. On the Truman and Eisenhower eras, see William Berman, *The Politics of Civil Rights in the Truman Administration* (Columbus, Ohio: Ohio State University Press, 1970); Barton J. Bernstein, "The Ambiguous Legacy: The Truman Administration and Civil Rights," in Bernstein, ed., *Politics and Policies of the Truman Administration* (Chicago: Quadrangle, 1970), 269–314; Alonzo E. Hamby, *Beyond the New Deal: Harry S. Truman and American Liberalism* (New York: Columbia Univ. Press, 1973); Robert Frederick Burk, *The Eisenhower Administration and Black Civil Rights* (Knoxville: University of Tennessee Press, 1984). On changes in the economy of the South, see James C. Cobb, *The Selling of the South: The Southern Crusade for Industrial Development, 1936–1980* (Baton Rouge: Louisiana State Univ. Press, 1982).
48. There are numerous studies on King, but see especially David L. Lewis, *King: A Biography* (Urbana: Univ. of Illinois Press, 1978); Stephen B. Oates, *Let the Trumpet Sound: The Life of Martin Luther King, Jr.* (New York: Harper & Row, 1982); and Hanes Walton, Jr., *The Political Philosophy of Martin Luther King, Jr.* (Westport: Greenwood, 1971). On the black struggle and black masses, see in particular August Meier and Elliott Rudwick, *CORE: A Study in the Civil Rights Movement* (Urbana: Univ. of Illinois Press, 1973); Clayborne Carson, *SNCC and the Black Awakening of the 1960s* (Cambridge: Harvard University Press, 1981); and Aldon D. Morris, *The Origins of the Civil Rights Movement: Black Communities Organizing for Change* (New York: Free Press, 1984).
49. Useful general analysis of the 1960s and the disintegration of liberal politics can be found in Allen J. Matusow, *The Unraveling of America: A History of Liberalism in the 1960s* (New York: Harper & Row, 1984); Godfrey Hodgson, *America in our Time* (New York: Doubleday, 1976); Frederick F. Siegel, *Troubled Journey: From Pearl Harbor to Ronald Reagan* (New York: Hill & Wang, 1984); and William H. Chafe, *The Unfinished Journey: America Since World War II* (New York: Oxford University Press, 1986).
50. A comparison of the ideas and politics of Bunche in the 1930s and those of Bayard Rustin in the last few decades would be especially enlightening.

Examples of some of Rustin's thought can be found in Rustin, *Strategies for Freedom: The Changing Patterns of Black Protest* (New York: Columbia University Press, 1976) and, " 'Black Power and Coalition Politics," *Commentary* 43 (September 1966): 35–40; "The Failure of Black Separatism," *Harper's* 211 (January 1970), 25–34; "From Protest to Politics: The Future of the Civil Rights Movement," *Commentary* 39 (February 1965): 25–31.

51. *New York Times,* 10 December 1971.

· 3 ·

CIVIL RIGHTS AND NATIONAL SECURITY: The Case of Ralph Bunche

Charles P. Henry

On 23 February 1963, Ralph Bunche delivered an address to the Virginia Council on Human Relations in Richmond. The speech was picketed by ten boys who belonged to the order of *Demolay,* a junior masonic group. They carried placards that read "Bunche for Communism" and "Free America."

This incident was significant in a number of ways. It reminded the general public of Bunche's national and international stature at a time when younger black leaders were the focus of national attention. The placards used to attack Bunche's radical past attracted the attention of the Federal Bureau of Investigation. They also pursued the pattern of red-baiting blacks who challenged the status-quo. Finally, the picketing, and the newspaper editorial that provoked it, drew an uncharacteristically emotional response from Bunche.

The day before Bunche's speech, the editor of the *Richmond News Leader,* segregationist James J. Kilpatrick, had accused Bunche of bias toward socialism and internationalism in an editorial. In supporting his charges, Kilpatrick dragged up "Dr. Bunche's procommunist record in the years previous to 1940." This record included his Marxist-oriented articles in the *Journal of Negro Education* and his booklet *A World View of*

Race, which was praised by black communist Abner Berry. Also mentioned was his role in founding the National Negro Congress (NNC) and his association with the Marxist journal *Science and Society,* the Institute for Pacific Relations, and Alger Hiss.

Denying that he had ever been a communist or a supporter of communism, Bunche attacked Kilpatrick's well-known belief in black inferiority. He went on to challenge those whites who would say he was isolated from racial discrimination because of his preeminence:

> They are surprised when I tell them that I am more directly and more emotionally involved with the problem of the status of the Negro now than I have ever been. Why? What they say about my daily contacts with the rougher impacts of segregation and discrimination is true, of course. Even so, when I go to Birmingham to speak, or to Atlanta, as I did for the NAACP last June, I can't get a hotel room (Dinkler Plaza) . . . Gromyko would be welcome, but I wouldn't.[1]

Bunche went on to recall many humiliating and degrading experiences in his past. Furthermore, he stated that he would not speak at the centennial celebrations of the Emancipation Proclamation because there was nothing to celebrate. He concluded with an imaginary dialogue between himself and a white listener, ending with the following lines: "And then, invariably, I stop and say, what the devil, it's all so utterly absurd. There's no place for reason here because it's all too irrational and emotional and nonsensical. . . . Anyone who exposes his prejudices to thought and reason, however, will soon see them dissolve."[2]

The Richmond incident illustrates the two major themes of this section. First, Bunche's radical, class-oriented perspective cannot be separated from his race or from the issue of civil rights. Secondly, by viewing race from a worldwide perspective, Bunche was able to achieve an international stature that seemingly placed him beyond the civil rights struggle in the United States. As in the case of Martin Luther King, it has become fashionable to glorify the later Bunche while ignoring his early radicalism. In fact, Bunche's views on race and human rights remained consistent, and only the strategies for achieving self-determination changed.

The Radical Bunche

From roughly 1929 to 1940, Bunche took a Marxist-oriented approach to racial problems, citing capitalism and imperialism as the basic causes of racial oppression. The most well-known expressions of these views are his "Critique of New Deal Social Planning as it Affects Negroes," which was first delivered at a conference at Howard University in 1935 and published a year later in the *Journal of Negro Education* and in his booklet *A World View of Race* (1936). The latter work was based on Bunche's award-winning Harvard dissertation, comparing the League of Nations' mandate system of colonial administration in Togoland to French colonial administration in Dahomey. Using an approach based on economic determinism, Bunche found little difference between the two types of administration. This finding would become important in shaping Bunche's views on self-determination as reflected in the trusteeship system he developed during the establishment of the United Nations. While there is some debate over the pioneering character of Bunche's approach, there seems to be little doubt that he used it for pragmatic rather than strictly ideological reasons.[3] According to Lawrence Finkelstein, economic determinism countered the prevalent myths of racial difference and racial hierarchy, which were firmly opposed by Bunche. The fact that Bunche relied on generalizations to counter these myths may explain his pursuit of anthropology in his postdoctoral work.

As early as 1929 Bunche had produced a sophisticated unpublished paper entitled "Marxism and the Negro Question." In it he labels the caste status of the American black as "essentially precapitalist survival, a 'relic of feudalism'. But such precapitalist survivals find a welcome place in the decaying structure of capitalism in its final imperialist monopolistic epoch." Along with Lenin, he viewed black Americans as a subject caste based on race. Often agreeing with Marx, Bunche said that the "ruling ideas of any age are the ideas of the ruling class." Thus, "race prejudice establishes its hegemony and is absorbed by the other classes of society," which accounts for the racism of white American workers and farmers.[4] Black society resembles "a colony or a subjected nation," but increasing class differentiation among Negroes is fortunately destroying "any possible 'racial unity' of all classes." Although Bunche called on the communist to defend the interests of black workers and peasants, he said their demands are in all respects akin to the classical ideals of the bourgeois—democratic revolution, the Great French Revolution, for example. Not a single one is a specifically socialist demand—not one necessarily implies the socialization of all the means of production.[5] In a 1936 speech to the City-wide Young People's Forum in Philadelphia, Bunche referred to W. E. B. Du Bois as "a tired, frustrated ex-radical whose racial chauvinism pitted black workers against white workers." Bunche cited his own membership in Local 440 of the American Federation of Teachers, which he regarded as a model of an integrated trade union that supported the black struggle. This union had already engaged in combat with the segregation policies of the National Theater in Washington D.C. and on the Ellenbogen rent bill.[6]

Buche's radicalism can be traced primarily to the influence of friends and colleagues at Howard University. Howard was a unique black institution in the thirties. Under the leadership of President Mordecai Johnson, a remarkable group of black scholars was assembled, and intellectual stimulation was supreme. Johnson was unlike many black college administrators of the day. His faculty members often had different life-styles or serious personal problems. And he was criticized by government officials for permitting Communists to speak on campus. The result was a "black Athens" that attracted such intellectual lights as Abram Harris, Sterling Brown, E. Franklin Frazier, Charles Thompson, Alain Locke, Charles Wesley, Ernest Just and, of course, Ralph Bunche. Harris, Brown, Frazier, Locke, Bunche, and Emmet Dorsey were particularly close and often met at Bunche's house, which was on campus. While Harris was seen as the intellectual leader of the group, Bunche was viewed as the most accessible to students. Bunche had been called a "democratic or British socialist" and an "intellectual Trotskyite"; however, his leftist views seemed far from orthodox. He and his colleagues at Howard distrusted the "black bourgeoisie," but they had no illusions about the masses or unions. Race and class were inseparable components of their approach.[7]

Student protest was not always viewed as favorably by the administration as intellectual curiosity (Howard was heavily dependent on federal appropriations). However, Bunche remained supportive of student actions on behalf of civil rights. These included, in 1934, protests against segregation in the House of Representatives' dining room and against the failure of the Attorney General to take action against lynching. Congress struck back. In 1935 it began an investigation of radicalism at Howard, and the students, inevitably, protested the investigation. Bunche's support of student demonstrations and his own activism, which served as an example for the students, made him the subject of governmental investigations as well. In fact, the Federal Bureau of Investigation conducted three major investigations of Bunche over a period of eighteen years.

The FBI Investigations

In 1942, apparently as a condition of his employment in the Division of Special Information of the Library of Congress, Bunche was investigated by the FBI under the Internal Security-Hatch Act. The results of this investigation showed that he was associated with various organizations listed by the government as communist fronts in the 1930s and 1940s. However, the report stated that Bunche had since resigned any affiliations with these groups.

The major findings of the investigation included the following meetings. In 1934 Bunche took part in a conference of the Civil Liberties Union that was attended by well-known Communists. It was also alleged that a year later, at Howard, Bunche participated in a student strike, opposed by university officials, against war.[8] In 1936 Bunche attended a meeting of the Scottsboro Defense Committee, allegedly questioning the role of the Supreme Court in dealing fairly with the Scottsboro case and commenting that a united front by the masses was the only means for achieving justice.[9] Also in 1936, Bunche attended a meeting of the National Negro Congress (NNC). (This meeting played a major role in subsequent investigations but was not given much attention in the 1942 investigation.) Bunche also attended a meeting of the Washington Committee for Democratic Action (WCDA) in 1939. Then, in 1942, he was identified as a member of the International Committee on African Affairs (ICCA).

Bunche's response to these allegations and findings indicated that he opposed the procommunist influence in these organizations and had resigned from further association with them. Specifically, he resigned from the National Negro Congress and the International Committee on African Affairs when Max Yergan assumed the leadership role in both.[10] Bunche said he had attended only one meeting of the WCDA in order to hear a discussion by the congressional sponsors of current anti-lynching and civil rights legislation.

In an interview with the FBI, Bunche cited his article "Triumph—or Fiasco?" in *Race,* which pointed out the contradictions in the National Negro Congress. He stated that he was out of the country on a Social Science Research Council Fellowship in 1936 and 1937 and had nothing to do with the NNC. Bunche stated that when he attempted to attend the 1940 national meeting to gather material for the Carnegie Study, NNC's Executive Secretary John P. Davis objected to his presence. Bunche then referred to his scathing attack on the NNC in the Carnegie Study and produced a Howard University news article on an anticommunist speech he had given on 16 July 1940.[11]

Several persons interviewed during the 1942 investigation said that while they had some doubts concerning Bunche's sympathies in the early or middle thirties, he was now a strong opponent of communism. The results of the report were given to the Librarian of Congress, Archibald MacLeish, who in May 1942 said Bunche "received complete exoneration."[12]

At the height of the McCarthy era, federal officials undertook a more intense and prolonged investigation of Bunche's radical past. In February of 1953, the FBI began an investigation under the United Nations Loyalty Program, mandated in Executive Order 10422 at the request of the Department of State. Bunche appeared before the Senate Committee on the Judiciary in March, 1953, and denied affiliations with the Communist party. The results of this probe were furnished to the Civil Service Commission in April 1953. On 28 May 1954, the investigation culminated in a sometimes heated hearing before the International Organizations Employee Loyalty Board that lasted nearly twelve hours. Bunche's was one of only thirty-two cases that were heard by the board out of the 1,700 Americans covered by Eisenhower's executive order. Bunche chose Ernest A. Gross, former deputy chief representative of the United States at the United Nations, to represent him. Shortly after the hearing the board rendered a "favorable loyalty determination" in regard to Bunche.

As with the investigation of 1942, most of the attention during the investigation seemed to focus on the role Bunche played in co-founding the National Negro Congress.[13] However, this time the investigation included the allegations of two former black Communists, Leonard Patterson and Manning Johnson, who placed Bunche at a meeting of the communist faction planning the NNC. At least one source stated that Bunche was introduced by the well-known black Communist Harry Haywood as a fellow Communist party member. This source also suggested that Bunche had worked undercover with top black leaders of the Communist party in order to gain greater black support and to avoid antagonizing NNC President A. Philip Randolph, a devout socialist.

These revelations led the FBI to consider a perjury charge against Bunche, on the grounds that he had denied Communist party membership in testimony before the Senate Subcommittee on Internal Security (the Jenner Committee) on 12 March 1953. On 2 July 1954, FBI and Justice Department officials met to discuss the perjury charge. Apparently, the testimony of John P. Davis and other former Communists supporting Bunche's denial prevented the FBI from going further. Investigators also found it difficult to get witnesses who were critical of Bunche to testify before the Hearing Board, because either these witnesses feared the reaction of friends and neighbors or did not want to destroy Bunche's career.

Several new charges were also leveled against Bunche during the 1953–54 investigation. He was listed as a contributing editor to the Marxist journal *Science and Society* from 1936 to 1940, although no actual contributions by Bunche to the journal were produced. Bunche was a 1940 candidate for vice-president of the AFL Teachers Union in Washington, which was considered communist-influenced. However, he ran on an anti-communist ticket against Doxy Wilkerson. And in 1947 a letterhead listed Bunche as a member of the District of Columbia committee of the Southern Conference for Human Welfare, which was founded in 1938 with the help of Eleanor Roosevelt for the purpose of alleviating the economic and social plight of poor blacks and whites in the South. From 1942 to 1945, Bunche was a member of the Institute of Pacific Relations and had been considered for a top staff position. Ironically, he had attended several of the institute's major conferences as a representative of the State Department. All of these organizations were identified by the government as communist fronts.

Perhaps Bunche's most damaging contacts involved persons he met in the State Department. The most well-known was Alger Hiss, whom Bunche had worked under in the early forties and had used as a reference when he moved to the UN. When Hiss was attacked for being a Communist in 1948, his former colleague wrote a strong letter of support. It said in part, "[T]he gallant fight you are making is on behalf of the integrity and reputation of every decent American . . . [and] I want you to know that I am in your corner." Sources said that Bunche later criticized Hiss and the damage he had done to the State Department. In his own defense, Bunche said he assumed Hiss was loyal since he had a higher secrecy clearance than Bunche himself.[14]

A similar event involving guilt-by-association occurred when a UN employee working with Bunche, Jack S. Harris, refused to answer questions before the Loyalty Board concerning his own possible communist ties. Bunche had worked with Harris at the State Department and had recommended him to the UN. Meanwhile, Bunche countered that he had hired Harris solely for his expertise.[15] Harris was eventually given $10,000 to compensate for his lost employment.

Despite Bunche's past associations, most of those interviewed described Bunche as a loyal American and a strong anticommunist. Among those attesting to Bunche's anticommunism was black communist leader Abner Berry, who contrasted the views of Bunche in 1950 with those in the mid-thirties, when he had praised Bunche. In a *Daily Worker* article he wrote that "[i]t is almost certain that if Dr. Ralph J. Bunche had fulfilled the promise of his brilliant and honest early years he would not be the proud possessor of the 1950 Nobel Peace Prize. In earning the Nobel Peace Prize for his service to the Western imperialist war makers, he has thoroughly exposed his retreat from the struggle for world freedom." He goes on to cite W. E. B. Du Bois when he said: "Perhaps then it was a counsel of perfection to have hoped that Ralph Bunche would have stood fast for justice, freedom, and the good faith of nations and his race—perhaps; but God knows I wish he had."[16] Bunche did little to assuage Du Bois' lament. On the contrary, he openly stressed the anticommunist tone of his writings. One notices a stronger anticommunist, pro-American emphasis in his many speeches following the Loyalty Board hearing. Of course, he remained opposed to McCarthyism and the hysteria it created.

A final investigation of Bunche was begun on 8 December 1960. The probe was requested by White House Assistant Lawrence O'Brien in connection with possible top-level appointments to be made by President Kennedy. If Bunche had lost such admirers as Abner Berry and W. E. B. Du Bois in the fifties, he added such notables as W. Averell Harriman,

John D. Rockefeller III, and David Rockefeller, all of whom believed Bunche a loyal American capable of performing any top-level assignment. In fact, Harriman stated that he suggested Truman appoint Bunche under-secretary of state. Among those interviewed was William Hastie, who had known Bunche since 1927 and had stated that Bunche was very critical of the Soviets and their leadership.

Another person interviewed in 1960 was Ernest Gross, who had defended Bunche at the 1954 Loyalty Board hearing. Gross contended that the 1954 hearing was brought about by persons who were jealous of Bunche's position and success. Harry Gideonse, president and chair of the board of Freedom House for twenty-one years, stated that Bunche had served as vice-president of that strongly anticommunist organization on several occasions.

No substantial new charges of communist links were uncovered in the 1960 FBI investigation. Ironically, the post Bunche was rumored to have been considered for was ambassador to the Soviet Union. Although Bunche was highly recommended by almost all of those persons interviewed, President Kennedy did not appoint him. It is impossible to determine whether Bunche's past associations and activities played a role in Kennedy's decision; nor is there any evidence that Bunche would have accepted the position if it had been offered.

The official investigations of Bunche confirm the impressions left by his early writings and speeches that he was heavily influenced by Marx. His early work also indicates a strong independent streak and distrust of any orthodoxy or party line. Any contact he may have had with the Communist party or front organizations was directed primarily at promoting the economic and political rights of blacks. When Communist party domination became apparent, Bunche withdrew his cooperation. It seems equally clear that by 1950, when he won the Nobel Peace Prize, Bunche had moderated his criticism of the United States and had intensified his anti-Soviet views. This transition, however, seems to have had little impact on the FBI, which seriously considered bringing Bunche before a grand jury on possible perjury charges.

A Worldwide Perspective on Civil Rights

By working for the United Nations, Bunche undoubtedly believed he was working for racial justice within a worldwide perspective. His speeches invariably link the international struggle for human rights and peace to the black struggle for civil rights. He had escaped limitations that would have been placed on him were he working for the U.S. State Department. Yet, in a very real sense, he had risen above race and was not viewed as a participant in the domestic struggle. Three examples will serve to illustrate this point.

In a speech entitled "Prejudice in World Perspective" delivered on 24 April 1954, in Grand Rapids, Michigan, Bunche recalled many racial incidents. One involved a dinner in New York, given by former UN Secretary-General Trygve Lie. Sitting next to Bunche was an American woman who was married to a European industrialist. They got into an involved conversation over the merit of equality for blacks. Finally she said, "You know Mr. Bunche, I've heard all that before. That's old stuff. I don't believe it and neither do you." She then said, "Let's get at the heart of this. A while ago you said you had two daughters. Now tell me, Mr. Bunche, would you wish your two daughters to marry Negroes?" When Bunche recovered from his astonishment, he said he could not object because he was a Negro and so were his daughters. Without a pause she said, "Yes, but you're different."

Another incident involved a speaking engagement at the University of Arkansas that Bunche agreed to only on the condition that the audience would not be segregated. After he spent two pleasant, integrated days in Fayetteville, one of his hosts told him how much trouble he had caused. He said that after they had agreed to Bunche's condition they realized that there were only a couple of hundred blacks in the whole county, "and they're sharecroppers and tenant farmers and they wouldn't come to hear Booker T. Washington, much less you, lecture." To avoid the embarrassment of having Bunche think he was tricked into speaking before an all-white audience, the faculty sent runners some 250 miles to Pine Bluff and Little Rock to round up blacks to attend Bunche's lecture. Bunche concluded that "those Negroes who had to travel over those hard Ozark mountain roads 250 miles each way to hear me lecture would probably be hating me for the rest of their lives."[17]

Recalling that Martin Luther King, Jr., said that Birmingham was the most segregated city in the South, one final example of Bunche's status is appropriate. On 13 February 1959, Bunche addressed the Periclean Club of that city. He recalled racial incidents from his youth and urged his listeners never to run from a fight for principles. There was, he said, no better place than Birmingham to point out that this is not a white man's world, that only one-third of it is white. And he said the country cannot afford any more Little Rocks and blacks had waited long enough. Thus, he criticized television newscaster Chet Huntley for urging blacks to stop their pressure and court appeals. Blacks are winning against the odds "because we are *right*." Bunche concluded by reaffirming his ancestry. Ironically, Bunche was refused a room at Birmingham's Dinkler-Tutwiler Hotel during his visit. Even more ironic, given Birmingham's segregation policies, was the mayor honoring Bunche with the key to the city.[18] Apparently it did not open hotel room doors!

On 3 March 1965, a slightly indignant Ralph Bunche responded to a letter from Margaret Allen and Agnes Cross, asking why he had not been more involved in the civil rights struggle. "For your information," said Bunche, "I have been involved in the civil rights struggle all my adult life, and I believe that there are only a few Negroes—and these were the leaders such as Du Bois, James Weldon Johnson, Walter White, A. Philip Randolph, Roy Wilkins, Martin Luther King, and James Farmer—whose voices were heard on the issue more than mine."[19] Indeed, the historical record confirms Bunche's assertion. In fact, Bunche's position was often given in advance of some of the leaders he cited. Moreover, not being the head of any rival organization, he was able to communicate with and support all of these leaders, except Du Bois.

Historical hindsight also reveals several shortcomings in Bunche's vision of the future. In a speech entitled the "Young Negro," delivered in Los Angeles in either 1926 or 1927, a very young Ralph Bunche attacked blind loyalty to either political party saying: "[The] New Negro . . . is thinking in terms of *men* and *merits!*" He castigated blacks who accepted separate parks, schools, and pools and, in language more appropriate to Los Angeles forty years later, states: "Whatever may be the attitude of you older people toward this dastardly practice of insolently slapping the Race in the face, I can tell in all sincerity that there is a violently smoldering fire of indignation among those of us who are younger in years and who have not yet become inured to such insults."[20] About that same time Bunche engaged in his first picket line.

During his radical days at Howard in the thirties, he took part in a well-publicized demonstration against the segregated seating policy of the National Theater in Washington. A temporary victory was achieved.[21] And under the auspices of the Washington Youth Committee of the NNC, Bunche chaired a united action campaign against the segregation policies of the Hecht Department Store in 1936.[22]

Bunche was aware of the Indian leader Mahatma Gandhi and the nonviolent methods he used long before Martin Luther King. During a panel discussion entitled "The Power of Non-Violence" sponsored by the Women's International League for Peace and Freedom in 1935, Bunche noted that minorities cannot use violence successfully. Even strikes were undependable when the government was used to break them. Moreover, complete noncooperation, said Bunche, was a new but unworkable tactic. A year later, at the City-Wide Young People's Forum in Philadelphia, he dismissed such tactics as violence, emigration, passive resistance, self-segregation, civil libertarianism, and goodwill. First, he said, one must fight *war* and *fascism.* Second, one must actively and energetically participate in developing a militant American labor movement.[23]

By 1950, as we have seen, Bunche's radicalism had mellowed; however, his view of rights remained broad. In a letter to Alma Booker he wrote, "I believe firmly in women's rights. I have often in my speeches emphasized that the status of women in most parts of the world is similar to that of an underprivileged minority group."[24] The following year, 1951, Bunche journeyed to Atlanta to address the forty-second annual convention of the NAACP. He stated that "no Negro however high he may think he has risen, no matter how much wealth he has amassed, is worth very much if he forgets his own people and holds himself aloof from the unrelenting struggle for full Negro emancipation." Bunche went on to argue that segregation by law "demeans the white southerner as well as the Negro." The white southerner, said Bunche, really did not know the "good Nigras" of the South. According to Bunche, the pace of progress had to be greatly accelerated. "It is not time that will solve the Negro problem; there is not time to wait, in any event."[25] That acceleration was to come faster than perhaps even Bunche anticipated.

Three years after his speech to the NAACP in Atlanta Bunche addressed the annual meeting of the NAACP again, this time in Dallas. Commenting on the momentous *Brown* decision by the U.S. Supreme Court, Bunche was unduly optimistic. He believed it would be implemented because Americans were law-abiding. In contrast to the views he had expressed while working on the Carnegie Study,[26] he now referred to the instinctive democratic impulses of southern whites: "I am quite convinced that there are a great many citizens of the South who are restrained only by the laws from giving expression to their instinctive democratic impulses as regards relations with their darker fellowmen." He added that "the problem of race is now less a problem of economics and politics than it used to be and more a problem of our minds, our thinking and concepts."[27]

Commitment to the Domestic Struggle for Civil Rights

Both Martin Luther King, Jr. and Ralph Bunche were overly optimistic about the role "good" southern whites would play in the coming struggle.[28] However, neither one withdrew from combat when white support failed to materialize. Shortly after a bus boycott began in Montgomery, Alabama, Bunche sent King a telegram that read in part: "I greatly admire and warmly congratulate you all. I know that you will continue strong in spirit and that you will stand firm and united in the face of threats and resorts to police-state methods of intimidation. Right is on your side and all the world knows it."[29] Bunche met King three months later when he introduced King as the main speaker at the NAACP Legal Defense and Education Fund's second-anniversary celebration of the *Brown* decision. In his introduction Bunche stressed the youth of King and the spontaneity of the rights movement, which consisted of ordinary people. He also contrasted King's bold leadership in social action with the traditional lack of such leadership, among blacks in the South, within the church.[30]

However, despite Bunche's public support for the Montgomery movement, he still had the same doubt about nonviolent direct action that he had expressed twenty years earlier. Meanwhile, Secretary of the Committee on Non-violent Integration A. J. Muste was supporting King in Montgomery and asked Eleanor Roosevelt for her support. Mrs. Roosevelt turned to Bunche for advice on what she should do. On 20 April 1956, he sent her the following reply: "1. I wonder if it is really necessary or advisable to set up an entirely new and separate organization" and "2. The use of the Gandhian 'nonviolent' slogan seems to me somewhat misleading and inappropriate in the context of the American Negro. In India it had application and there were those who advocated it. In India, therefore, there was a nonviolent alternative. There is none here, although the use of 'nonviolent' would seem to imply that there is."[31]

A year later Bunche called the 1957 Civil Rights Act "disappointingly weak." By 1960 he was supporting the student sit-ins that swept the South. Perhaps the fullest expression of Bunche's views on the civil rights movement appeared in an Associated Press interview in newspapers across the country during the Birmingham campaign. He called Birmingham chief of police "Bull" Conner a fascist and said neither the local, state or federal government had done enough to defend civil rights. Stating that the black struggle was in its climactic phase, he defended the use of children in demonstrations. Blame for the violence, said Bunche, rested on the police and not the protestors, nor the general white population. He added that the potential for the expression of violence on the part of impatient blacks could occur in the North as well as the South. In response to another question, Bunche said the appointment of a black to the president's cabinet was long overdue, as it was to the Supreme Court (and suggested his friend William Hastie). He also condemned Adam Clayton Powell's proposed boycott of the NAACP as well as the program of the Black Muslims.[32]

Perhaps more interesting than the released interview were those parts of the original that were not printed. When asked if race had impeded his academic career Bunche responded that few, if any, white institutions would have hired him when he left graduate school. Bunche added that he had declined President Truman's offer to appoint him assistant secretary of state because of pervasive segregation in Washington, D.C. But he also concluded that there was much more understanding, sympathy, and active support from white people than ever before.[33]

In a press statement of 8 July 1963, entitled "Why I Went to Jackson," Bunche explained his "pilgrimage" to Medgar Evers' funeral. He said "I went to Jackson to thank a dedicated and courageous man, who died for a cause as righteous as any cause can be, and who was a hero and is a martyr in the truest and noblest sense. . . ." During that same trip, Bunche attempted to visit seven female students from Tougaloo Southern Christian College who had been jailed for trying to worship in white churches in Jackson, Mississippi. Although he was unsuccessful in reaching them, he delivered a blistering speech at the college and criticized former President Truman for his comments about "Northern busybodies." Bunche also said Mississippi was more in need of the UN than South Africa.[34] This speech drew a tremendous reaction from the press, and Governor Ross Barnett accused Bunche of slandering Mississippi.[35] One local newspaper ran a story featuring all of the old communist charges against Bunche.

On the tenth anniversary of the *Brown* decision, Bunche spoke at the NAACP Legal Defense Fund celebration and also introduced Martin Luther King. Bunche said that the most significant development since World War II had been the black's loss of fear. He now fully embraced the technique of direct mass and action. "King," he said, had "understood the nature of the weapon of direct, mass nonviolent action" and how to use it. According to Bunche, "these are tactics and not ends," and they must be planned well, timed well, and used judiciously: their reason and objectives clear; their targets unmistakable." As an example of the misuse of such tactics, he cited the "so-called stall-in last month on [the] opening of [the] World's Fair."[36]

Having finally accepted nonviolent, direct action as a tactic, Bunche chose the march from Selma to Montgomery as the opportunity to join King in the frontline. An FBI report to the Secretary of State and the President on his activity indicated that Bunche could not walk more than one and a half hours and that he needed a private room because "he lives on the needle." No mention was made of the fact that Bunche suffered from diabetes and phlebitis. On aching legs from the steps of the state capitol, he addressed the crowd: "Governor Wallace and some others denounce many of us who are not Alabamians for being outsiders and meddlers, and that includes me[.] I stoutly deny this. I am here as an American, an American with a conscience, a sense of justice, and a deep concern for all of the people and problems of our country. I came here to identify with the just cause of the right of Alabama Negroes to vote, as our president himself has said every good American should[.] I say to Governor Wallace that no American can ever be an 'outsider' anywhere in this country."[37] Though this speech brought Bunche much hate mail, it also brought him inside the civil rights movement. He was no longer Ralph Bunche, the radical outsider, criticizing the NAACP; nor was he Ralph Bunche, the world diplomat, who was above the race struggle. He was now Ralph Bunche, the civil rights leader.

Conclusion

Growing up during the time of the "New Negro," and radicalized by the Great Depression, Bunche was proud of his race. He also realized that economic injustice was the basic cause of black inequality. In fact, the problems of economic injustice that confronted Bunche in the early thirties were the same ones that faced King in the sixties. Ralph Bunche soon lost any faith that he might have had in the Communist party's willingness to place black interests on a par with those of the Soviet Union. As fascism developed in Europe Bunche feared its consequential development in the United States. Seeing the racial limitations on government service in the United States, he directed his energy, in the United Nations, toward promoting human rights, specifically the ending of colonialism. His success at the UN gave him a status that had never before been achieved by a black American. However, this status often served to distance him from leadership in the civil rights struggle; and in spite of it, the government also, as represented by the FBI, never fully trusted Bunche because of his radical past, his internationalism, and his commitment to civil rights.

Perhaps the consistency in Bunche's goals and values may be appreciated in a statement on the occasion of his death, from an unlikely source, the Institute of the Black World:

> Contrary to white propaganda, Ralph Bunche was not "a man without color," but a man without a country. The country which should have been his now has to conceal the truth of Ralph Bunche in order to conceal the truth about itself. And the truth is that everything Bunche stood for, America stood against. Bunche stood for peace, whereas his country stands for war; he stood for honesty, whereas his country stands for duplicity; he stood for justice, whereas his country stands for power; and he stood for mankind, while his country stands for race master.
>
> What also distinguishes Bunche from his country is the contrast between their notions of public service and responsibility, indeed their very notions of the nature of man. Bunche was a moral stranger in this immoral land, a prophet without honor, a man whose principles were rejected as a way of life by the land he so diligently tried to serve, but with which he could find no real common ground. So America exported Bunche to other pastures where his ideals would not prove a constant embarrassment to it, an obstacle to its running of the world.[38]

For Ralph Bunche there could be no national security without civil rights, and there could be no international peace without human rights.

Notes

1. Speech before the Virginia Council on Human Relations, 23 February 1963, Box 56, Ralph Bunche Papers, University of California at Los Angeles (UCLA). See also Federal Bureau of Investigation documents of the same date.
2. Ibid.
3. See the presentations in this volume by Martin Kilson and by Nathan Huggins, who contend that Bunche's approach to Africa was far in advance of its time. Lawrence Finkelstein, on the other hand, takes the position that economic determinism was in fashion at the time. All agree that Bunche was very pragmatic in his approach to the problem of colonialism in Africa.
4. "Marxism and the Negro Question," Ralph Bunche Papers, UCLA, Box 133, folder #4 (n.d.).
5. Ibid.
6. "Realism and the Negro Problem," Ralph Bunche Papers, UCLA, Box 43, 22 March 1936.
7. Mrs. Ralph Bunche, Robert Weaver, and Robert Martin all cite Howard as the source of Bunche's radicalism. There is no sign of Marxist views at UCLA, and Weaver, who was at Harvard with Bunche, says it certainly did not come from there. Weaver, who was a socialist at the time, stated that Bunche and his Howard colleagues were not class-oriented in the traditional sense. Interview with Dr. Weaver on 6/6/86; with Dr. Martin on 4/11/86; and with Mrs. Bunche on 10/18/85.
8. Later investigations produced conflicting testimony. One interviewee said Bunche escorted students who used violence against the strikers to the Dean's office. Other persons interviewed said Bunche was not involved in the strike.
9. Bunche's position advocating mass action was that taken by the International Defense Fund in contrast to the NAACP position calling for legal action only. These tactics in the Scottsboro case are discussed in Mark Naison, *Communists in Harlem During the Depression* (New York: Grove, 1983).
10. Max Yergan became a well-known communist spokesman when he returned to the U. S. in 1936 after fifteen years as a director of YMCA work in South Africa. When Yergan assumed the leadership role in both the NNC and the International Committee on African Affairs in 1940, Bunche resigned. Bunche is extremely critical of the NNC's communist direction in his "Critique of the National Negro Congress" in the *Extended Memorandum on the Programs, Tactics, and Achievements of Negro Betterment and Interracial Organizations* from the Carnegie Survey of the Negro in America, Ralph Bunche Papers, UCLA.
11. FBI interview with Ralph Bunche, 26 February 1942.
12. FBI report on Bunche to Lawrence F. O'Brien, 29 December 1960.
13. For a comprehensive discussion of Bunche's role in founding the NNC, see John B. Kirby, *Black Americans in the Roosevelt Era,* chapter 7; Raymond Wolters, *Negroes and the Great Depression,* pp. 353–82; Harvard Sitkoff, *A New Deal for Blacks;* Mark Naison, *Communists in Harlem,* chapter 7; and Lawrence S. Wittner, "The National Negro Congress: A Reassessment," *American Quarterly* 22 (Winter 1970): 883–901.
14. FBI Memo from D. M. Ladd to the Director (Hoover), n.d.

15. FBI Memo from C. H. Stanley to Mr. Rosen, 27 May 1954.
16. Abner Berry's earlier praise of Bunche and his work in the *Daily Worker* had been a subject of FBI and conservative concern. The relationship between Bunche and Du Bois grew cool after Du Bois publicly attacked Bunche's handling of the Palestine negotiations. In 1951, Bunche refused E. Franklin Frazier's invitation to sponsor a testimonial dinner for Du Bois, citing this "personal" attack on his character.
17. "Prejudice in World Perspective," Fountain Street Church, Grand Rapids, Michigan, 24 April 1954; Ralph Bunche Papers, UCLA, Box 50.
18. "Remarks before the Periclean Club," Birmingham, Alabama, 13 February 1959; Ralph Bunche Papers, UCLA, Box 53.
19. Letters to Margaret Allen and Agnes Cross, Ralph Bunche Papers, UCLA, Box 127. Bunche always states that he did not consider himself a leader and that there were too many "self-appointed" Negro leaders. Still be believed that his views represented those of a large majority of black Americans.
20. "Young Negro," n.d., Ralph Bunche Papers, UCLA, Box 43, p. 6. Many years later, Bunche was to condemn the violence in Watts as detestable, and an action that Negroes will have to pay for. He mentioned that all of his close blood relatives still lived there, and he understood the conditions that produced the violence. The only remedy, he said, was "city, state and national authorities must quickly show the vision, the determination and the courage to take those bold—and costly —steps necessary to begin the dispersal of every black ghetto in this land." Press Statement, 17 August 1947, Ralph Bunche Papers, UCLA, Box 127, folder 58.
21. Lawrence Finkelstein relates that Bunche was very frustrated by the timidity of Washington's black residents who asked him to pick up their "integrated" theater tickets for them rather than appear in person at the box office. At this point, says Finkelstein, Bunche decided to become "more of a model and less of an activist." Conversation with Finkelstein on 5/6/86.
22. Ralph Bunche Papers, UCLA, Box 43.
23. "Realism and the Negro Problem," Ralph Bunche Papers, UCLA, Box 43. Elsewhere Bunche said that Gandhi's tactics appealed to Hindus but would not attract blacks; black Americans were not inherently nonviolent.
24. Letter to Alma Booker, 4 May 1950, Ralph Bunche Papers, UCLA, Box 127. Ms. Booker responded by objecting to Bunche's use of the terms "man" and "brotherhood" and his focusing on female rights in Palestine rather than the United States.
25. Address to NAACP 42nd Annual Meeting, 1 July 1951, Ralph Bunche Papers, UCLA, Box 47. Bunche replaced Charles Houston on the NAACP's Board of Directors on the latter's death.
26. His memorandum has been published as *The Political Status of the Negro in the Age of FDR*, ed. Dewey W. Grantham (Chicago: Univ. of Chicago Press, 1973).
27. Address to NAACP 45th Annual Meeting, July 4, 1954, Ralph Bunche Papers, UCLA, Box 50, p. 3.
28. *In Stride Toward Freedom*, King expresses his faith in the good will of most white Southerners. By 1963, he has become more cynical towards their support as he indicates in "Letter from a Birmingham Jail." In his last book, *Where Do We Go From Here*, he attacks Northern white liberals as well for their

lack of support. King's writings and those of his biographers such as Stephen Oates document King's great admiration of Bunche.

29. Telegram, 22 February 1956, Ralph Bunche Papers, UCLA, Box 127.
30. Introduction, NAACP Legal Defense Fund Dinner, 17 May 1956, Ralph Bunche Papers, UCLA, Box 52.
31. Letter to Mrs. Roosevelt, 20 April 1956, Ralph Bunche Papers, UCLA, Box 127, folder #38.
32. Interview with Associated Press reporter William Oates, 9 June 1963, Ralph Bunche Papers, UCLA, Box 58.
33. Ibid., 31 May 1963.
34. "The UN in 1963," 23 October 1963. Ralph Bunche Papers, Box 56. He also indicated in this speech that his daughter Joan was involved in voter registration efforts in the South. His son had been involved in the famous West Side Tennis Club incident in 1959. Bunche had also encountered problems in enrolling his daughter in a private Quaker school in Pennsylvania.
35. *New York Times,* October 26, 1963, Ralph Bunche Papers, UCLA, Box 56.
36. Introduction, NAACP Legal Defense Fund Dinner, 28 May 1964, Ralph Bunche Papers, UCLA, Box 56, pp. 3–4.
37. "March on Montgomery from Selma," 25 March 1965, Ralph Bunche Papers, UCLA, Box 57.
38. Institute of the Black World, "Ralph Bunche: The Man Without a Country," *Monthly Report,* 1972, p. 2.

PART II

AFRICANIST AND DECOLONIZER

· 4 ·

RALPH BUNCHE THE AFRICANIST

Nathan Irvin Huggins

History has a way of playing tricks on us. Looking back on a life such as that of Ralph Bunche, we are inclined to imagine a certain reasonableness about the outcome. In professional terms, things turned out so right for him: he found himself in a profession and career for which he seemed perfectly prepared; he found himself—when the events of history called—to be perfectly suited for the role he was to play. One would expect there to have been a plan all along, a boy and man purposefully preparing himself for the result we now see. So right, so condign was it, that we are tempted to think it in the cards, so to speak.

We tend to ignore, therefore, the accidental and contingent aspects of that story; how, by subtle and also reasonable alternate choices, the story might have been different. After graduating high school, for instance, Bunche thought momentarily of continuing and developing a carpet-laying business that was moderately successful and had already helped him through school. It did not take much persuasion from his grandmother and aunts for him to choose college at the newly opened southern branch of the University of California. He might well have made the other choice, without profoundly shocking family, friends, or his own realistic sense of future.

He thought, as well, about a career in law. That, too, would have been reasonable. One of his best friends, Charles Matthews, did follow the law and made a quite successful career at it. Instead, Bunche went to Harvard graduate school after UCLA, apparently with law still as a probable option. Yet, he decided on a scholarly career rather than the law. He chose political science, and he chose to work on public administration in a non-American, African, field. The point is that none of these choices were deliberate and planned, however reasonably they turned out.

The same could be said of any life: that despite contrary appearances lives and careers are contingent. With Bunche, it is important to keep the obvious in mind. We might otherwise gloss important and perplexing questions. We would be apt to lose the importance of race as a weight on the scale. Apt to miss how rare men like Ralph Bunche were, how unlikely it was when events called to find him—a black man—trained as an Africanist, ready to serve the State Department and OSS, and ready to serve as an architect of the United Nations.

Few clues from his school and college days would have predicted Bunche's course as an Africanist. He showed no notable interest in Africa and little at all to suggest he even knew what an academic career might be. College certainly made sense. The household in which he grew up had a strong commitment to education. Also, in his youth education had a nearly obligatory character for blacks who aspired and were race conscious. His maternal grandfather, who died before Ralph was born, had been well educated and worked as a teacher and principal in schools in Fort Dodge, Kansas, and Waco, Texas. His maternal grandmother, who raised him, and his aunts who shared the household, were educated beyond the high school level. He was, himself, a bright young man and an exceptional student. He earned membership in his high school's honor society, a membership that was denied to him because of race.[1] His work in college was of similar high quality and he was chosen to give the valedictory address at his commencement in 1927.

He had shown, both in high school and college, a keen interest in foreign countries, though not foreign cultures, and international relations. In high school, he became proficient in French and was fluent by his freshman year in college. Except for athletics, his main extracurricular interest was in an international relations club. Yet, he majored in philosophy, and the teacher who had the greatest influence on him while in college was Dean Rieber, something of a scholar of Romantic philosophy. And, despite his valedictory address of 1927, charging his class to work for world peace, and assuming its best hope to be in international organization—despite that strangely prescient speech, there is little else to suggest how his career interests would evolve.

The reason I make so much of this is that I think it is unusual that a very bright, black young man, graduating from UCLA in 1927, would have chosen an academic career without first giving it a lot of anxious worrying. Beyond the southern black colleges and universities, there was little hope for a black man or woman to follow an academic career—not at least until after World War II. What work there would be, therefore, was in the South. Except for Howard, Fisk, and the Atlanta colleges none of them could have contained the intellectual energy and brillance of Ralph Bunche. Yet he seems to have had no such anxiety. Just as there is no sign of conscious and deliberate intent, there is no sign of his doubt.

It is as if he just moved as his intellectual interests, talents, and opportunities directed him, without much conscious attention to where it would all lead and with a genuine faith that it would come out well. (There is much to be said for a compelling faith based on romantic assumptions of self-reliance, the fundamental goodness of life and history—an Emersonian optimism.) Surely, he must have heard the lore of black doctors of philosophy, pushing brooms in the post office. All black youth had, but it did not matter to Ralph Bunche. And growing up on the West Coast, he had not, as southern youth did, seen around him evidence of black men in academic institutions. Had he the chance to have seen the provincial and intellectually cramped life characteristic of black colleges and universities, he might well have chosen otherwise.

Some faculty at UCLA, especially Dean Rieber, inspired and encouraged Bunche in his view of himself and in his possibilities, despite all the evidence in society that seemed to deny hope of fulfillment and achievement. When the opportunity to go to Harvard came, it was unthinkable to say no. It might be nothing more than a year of graduate school and, maybe, law school at Harvard or in the West, but what would be lost? Meanwhile, the one year gradually was extended. Philosophy was abandoned for political science (or government, as it is called at Harvard), and in a matter of six years he would complete a Ph.D. dissertation on French colonial administration in Togoland and Dahomey.

In those years—from 1928 to 1935—there was little if any instructional offering at Harvard on Africa. Some believe there still is not. Bunche could have had nothing in course work, and the scholarly literature on Africa was sparse, to say the most. Years later, when he was asked to name the best teacher he knew at Harvard, he said Charles Howard McIlwain,[2] an odd choice, as McIlwain taught political philosophy and was in no clear way instrumental in Bunche's professional training.

Three Harvard teachers were, however, and only one of them, Rupert Emerson, would find Africa to be central to his scholarship, and that was to be years after Bunche left Harvard. The other two were Arthur Holcome who, in those years, worked principally in American government, and John Freeman Sly, who was in public administration and finance. From correspondence it would seem that of these three Sly was the closest to Bunche. In fact, they exchanged letters for years. These letters were warm and somewhat personal, with little of the Harvard reserve found in those of Holcome and Emerson. Holcome directed his dissertation, however, not Sly, who had moved to Maryland, and not Emerson who served as a second reader.

There was some uncertainty as to what subject Bunche would write on for the dissertation. Topics bounced about. He thought for a time of working on something in Brazil. All of this is to say that until he chose the Togo-Dahomey topic, Africa was by no means a certainty. It is clear, however, that a controlling factor in his choice was that he could get support for the African topic from the Rosenwald Foundation. Money is always important in these matters, but in the early 1930s a black scholar could only expect to get funding from two or perhaps three sources: Rosenwald, the General Education Fund, and Phelps-Stokes.

French Administration in Togoland and Dahomey

In the winter of 1932–1933, Bunche spent slightly more than three months in West Africa, studying French administration in Togoland and Dahomey. His dissertation, the product of this research, reveals something much more than a mere academic or scholarly concern with the subject. As he writes in the preface, the "study . . . is stimulated by a deep interest in the development of subject peoples and the hopes which the future holds for them."[3] The work is written from that point of view. It accepts subject status as a reality but assumes self-determination as morally right and ultimately possible, and it is ready to accept indigenous culture, traditions, and institutions as viable and sufficient bases on which to build independent nations. In short, it views the European presence as an unnatural intrusion, necessary perhaps, but a superimposition on native cultures that must ultimately find their own way into the modern world.

Togoland and Dahomey invited comparison. Dahomey was a colony in the French West Africa system. Its neighbor, Togoland, had been a German colony until the Versailles Treaty and the League of Nations placed it as a mandate territory under French administration. Bunche's study, then, permitted a comparison between the European administration of African peoples, who were not only under conventional colonial rule but also under the mandate system of the League of Nations. Since they were neighboring territories of comparable circumstances and administered by the same European power, a comparison between them might be all the more trenchant with regards to the effect of international involvement in colonial administration.

In principle, mandate territories were under the protection of the League, and the Mandate Commission was to oversee their administration so that they would not be treated as a colony, that is to say, exploited like a colony. It is fair to say that the mandate system was designed as a instrument of reform of the colonial system. Subject peoples were to be under the tutelage of a mandate power that was technologically and, as they would see it, culturally advanced, with the ultimate aim of self-government and independence. That independence might be far in the future, but the administration was to work toward that end. The mandate was the white man s burden, idealized and institutionalized in the League of Nations.

The mandate power was to establish and maintain order, help to establish a basis for economic viability and for self-government at some indefinite, future time. While the mandate power would have the right to recoup the costs of its administration from the territory itself, for example, through taxes and trade, it was not supposed to exploit the territory for gain or profit. Of course, there were no such constraints—real or ideal—on the administration of colonies.

Bunche's study shows there to be differences in the administrations of the two peoples, but these differences were slight and most often owing to procedural demands of the Mandate Commission. Most of the marginal differences between colony and mandate were only grudgingly maintained under League oversight and had little effect on the natives. "In general," Bunche wrote, "it can be said that there is slight difference in the treatment and status of the natives under the Togo mandate, and that of their neighbors in the colony of Dahomey."[4]

Bunche's interest, however, goes to that narrow question. He analyzes the differences between the philosophical approaches of the British and the French. The British, denying the possibility of Africans becoming assimilated, tolerated (even sustained) the maintenance of native institutions, coexisting but subordinate to the colonial administration. The French, assuming the possibility of assimilation, and later association of African and French and denying in principle the weight of color difference, undermined native institutions and culture as primitive and illegitimate. Bunche would point to the corrupting influences of both attitudes on native culture and institutions and suggest that neither would lead to self-determination without native unrest and threats of disorder. Basically, he would find that either system was at bottom exploitative. The need was to extract the European determined value from Africa, and that would mean getting Africans to work to produce that value.

The strategy was simple. As Bunche would write with irony: "In order to 'liberate' the African from his thralldom of economic freedom therefore, the colonial and commercial interests have adapted three general devices." First were taxes, to be imposed directly or by work. To pay them, the native would either cultivate the land for the market or work for wages. Second, new needs were to be stimulated, such as for clothes, tools, tobacco, and the like. And third, there was to be force. "In a sense, there is no labor problem in Africa for the African, but only for the white man."[5]

The full significance of extending the Industrial Revolution to Africa seemed to imply the breakdown of primitive communal life and the development of a new and different communal bond among the natives, thus detribalized, "a bond which in South Africa already takes the form of native trade unionism."[6] Furthermore, Bunche argued:

> The present-day labor problem in Africa, therefore, is not greatly different from our own in the early years of our industrialization. In most parts of West Africa, the demand for labor exceeds the willing supply, a condition, which, however, has not afforded the African any . . . advantage in bargaining power. . . . The African "boy" who pulled the writer about Conakry in a rickshaw owned by the French Syndicate, identified himself with wage-earners throughout the world, when he complained . . . "much work little money."[7]

TAXATION

It was through an elaborate system of taxation, Bunche found, that the French administrations in both territories were able to use native labor for their own ends. By obliging natives to pay taxes in money, they were also being forced to work for wages. These were labor taxes or prestation, the practice of exacting four to ten days of labor per year on public projects. As Bunche would see it, this practice amounted to "forced labor for local public purposes."[8] The French insisted, before the Mandate Commission, that prestation was a fiscal matter and not forced labor, a form of "taxation in kind." For the native lacking money to redeem the obligation, however, it was forced labor. Despite the French argument that "all taxation . . . may be regarded as 'forced labor,'" the Mandate Commission disagreed with the French.[9]

Bunche also found an assortment of other, direct taxes, imposed with slight differences, on both Togo and Dahomey. There were head taxes for all residents. French and other Europeans paid a fixed rate of 120 FF (French francs) a year in 1929. Native rates varied from 5 FF to 30 FF per year. In 1929, this head tax netted the Dahomean administration 13,095,918 FF, of which only 97,900 FF was contributed by French and other aliens. In addition to head taxes, there were license fees such as professional, manufacturing, and business fees. There were also taxes on firearms and automobiles, as well as property stamp taxes for official registrations.

More troubling to Bunche were the onerous methods of collection. Native chiefs, whom the French had stripped of all other authority, acted as tax-collection agents for the administration. Since they received rebates on what they collected, they had an incentive to keep taxes high; and they had no incentive to maintain an accurate census. "The native soon learns in his contact with the European," Bunche wrote, "that white government, if good, is expensive and that sometimes it is merely expensive."[10]

The Togo natives were only slightly less burdened than the Dahomean. The Mandate Commission questioned, nevertheless, the burden they bore, "particularly in view of the fact that there have been recurring surpluses in annual budgets, which . . . exceeded thirty million francs." While the French said they were saving to build a railroad, the commissioners questioned whether railroad construction was entirely in the interest of Togo natives. There was concern about the flight of natives of Togo to the Gold Coast because of their tax burden. But the French defended direct taxes, pointing out that with head taxes the native " 'is induced to work in order to pay his tax . . . just as the goods in a depot incite him to work in order to procure them.' "[11]

The Mandate Commission also complained that while natives paid a lower maximum tax rate than French residents, the French were much better able to pay their rates than the natives were theirs. The French, however, described the European residents as chiefly petty administrators or trade employees, declaring that " 'they are less well-off than the natives who paid at most 115.15 FF. . . . It should not be forgotten,' continued M. Bonnecarrère, 'that a native cocoa-planter was a multimillionaire, while the official or the European employee had only his pay or salary. Nearly all well-off natives had automobiles, while the officials or the employees were compelled to go on foot or bicycle.' " Bunche found little support for this claim.[12]

EDUCATION

While education was the key to the Africans' economic, political, and social future, Bunche found the European administration deeply divided on educational policy. Some wanted to keep Africans uneducated. "Some," he said, "attempt to hide behind the romantic sentimentalism that the African must be left entirely to his own devices, in a foolish and not always honest glorification of the noble savage." The problem posed for the colonial powers, he went on, "is not whether the African shall be educated, but how may the inevitable education, which the African will acquire, be controlled and to what objectives shall it be directed?"[13]

He saw four basic possibilities: to train a few leaders; to teach the masses enough to make them more useful and to "know their place"; to train a cadre of more-or-less expert artisans; and finally to train "good citizens," or collaborators in the colonial administration, with the possibility of eventual self-rule. He quoted with approval from the work of

A. Victor Murray: "'What we think his future will be determines his present. If it is true that Africa of today conditions Africa of tomorrow, it is no less true that our hopes or fears for Africa of tomorrow condition Africa of today.'"[14] If the standard were eventual self-rule, Bunche saw no evidence of that intent on the part of the administration.

Everywhere he found colonial education limited, "rarely go[ing] beyond the stage corresponding to our primary instruction." It was conditioned by self-interest: the French first, and the native second. He was especially critical of efforts by both the French and British to adapt educational plans used elsewhere to Africa. Particularly troubling was the attention paid to a report by Dr. Thomas Jesse Jones, of the Phelps-Stokes Fund. Jones had been considered by the administration as authoritative because he boasted a background of valuable experience with the black American population in the South. The Jones report recommended applying to African education a model similar to that of Booker T. Washington's Tuskegee model. This model was to use a formula of industrial and agricultural training, considered to be the type of education most suitable for Africans. Bunche was very critical of such schemes. They rested on the non sequitur that what was thought to be good for black Americans would be good for Africans. He pointed out that Booker T. Washington's ideals were not embraced by an important body of Afro-American opinion:

> As the urbanization of the Negro has intensified, along with his struggle for political and economic equality, these views have progressively lost support among intelligent Negro population.[15]

Also, such a plan failed to take into account the heterogeneity of the African peoples. Furthermore, educated Africans reject such a model of education, recognizing that it is not prevalent in the western world for the dominant population.[16]

The French proclaimed that native education was a matter of "duty and mutual benefit." Yet its commitment to a colonial policy of "association" raised profound questions: What was to become of native languages? Was there a native culture worthy of transmission? Would the educated native in fact become a "Frenchman"?

There was little question where the French administration stood on these questions: nothing of native culture was worthy of teaching; one indulged it only for pragmatic reasons. The assumptions on which this policy rested were shared by most in the West. Thomas Jesse Jones of Phelps-Stokes, for instance, wrote:

> In the advanced courses where great emphasis is placed upon "moral" education, the native language is generally found inadequate to express the delicate

nuances necessary in the development of upright, loyal character on the Western plan. It is held essential that the native leaders know one European language "as a means of access to the great accomplishments and inspirations of civilization."[17]

Bunche found that French educational policy and administration were parallel in Togo and Dahomey. In both, there was a suppression of native languages, as well as suppression of the initiative of missionary schools to support native culture. Both forms of suppression were intent on creating class divisions. Bunche would conclude:

> However honest the French motives may be, the existing policy justifies the suspicion that the objective is the suppression of the native culture in favor of French culture. But since it has been quite generally agreed among the French writers and high colonial officials that the natives cannot be readily assimilated to the French culture, this attitude in respect to language and curriculum seems to present a paradox.[18]

NATIVE AND JUDICIAL PROCESS

Bunche located the area of the greatest weakening of native institutions in the administration of justice.

> Deprived of its [judicial power], the tribal chief loses his greatest power, and its loss becomes virtually fatal to traditional native institutions. The French have tended to ignore these important considerations in West Africa with serious consequences for both themselves and the native society.[19]

Furthermore, there was confusion caused by imposition of European codes and administration. Bunche found a lack of penal codes, except in Togo, inadequate courts, and an abuse of power. Basically, there was a difference in status. Since there was understood to be a difference between *citoyen* and *sujets*, the Europeans and the few native *assimilés* who had gained French citizenship constituted a favored class.

The law of 15 May 1791 had admitted free blacks to French citizenship on the same basis as Europeans. The law of 24 April 1833 gave to all persons in the French colonies who were born free, or who had legally obtained their liberty, both civil and political rights. "The French law of today retains this principle but withholds its application from all but the 'chosen few.'"[20] Strict procedure in Dahomey resulted in only ninety-seven natives being admitted to French citizenship between 1912 and 1932. Bunche observed great bitterness over the imposition of trivialities, such as the two categories of status for children of naturalized natives: citizenship for children born after naturalization and subject status for those born before.

According to the League of Nations resolutions (22 April 1923): native status was distinct from that of the nationals of the Mandatory Power, and natives were not to be assimilated by general decree; natives would not acquire the nationality of the Mandatory Power as a result of the protection they received; individuals were to voluntarily obtain nationality, according to the Mandatory Power's regulations; and the Mandatory Power was to designate the status of natives. The natives of Togo were neither subjects nor *ressortissants* of France. There were provisions by which they could obtain citizenship, but none had done so.

Bunche found the mandate system mixed at best, with little significant difference between native life under colonial or under mandate rule. He was prepared to grant that the mandate principle had "operated generally to liberalize and humanize the policies of the colonial powers." To the extent that was true, some praise was deserved. But, he was quick to add, this was only the beginning of a "great work."

> It is not so important that the territories under mandate be better administered than the colonies of the world, but it is important that the mandate principle assure to these territories an unselfish, helpful administration, which will afford them an opportunity to properly prepare themselves for the eventual day when they will stand alone in the world. The African is no longer to be considered a barbarian, nor even a child, but only an adult retarded in terms of Western civilization.[21]

Academic Research and Fieldwork

Bunche's dissertation was very successful in almost every respect. It was awarded the Toppan Prize at Harvard for the best dissertation in political science. It was a thoughtful, well-written analysis of colonial administration, and it remains one of the earliest serious works on this subject. One is only surprised, now, that it was never published as a book. It seems that Ralph Bunche made very litle effort to publish it, in whole or in part. Normally, there would be correspondence between an advisor and student, discussing the prospects of publication. There is none, in this case.

It is my view that Bunche was not quite satisfied with the work. This is based not on anything really substantial. It merely seems, on reading the work, that the kinds of questions Bunche wanted to ask and to answer— questions about Africans rather than their European administrators— could not be satisfied by the subject of this dissertation.

After all, he was writing a dissertation in public administration. And while it dealt with an African subject, the questions it addressed were focused on the internal dynamics of French administrations that functioned within and without League of Nations constraints. The role of the native population was only incidental. It was as if the topic itself had forced Bunche to view the African through the frames of reference constructed by the French and the League's Mandate Commission.

He tells us as much in the preface. He remembers the research trip to include "a never-to-be-forgotten jaunt of one month's duration into the interior of French Mandate Togoland and the adjacent colony Dahomey."[22] There was no place in the dissertation to use his impressions of that jaunt. Further, it is fair to say, his training as a political scientist had not prepared him to deal adequately with a native culture and its institutions. Perhaps the trip to Africa, and the experience of writing the dissertation inspired him to do a different kind of study, to deal with Africans themselves; for during the years following the dissertation, Bunche retrained himself. He traveled regularly to Northwestern University, where he took courses in anthropology, and he established a close personal and professional relationship with the anthropologist Melville Herskovits.

In the academic year 1936–1937, Bunche took a sabbatical from Howard University and, with a grant from the Social Science Research Council, began a research trip in southern and eastern Africa. He arrived in Cape Town on September 29th, spending a little over two months in South Africa visiting several cities and regions. He moved on to Tanzania, Kenya, Zanzibar, leaving Africa in May to continue a trip through the Pacific and then home.

It is impossible to describe fully the results of this trip. They are contained in several boxes of notes, handwritten and unorganized. They are his records of the political and cultural phenomena he observed. They are also reports of interviews of Africans and Europeans of all degrees and classes. Bunche had a clear interest in indigenous institutions and resources that might bring blacks and coloreds in South Africa into power. He was keenly interested in the interplay between the native culture and the pressures and laws of the European administration. These notes, unlike the contents of the dissertation, provide evidence from the native point of view. It was—as American historians would say—writing the story from the bottom up.

The notes consist of typed notations on 5 by 7 cards, more or less randomly gathered in three file boxes. They are notes of observations, conversations, factual information. The material from South Africa is especially concerned with political matters: incipient political parties organized by blacks; color and racial divisions (not simply legalistically, but in practice and attitude); labor organization, and the like.

The following random notes from this collection give an idea of Bunche's areas of interest at that time.

Politics

African National Congress—organized 1912. (see Thema in Johurg[*sic*]).

At beginning a collection of tribal organizations, burial societies, etc. Founder was Dr. Seme—who, tho a natural South African, (Swazi) had studied in U.S. (England?). First meeting at Bloemfontein—representatives from all over the country. Came into being on eve of Land Act of 1912–13—sent delegation to England to protest vs. their Act. Unsuccessful. War broke out and they had to return. Two delegations were sent. Most of leaders were liberals and strung along with government during war. Engaged in nothing to embarrass government during war. But agitation by some of young members began in 1917, leading to strikes in Johurg, accompanying the first pass-burning demonstration. Mine workers shot. The Congress responsible for all these early disturbances.

Government stool pigeons led to breakup of the Congress and whole thing collapsed.

but it reached thousands of people in its active years; many chiefs supported it. The organization received a great deal of money from the people. It also suffered from graft.

After 1916, African National Congress subsided, and began to lose its indus. interest and more and more to enter and confine itself to political matters.

African National Congress divided into several factions today. Seme head of what is called the "official" Congress.

There were questions, observations, and conjectures.

Basutoland

Question continually in my mind: How can this handful of whites keep these millions of blacks down?

The blacks can't be but so dumb—they show too much adeptness at handling the white man's contraptions—bicycles, cars, carpentry, forges, football, cricket, languages, etc.

Cape Town

September 29

All hues and shades of dark faces on streets—in mixture resemblance is similar to U.S., only Malay and Indian strains here account for more straight black hair.

Watched more or less full-blood cut capers for a crowd on the Parade. Had his woman with him—they sang a little, and then he would walk and dance on his hands. Negroes enjoyed it. Two drunk whites lounging and watching. One kept asking the Negro to pose on his hands for snapshot and then would snap the camera with his hand covering the lens. Natives and colored saw his drunken mistake and were immediately tickled. One very bad looking drunken mulatto staggering all over the place. No jim crow on buses for either colored or natives.

September 30

Listened to a black man, a Garveyite, haranguing a crowd of colored and natives in the Parade. Had a U.N.I.A. button on his lapel. Held copies of the "Pittsburgh Courier," "The Bantu World" and "The Black Man" in his hands as he spoke a fairly good English.

The character of these notes is perhaps a clue to the kind of work on Africa Bunche wanted to do, mixing anthropological techniques of observation and tribal and cultural life with his abiding interest in politics and political movements. He was defining himself as an Africanist. Significantly, what was published from his trip was a discussion of circumcision rites in Kenya, hardly one might say, the work of a political scientist.[23]

It was, however, 1937 when he returned. He began trying to get funds so that he could collect his notes and write his new study, and he was successful. In the meantime, however, the Carnegie Endowment had commissioned Gunnar Myrdal to do a study of the problem of race in the United States, and Ralph Bunche was to be drawn into that enterprise as Myrdal's principal aide. It was totally absorbing research, permitting the kind of anthropological fieldwork that might help discover political issues among the powerless. Bunche would not have time, though, to return to his own work.

Myrdal's attention was divided after the outbreak of World War II in Europe, and Ralph Bunche took up more of the responsibility of converting the draft studies into actual reports. Still, he wrote of returning to his notes on Africa. With America's entry into the war, Bunche was brought into the Office of Strategic Services and then into the State Department. The rest of the story is familiar. However, it was Bunche's training as an Africanist that prepared him for service in the war years. And it was that very direct knowledge of the mandate system that informed him in his development of trusteeship concepts in the United Nations.

Notes

1. Ralph Bunche Papers, UCLA, Special Collections.
2. Letter to Josephine Cook, 15 February 1956, Ralph Bunche Papers, UCLA.
3. Ralph J. Bunche, "French Administration in Togoland and Dahomey," (Ph.D. diss., Harvard University, 1934).

4. Bunche, "French Administration in Togoland and Dahomey," p. 425.
5. Ibid., p. 258.
6. Ibid., p. 26.
7. Ibid.
8. Ibid., p. 290.
9. Ibid., p. 294.
10. Ibid., p. 298.
11. Ibid., pp. 304–305; and Bunche quotes from Permanent Mandate Commission, 18th session, 1930, Minutes, p. 86.
12. Ibid., p. 307.
13. Ibid., pp. 309–310.
14. Ibid., p. 311. Bunche quotes A. Victor Murray, *The School in the Bush* (New York: Longmans, Green, 1929), p. 5.
15. Ibid., p. 317.
16. Ibid., p. 318.
17. Ibid., p. 327. Quotes Thomas Jesse Jones, *Education in Africa*, Report by Phelps-Stokes Fund for African Education Commission (New York: Phelps-Stokes Fund, 1922), p. 25.
18. Ibid., p. 364.
19. Ibid., p. 366.
20. Ibid., p. 393.
21. Ibid., pp. 41–42.
22. Ibid., "Preface."
23. Ralph J. Bunche, "The Irua Ceremony among the Kikuyu of Kiambu District Kenya," *The Journal of Negro History*, XXVI (January 1941): 46–65.

· 5 ·

RALPH BUNCHE'S ANALYTICAL PERSPECTIVE ON AFRICAN DEVELOPMENT

Martin Kilson

A Progressive Pragmatist

It is apparent from Ralph Bunche's earliest professional writings that his ideological framework for dealing with the modern world is best described as "progressive pragmatist."[1]

Bunche was progressive in the basic sense of that term. He accepted the values and norms of the Enlightenment, values that defined the parameters of the knowledge revolution and the economic revolution through which the modern nation state has traversed since the seventeenth century. He considered the metamorphosis from the feudalistic era a momentous opportunity for advancing humanitarian and equalitarian processes for all people, regardless of race, religion, gender, or political origins. In his first published book, *A World View of Race* (1936), Bunche warmly embraced the Enlightenment legacy. "The concept of human equality and the doctrine of natural rights were," he remarked, "cradled in the modern Western World."

These ideals embodied the political promise of the future; indeed, they formed the warp and woof of the most modern political institutions. There was no limit to the promise which such doctrines held forth to peoples and classes which had been abused and oppressed for centuries. The "civilized" West of the nineteenth and twentieth centuries became a great testing ground for these principles which were counted upon to free the great masses of people from suffering and bondage.[2]

This regard for the values and structures of progress of the Enlightenment legacy was not, however, uncritical or one-dimensional. Quite the contrary. Bunche, throughout his intellectual and professional career, had a natural gift for what I call the *contra-posture*, the critical, and thus for the *realpolitik*. If not fully evident at the initial encounter with a new idea, policy, or system, this *contra-posture* would nonetheless soon surface, in Bunche's views and behavior. This, then, is the pragmatic side of Ralph Bunche. Accepting as he was of the basic importance of the Enlightenment legacy, Bunche's *contra-posture* and sense of *realpolitik* regulated his fidelity to this legacy.

Thus, for Bunche, the realities of the world required that the Enlightenment legacy be measured against here-and-now social and power patterns. And it is in the evaluation process where distortions of the Enlightenment legacy can occur, sometimes bidding to supplant the legacy itself. This is precisely what Bunche had in mind when he observed, for instance, that "the practical history of our modern world [shows that] the ideal doctrine of the 'equality of man,' (along with most of its ideals), has fallen upon hard times."

> True, we continue to pay lip service to the "sacred" concept of the "natural rights of man" and its international corollary, the "rights of peoples." But the dominant peoples and powerful nations usually discover that such concepts cut sharply across their own economic and political interests. So, with those favored groups, who know well how to use them for their own profit, such doctrines come to assume a strange role.[3]

I might add that the theme of a conflict between ideals and power-realities engaged Bunche at many levels. For instance, at his initial encounter with versions of Marxism-Leninism in the 1930s, Bunche's *contra-posture* was not always alert. This can be seen, for instance, in a concluding observation Bunche makes in *A World View of Race*. Here, he predicted, rather naively, that if racial groups were to turn to Soviet variants of humanitarian and equalitarian values they would awaken to the disutility of racial or ethnic self-definitions, replacing them with class self-definitions and thus presumably with revolutionary identities. As Bunche puts it:

> If the oppressed racial groups, as a result of desperation and increasing understanding, should be attracted by the principles of equality and humanitarianism advocated by the Soviet Union (and it is both logical and likely that

they will) then racial conflict with become intensified. In such a case, however, racial conflict will be more directly identified with class conflict, and the oppressed racial groups may win the support of . . . previously prejudiced working-class groups within the dominant population.[4]

This pushing-and-pulling between the ideal and *realpolitik* elements, in Bunche's analytical perspective, was to tantalize him throughout his career. In practical terms, it meant sometimes leaning toward leftist-naiveté, sometimes toward bourgeois-naiveté, and sometimes toward overconfidence in the hegemonic aura of established power centers (such as capitalist colonial power, communist colonial power, international agencies, and the like).

These tendencies impinged upon Bunche. For instance, these tendencies were to harass Bunche's effort as a social scientist to strike a progressive-pragmatist stance toward the imperialistic mode of transferring a modernizing political economy—the capitalist political economy—to African societies. This same tugging among the constituent parts of Bunche's world view was to appear as well in the early 1960s when, as international diplomat and crisis manager (the twentieth century's first such black figure), Bunche was to be a key operative in the United Nations' intervention in the Congo crisis.

Colonialism as Modernization: Costs and Benefits

There are two stages in Ralph Bunche's interaction with the politics of modern colonialism and its global implications. One is the political-analyst stage (1930s–1940s) and the other is the crisis-manager diplomat stage (1940s–1960s). This study concentrates on the first stage.

Throughout the political-analyst stage, Bunche's perception of the modernization of the colonial state vacillated between emphasizing the price exacted by the state (his progressive or leftist outlook) and the objective advantages transmitted to it (his pragmatist or functionalist outlook). When characterizing the colonial state, Bunche was sometimes strident but always incisive. From the late nineteenth century onward, the imperialist process crudely categorized the peoples of the world as "advanced" or "backward," the latter helplessly backward and incapable of "keeping step with the modern industrial world." To Bunche, such classification was mere deceit, an attempt "to mask [imperialist Europe's] cruelly selfish motives under high-sounding titles."[5]

The rhetoric of power is seldom the reality of power. The essence of the colonial state is, then, plain enough: "Powerful industrial nations have raped Africa under the false pretense of shouldering 'the white man's burden' . . . to convert [Africans] to the Christian religion and to expose them to the benefits of an advanced European culture." But come the post-conquest process of sustained colonial governance, "the backward peoples bitterly learn that the 'blessings' consist of brutal suppression, greedy economic exploitation of the natural and human resources of a country which is no longer their own, forced labor, the introduction of previously unknown diseases, vice and social degeneration."[6]

Why the imperialism and the colonial state in the first place? Bunche-as-progressive found this query easier than did Bunche-as-pragmatist. Evidence of Bunche's leftist posture toward colonialism in the 1930s is found mainly in his published writings (especially in *A World View of Race*, but also in magazine articles), while evidence of his pragmatist posture is found in his unpublished writings (in his doctoral dissertation specifically, in his correspondence and official memoranda).

To illuminate this query about imperialism, Bunche, as a leftist in the 1930s, resorted to the conventional Marxist-Leninist wisdom. "Imperialism is an international expression of capitalism," he observed:

> The rapid growth and expansion resulting from the development of industrialism and capitalism led the peoples of industrial countries to seek raw materials and new markets all over the world. This led to more general group contact, and because of the base motives of imperialism, to more widespread racial conflict. . . . The accumulation of "surplus capital" and the resultant demand for overseas investments, all tended to force European imperialist nations to invade completely the African continent.[7]

When the same query, as to why the colonial state and its imperialist process, was faced by Bunche-as-pragmatist, his response was more reflective. That is to say, it was less strident, less ideologically assured, evincing some openness toward colonial modernization.

At the core of Bunche's pragmatic perspective on the colonial state was his belief that, despite its clearly self-serving purposes (in expanding its wealth and in transferring its technology) the colonial state had enough flexibility to allow for institutional variability and experimentation. As Bunche said:

> Perhaps its [the colonial state] greatest significance is found in its possibilities as a fine proving ground in human relations—social, economic, and political. Here is one place in a troubled world where mistakes previously committed may be corrected, where, indeed, a new, a better civilization may be cultivated, through the deliberate application of human intelligence and understanding.[8]

It is no surprise that Bunche resolved the seeming contradiction between his leftist and pragmatist perceptions of the colonial state by applying rationality-and-knowledge (what he calls "intelligence and understanding") to modern problem-solving. In the 1930s, Bunche was, after all, a peer of the second generation of Afro-American intellectuals who, along with cosmopolitan, liberal, and leftist white allies, committed themselves to scientific, problem-solving responses, rather than revolutionary ones, for resolving America's vicious racist practices.[9]

Thus, for Bunche, those colonial elements that were prone to institutional experimentation would surely fail unless they recognized *the salience of Africans as human beings*. The naked forms of exploitation of Africans in some colonial states (such as South Africa, Rhodesia, and the Congo), discarding the salience of Africans as Africans, would doom the colonial state's modernizing role; for "after all, great though her natural resources are, the vital wealth of Africa is in the humanity that dwells within the sweltering continent." Thus, Bunche was convinced that in order for colonialism to supplant its self-serving, authoritarian realities the colonial ideology would have to maintain a status of parity between Europeans and Africans. Or, as Bunche put it: "The solution of the problem of the future of Africa is to be found in the determination of the eventual relationships that will prevail between the Africans and other [European] peoples."[10]

Precisely how do the dynamics within the colonial state, apart from the self-serving or power-appropriating dynamics, serve the development of an equitable modernization under colonialism? For American analysts of colonialism like Ralph Bunche and Rupert Emerson, this query was not easy to assimilate.[11] In particular, grappling with the pragmatic response to the open-ended options within the authoritarian colonial state could not have been easy for Bunche, owing to his leftist links. Along with sociologist E. Franklin Frazier, Bunche was, for example, on the editorial board of a major Marxist journal, *Science & Society: A Marxist Quarterly*. Thus, how would a leftist not only debunk but also accommodate change in colonialism?

Ralph Bunche partially resolved this dilemma by cultivating two system-remedial dynamics within the colonial state. One system-remedial dynamic centered on the role of the educated elites, the emerging black African bourgeoisie. The second system-remedial dynamic concerned the accountability process, such as the participatory practices within the colonial state and the role of international organizations (such as the World Court, the League of Nations—later the United Nations—foreign policy instruments). Yet, prone to chasten his pragmatic optimism, Bunche was cautious regarding the outcome of these system-remedial options.

Though the time when the West African will be able, in the words of the League Covenant, "to stand alone in the strenuous conditions of the modern world," *is probably many generations removed from the present day,* [italics added] he should be serving an apprenticeship in the art of self-rule under the tutelage of his immediate rulers. . . . It must be made possible for him now to acquire the experience and develop the leadership essential to sound government everywhere.[12]

The Educated Elites and the Politics of Accountability

Whereas Bunche-as-leftist strained to concede a positive outcome for the colonial state in Africa, Bunche-as-pragmatist contemplated hopeful options for colonialism. As a progressive, Bunche was quite certain that the governing precepts underlying the African colonial state were both mistaken (as models) and unworkable (as blueprints). Asking himself, "By what devices is the African governed?" Bunche responded rather critically:

> Two extremes of policy have been applied to him. The one, based entirely on greed, regarded him as the essentially inferior, subhuman, without soul, and fit only for slavery. The other, based entirely on sentiment, regarded him as a man and brother, extended to him the equalitarian principles of the French Revolution and attempted to "Europeanize" him overnight. Both were unscientific and devoted little attention to the needs and desires of the African.[13]

Not only were the governing precepts flawed as such; but *they never even contemplated an end-game scenario*. For Bunche, the importance of an end-game scenario was that *it predisposed steps and stages, however miniscule, through which a terminus point might be reached*. Anything else was a political recipe for systemic confusion ("policies . . . remain so vague as to the actual objectives aimed at")[14] or systemic breakdown. Moreover, for Bunche-as-pragmatist, the risks of systemic confusion were clearly to be avoided. For one thing, they threatened the long-run interests of a global political economy. They threatened, too, the prospects of bringing African societies into a status of parity within the global political economy. Nonetheless, for Bunche-as-leftist the realization of a viable endgame scenario for colonialism was at best problematic. As he said, the "French and English alike are in Africa primarily for economic exploitation and not from motives of philanthropy. . . . Both powers intend to retain control of their respective possessions and their subject populations indefinitely."[15] Yet, Bunche-as-pragmatist perpetually qualified Bunche-as-leftist. So, within the very same sentence Bunche chastized "England and France [for] not thinking in terms of native independence or self-government for the West Africans. . . ," but also deferred to a pragmatic ally, ". . . except in its [self-government] most meager local sense."[16]

Thus, as long as Bunche entertained an end-game scenario for the colonial state, which he did for the duration of his left-wing ties, the pluralistic imperative that shaped his pragmatism compelled him to contemplate nonideological options. These options required at least one basic component. They were to

> exhibit a definite program for native development which will lead the native toward an ultimate specific political and social status. . . . The only sound objective of African colonial policies should be to prepare the Africans for membership in the community of the civilized world, not as individuals but as communities.[17]

In considering end-game scenarios for colonialism, Bunche was both realistic and pragmatic-utopian, but he was not self-contradictory. He was not because his dialectical way of thinking informed him that power, realism, and accountability might just as readily be *reciprocal* to one another as they might be *antithetical.*

It seems that the perpetual tension between the leftist and the pragmatist in Bunche reached its apex when he endeavored to reconcile, analytically, the cleavage between the colonial state's greed and its accountability. The reason for his endeavor was that Bunche now had to identify a group, within colonial society, reasonably capable of mediating the greed/accountability cleavage toward a viable end-game option for the colonial state. Bunche selected the emergent educated class of Africans to shoulder the task of resolving the greed/accountability cleavage, because this class's own development depended upon such a resolution.[18]

From the observations of his fieldwork in West Africa in the 1930s, the African sources of the educated elite were quite apparent to Bunche. These sources come, he observed, from "all notable members of the native community—chiefs, wealthy merchants, government clerks, members of the [traditional] village councils of elders. . . ."[19] Less apparent *prima facie* was why the colonial state facilitated the emergent educated elite, an incipient black bourgeoisie and governing class.

According to Bunche's analysis, there were several reasons for the formation of an African elite within the colonial state. The primary governance of the African colonial state was through overrule, using foreign personnel to control the central bureaucracy and decision making, though a variety of tasks were allowed to Africans. While opposing the idea of colonialism, most Africans acquiesced and accepted governing roles. As Bunche put it, under colonial *overrule* the African's "immediate problem . . . is only to prepare himself ably to assume the meager share in his own administration delegated to him by rulers in the selection of which he has had no voice."[20]

Furthermore, the French in particular encouraged openness in racial matters, thus assisting in the formation of the African elite. "Beyond doubt," observed Bunche, "the French know the native better, they come into closer contact with native life, while the English stand aloof."[21] Bunche articulated this perspective even in the leftist-oriented *A World View of Race*, characterizing the French as possessing "a measure of sincerity. There is no real color line in France and none in her colonies, though individual instances of prejudice and discrimination may be encountered in both places."[22]

The French colonial state also gave a select few access to important administrative posts. These posts ranged from seats on municipal councils and functional commissions (such as water commissions and school and sanitation boards), to what Bunche termed "subaltern positions" in central government departments, representation in decision-making colonial assemblies, and executive posts, such as undersecretary for colonies in Paris, which several blacks held during the interwar era.[23]

Endgame Scenario: Transforming Colonialism

Thus, with some measure of African elite-formation conceded by the colonial state, Bunche entertained an end-game scenario for the colonial state that involved a major contribution by the African educated elite.

Throughout his African writings in the 1930s, Bunche was concerned about the role of the educated elite in transforming the colonial state. "The formation of the elite is at once the most cardinal and the most debatable point in the present French policy,"[24] Bunche observed in 1934. The root of the quandary over the educated elite was simple enough for Bunche. "The members of this elite above all others are to be bound to the French state and, through absorption of French culture, will become *assimilés*."[25] Indeed, Bunche even speculated that "the presence of an elite group in the native community . . . may be a condition viciously inimical to the best interests of the masses of the natives."[26]

Bunche's anxiety about "the elite native [becoming] a black Frenchman . . ."[27] was expressed in a testy discussion of Blaise Diagne, a leading Senegalese administrator and under secretary for the colonies, who was given to gross hedonistic display of the wealth and power he derived from his French connection (an African-elite pattern, by the way, quite common over the past twenty-five years of independent states). From Bunche's perspective, "It is a matter of serious doubt that the celebrated Senegalese Diagne now has much honest concern with things African extending beyond the African bric-a-brac of his elaborate and ornate Paris apartment."[28] Somewhat unfairly, Bunche resorted to a writer with a black Communist magazine, published in Paris, in order to label Diagne as illegitimate: "Already many of his native constituents have hurled the epithet 'traitor' at him," Bunche noted.[29]

It was, then, the loss of an autonomous, relatively self-defined, African educated elite that Bunche feared. Bunche suspected, and rightly, that an African elite autonomy might enhance the realization of a redefinition of the colonial state. Thus, Bunche's keen political intuition identified several domestic and international dynamics that possibly might be favorable to this outcome.

First, Bunche was aware of a growing dissidence among some educated elite who, "endowed with the white man's training, are hungry for positions that carry the white man's dignity."[30] The French colonial oligarchy noticed this potential dissidence too; for they continually recast the colonial educational system in hope of "avoiding the impending danger of the development of an intellectual proletariat in Africa."[31] This whetting of appetites toward the modernization of the African educated elites along one axis, that of skills, technology and administration, but withholding fruition along the power-appropriating axis, was viewed by Bunche as a recipe for restructuring the colonial state.

Precisely when this would actually translate into a metamorphosis of the colonial state Bunche hesitated to guess. Rather, his concern was with *process*, not *events*. So, he turned his analytical acumen toward other dynamics, domestic and global, that might induce the colonial-state transformation. One dynamic concerned the slowly *evolving corporateness of the African educated elite,* a situation that Bunche delineated when remarking that "the educated African is rapidly acquiring a zest for . . . political fetishes of the Western world."[32] In language that anticipated that used by analysts two decades later, Bunche captured this incipient *corporateness* of educated Africans in the following observation: "Sooner or later, as the educated class of natives increases in numbers, the French will be confronted with the difficult problem of the colonial administration of backward peoples, viz., *that there is no apparent peaceful means of transition to full self-control.* This condition is already looming larger on the horizon in neighboring British Gold Coast."[33]

Keenly perceptive and prophetic, Bunche realized the importance of attenuating the ethnic or tribal boundaries with this early stage of *corporateness* among educated Africans. In his observations, Ralph Bunche anticipated Karl Deutsch's famous thesis on social mobilization, explaining postwar nationalist dynamics in developing countries. As Bunche observed in 1934:

Tribal lines are being cut across as a result of improved means of communication and travel, and tribal authority has been broken down deliberately by the French. This may prove to be a blessing in disguise to the native however, for it will make it possible for him to ultimately present a united front in his demands for an increasing share in the control of his own country. This he could not do so long as tribal rivalries, jealousies, and isolation persisted.[34]

Another dynamic that Bunche identified as fundamental to the transformation of the colonial state concerned popular society, or the masses. Here Bunche's analytical projections are a sophisticated synthesis of the ideas of social analysts of modernization like Marx, Weber, and Schumpeter, all of whom Bunche had read.

Basic to Bunche's projections for popular society was his proposition that "probably the greatest error [among social analysts] is the mistake of assuming *ipso facto* that the African and his problems are essentially different from the Western world. Basically the African is confronted by the same difficulties which any people in process of evolution encounter."[35] Convinced that "there is nothing particularly unique about either the African or his [modernization] problems," Bunche analyzed the problems of African modernization squarely within a comparative-global context. In so doing, Bunche anticipated Wallerstein's analysis. "The African native today," Bunche remarked in 1936, "is comparable with the peasants and workmen of England and France of a century ago and with other workers and peasants today in less advanced countries of the modern world."[36]

Bunche's global perspective on the modernizing stresses of African popular society in the 1930s was not only anticipatory but perceptive. Perceptive as well was his suggestion that popular society might reject the colonial state's effort to slacken modernist exposure as a means of political control. As Bunche stated: "[The colonial state] cannot limit the experience and sophistication which inevitably come to the native along with the exploitative forces of Western civilization; these lead him to desire independence and self-assertion, making him 'troublesome' to the administrators."[37]

Clearly, however, Bunche was aware that popular society's ultimate role in colonial-state metamorphosis, while important contextually, required skillful elite superintendence. Bunche's final projections on how the elite role influenced a remedial colonial state were as foresighted as his projections regarding popular society.

Just as he had suggested a comparative-global context for the possible dynamics that might shape popular society's role, Bunche did the same for the elite. The observations of his fieldwork (and a first-rate field-worker he was) had brought home to him that the African educated elite "have news of the powerful weapons of effective resistance to abuses, employed by the oppressed in the Western world." Among these "weapons" Bunche noted "the boycott" and "the general strike," all of which could be calibrated through "a strong movement of passive resistance [that] could make the white man's presence in West Africa futile."[38] This transnational flow of political ideas and methods would, in fact, prove fundamental to postwar African nationalism, illustrating the depth of Bunche's end-game scenarios for the colonial state.

Conclusion

At the end of what is referred to as Bunche's end-game scenario, he clearly anticipated the postwar nationalist parties and movements, though he did not actually use the words *nationalist movement* or *nationalist party*. Once, in *A World View of Race*, Bunche referred to "the Pan-African nationalists," less in regard to the end-game scenarios for the colonial state than to what Bunche considered to be the pathological uses of ethnic and racial xenophobia. Bunche opposed using xenophobia in order either to redress global-power imbalances or to protect existing imbalances. He had in mind, of course, the Nazi use of anti-Semitism and race genocide in Europe and demonic elements among white racists in America, such as the Ku Klux Klan.[39]

As an outgrowth of his rationalistic pluralism and pragmatism, Bunche was contemptuous of all ethnocentric manipulation of global-power imbalances, even by blacks. In his words: "There are those, like the Pan-African nationalists, who feel that the darker peoples of the world must band together and gird their black and yellow loins for the oncoming world conflict between the races; the stakes in this little fracas are supposed to be world supremacy."[40] Notice the rather primitivistic allusions of his phrase, "gird their black and yellow loins," and his sardonic concluding phrase, referring to possible victors but victors in a "little fracas."

So Bunche's ultimate response to redressing global-power imbalances rested on the reflective side of leftist wisdom, not a bad place on which to rest this momentous issue. Thus, to the ethnocentric manipulators of power imbalances, domestic or global, Bunche retorted:

> They carefully avoid the fact that for either a White or a Black man it is scarcely more pleasant to be exploited and oppressed by privileged members of one's own race than by members of some other race. . . . Race issues [are real] but tend to merge into class issues. . . . The titanic conflicts of the future will be the product of the uncompromising struggles between those who have and those who have not. These conflicts now wage within all groups, racial and national.[41]

Thus it is clear that Bunche's analytical perspective was intricately dialectical, moving between pragmatism and idealism. Bunche's route to an end-game scenario for reforming the colonial state in Africa was sophisticated and essentially accurate. Follow it in the 1930s and you will arrive at the Africa of the 1950s and onwards. Even some of the systemic distortions in today's African regimes, such as pathological corruption, authoritarian abuses, and a gap in wealth between elites and masses, will be familiar. Nowhere does Bunche's analytical guide to African development suggest that such distortions were unlikely; indeed, he clearly foresaw some of them, such as pathological corruption. Bunche's analytical map of African development also anticipated possible solutions to current crises within the African states. In particular, he would certainly identify popular society—the masses—as a source of reforming initiatives. For though popular society's appetite for modernity has been stimulated by developments thus far, the standards and expectations of this appetite are still to be met. Furthermore, Bunche's analysis also emphasized the role of global dynamics in African development and state metamorphosis, dynamics that are far from being spent.

Notes

1. Among Ralph Bunche's earliest professional writing is his superb doctoral dissertation. It is perhaps the first analysis of political science fieldwork of colonial governance by an American graduate student. This study was directed at Harvard in the late 1930s by Arthur Holcombe and Rupert Emerson; it remains unpublished. Fortunately, the Columbia University historian Dewey Grantham has published nearly 700 pages from the thousands of pages of memoranda that Bunche wrote, again through fieldwork, for the Carnegie Corporation on the political status of Afro-Americans. See Ralph Bunche, *The Political Status of the Negro in the Age of F.D.R.* (Chicago: University of Chicago Press, 1973). See also Gunnar Myrdal, *An American Dilemma* (New York: Harcourt Brace, 1944).
2. Ralph J. Bunche, *A World View of Race* (Washington, DC: Associates in Negro Folk Education, 1936), p. 1.
3. Ibid.
4. Ibid., p. 36.
5. Ibid., p. 38.
6. Ibid., p. 39.
7. Ibid., pp. 40, 42.
8. Ibid., "French Administration in Togoland and Dahomey" (Ph.D. diss., Harvard University, 1934), pp. 1–2.
9. See, for example, John Hope Franklin and August Meier, eds., *Black Leaders of the Twentieth Century* (Urbana: University of Illinois Press, 1982). For a case study of a social-engineering black intellectual and colleague of Bunche at Howard University, see Genna Rae McNeil, *Groundwork: Charles Hamilton Houston and the Struggle for Civil Rights* (Philadelphia, PA: University of Pennsylvania Press, 1983). See also Gunnar Myrdal, *An American Dilemma*.
10. Bunche, "French Administration," p. 2ff.
11. Emerson spent much of his intellectual career reflecting on this issue. See his monumental book, *From Empire to Nation: The Rise to Self-Assertion of Asian and African Peoples* (Cambridge, MA: Harvard University Press, 1967).
12. Bunche, "French Administration," p. 388.
13. Bunche, *World View*, p. 46.
14. Ibid.
15. Ibid., p. 47.

16. Ibid.
17. Ibid., pp. 46–47.
18. Ibid., pp. 46–65. See the discussion of the educated class.
19. Ibid., "French Administration," p. 96.
20. Ibid., p. 388.
21. Ibid., p. 129.
22. Ibid., *World View,* p. 52. Bunche offers a vivid account of his sea voyage to West Africa in the 1930s in order to illustrate French racial openness. "This French attitude," he observes, "is strikingly evident on the boats of the French lines. . . . Here there is to be found a genial cordiality among the French and their elite associates of the darker races. . . . The genuine warmth of the associations between these groups of upper-class Black and White, the apparent lack of any race consciousness on the part of either, is quite startling when contrasted with similar groups on board the English and German vessels engaged in the same service. On the latter, most of the practices of segregation and aloofness common to the United States in its attitude toward its Negro population are in evidence."
23. Bunche discusses African elite-formation in several places. See "French Administration," pp. 95ff, 103 ff, 318 ff, 388ff. See also *World View,* pp. 46–65. There is some overlap within these two discussions since Bunche used sections from his dissertation for *World View.* However, the analysis in the latter is consistently more leftist than in the dissertation.
24. Bunche, "French Administration," p. 95.
25. Ibid., p. 96.
26. Ibid., p. 97.
27. Ibid., p. 98.
28. Ibid., pp. 95–105, 131 ff.
29. Ibid., p. 131.
30. Ibid., p. 389.
31. Ibid., pp. 315, 318.
32. Ibid., p. 392.
33. Ibid., p. 422. See also *World View,* pp. 58–61.
34. Ibid., p. 422. Cf. Karl Deutsch, *Nationalism and Social Communication* (Cambridge, MA.: M.I.T. Press, 1953).
35. Ibid., p. 128. See also *World View,* p. 63. Notice Bunche's recasting of this observation, anticipating the language of the postwar analysts: "In truth, the African is confronted with the same difficulties encountered by any people in process of social development."
36. Ibid., *World View,* p. 63. For Wallerstein's perspective, see, for example, Peter Gutkind and Immanuel Wallerstein, eds. *The Political Economy of Contemp. Africa* (Beverly Hills, CA: Sage Publications, 1976).
37. Ibid., "French Administration," p. 421. Cf. Martin Kilson, *Political Change in a West African State* (Cambridge, MA.: Harvard University Press, 1966). See also Martin Kilson, "Anatomy of African Class Consciousness: Agrarian Populism in Ghana," in Irving Markovitz, ed. *Studies in Power and Class in Africa* (New York: Oxford University Press, 1987).
38. Ibid., p. 423.
39. Ibid., *World View,* pp. 92–96.
40. Ibid., p. 95.
41. Ibid., pp. 95–96.

· 6 ·

RALPH BUNCHE:
An African Perspective

W. Ofuatey-Kodjoe

During the first half of this century, black intellectuals and social scientists spent a great deal of their energies writing about the problem of race in society. In a sense they had no choice. The condition of their people as a racially oppressed group left them no alternative other than to use their intellectual talents to try to explain the condition of their people in society. Thus the writings of these thinkers are replete with analyses of the role of racial ideologies and racist policies in society, the effects of these ideologies on the condition of black peoples, and strategies that could combat the pernicious effects of racism. Some dealt with the issue of race on a parochial basis. For instance, Booker T. Washington was mainly concerned with the condition of blacks in the U.S.[1] Others, like W. E. B. Du Bois, sought to analyze the issue in its global manifestations.[2]

As a professional academic, Ralph J. Bunche was part of this tradition of black scholarship. As a black political scientist living in a racist world, he had an analytical and activist interest in the condition of black people. Like Du Bois, Ralph Bunche was one of those who chose to deal with this issue from a global perspective. Thus, as a scholar, his central intellectual preoccupation was the question of race in the political economy of the world. Thus, in *A World View of Race* he notes that

> The concept of race plays an increasingly dominant role in the political and economic affairs of our modern world . . . careful analysis of the role played by race affords us an important clue to world affairs.[3]

Bunche's globally-focused scholarship on race has two interrelated aspects. One aspect involves an examination of the condition of blacks in American society. It is this aspect that produced Bunche's contribution to Gunnar Myrdal's monumental work, *An American Dilemma: The Negro Problem and American Democracy,* some of which was later published as Ralph Bunche, *The Political Status of the Negro in the Age of FDR.*[4] The second aspect of this scholarship is an examination of the condition of Africans under French rule in Togoland and Dahomey. This work not only earned Bunche a Harvard doctorate but the distinction of being the first black in the United States to be awarded a Ph.D. in political science.[5] It is on this second aspect of Bunche's scholarship that this paper will focus because it became the foundation and impetus for his subsequent national and international career.

In his earliest research on Africa, Ralph Bunche examined the condition of Africa in the context of global political and economic realities; the causes of Africa's situation; and the consequences of this situation for Africans and for the world. In this effort, Ralph Bunche was less concerned with African society per se. Rather he was more interested in Africa as a region under European imperial subjugation and exploitation. To him, "Africa is imperialism's greatest and most characteristic expression,"[6] and he wanted to study the impact of imperialism on the Africans.

Bunche concluded that the characteristic pattern of imperial domination was the establishment of a colonial government that had "a makeshift system of administration,"[7] designed to meet the needs of Europeans with little regard for the welfare of the native population. The structures of domination were established after the Europeans had conquered and "pacified" these areas by force.[8]

There were two reasons for the European conquest and partition of Africa. One reason was that the level of capitalist economic development in Europe caused a need for raw materials and markets in Europe. This need could be filled in Africa.

> The need of industrial countries for expanded markets, for raw materials found in the tropics and subtropics, the accumulation of "surplus capital" and the resultant demand for overseas markets, all tended to force European imperialist nations to invade completely the African continent.[9]

The other reason was the fact that the ravages of the slave trade had diminished the ability of the African countries to resist European aggression. In addition, Europe had made significant advances in the technology of warfare, which made it possible for it to overcome the African resistance.

> Africa, and particularly West Africa may be taken as an excellent illustration of how dominant and "superior" races of Europe have conquered peoples less expert in "civilized" methods of warfare.[10]

In order to facilitate the plunder of Africa, the Europeans constructed an elaborate ideology designed "to mask its cruelly selfish motives under high-sounding titles" and "to make the exploitation of the conquered peoples more acceptable to them."[11] This imperial ideology, known as "the civilizing mission," was based on the notion that the European is superior while the African is "a docile primitive with the mind of a child" and that it was "the particular mission of the dominant peoples to bring civilization to the backward peoples of the earth; to convert them to the Christian religion and expose them to the benefits of an advanced European culture."[12]

One of the significant aspects of the strategy of colonial subjugation was the development of a small cadre of a "native elite" that would accept and legitimize the colonial system. The differences between the British colonial philosophy of Indirect Rule and the French philosophy of "assimilation," later abandoned in favor of "association," was such that the "native elite" was more highly developed in the French than in the British colonies. However, the significance of this fact, as it related to the fundamental aspects of imperial ideology and administration, was minimized by the equal commitment of both the French and the British to the exploitation of the colonies and their adamant intention to maintain perpetual domination of their colonies.[13]

Next, Ralph Bunche turned his attention to studying the effect of colonialism on the African people. His judgment was that in spite of the pronouncements of imperial propaganda to the contrary, colonialism had had a devastatingly pernicious effect on the African people. The characteristic effect had been, in his own words, "brutal suppression, greedy economic exploitation of the natural and human resources of a country which is no longer their [the Africans'] own, forced labor, the introduction of previously unknown diseases, vice and social degradation," all this "leading to great decimation of population in many parts of Africa and the breakdown of African civilization."[14]

On the basis of this analysis, Ralph Bunche predicted that the colonial situation had within it the seeds of tragic violent conflict. The difficulty would be caused by a collision between the interests of the colonial powers and the emerging African elite. The colonial powers were determined to maintain control over their territories. On the other hand, the educated African elites . . . were becoming increasingly resentful of the limitations on their political, economic, and social advancement, in spite of their European education and acculturation.[15] In addition, there was "much smoldering resentment among the native masses which may some day break out in violent conflict."[16] These are the raw materials for political unrest in the colonies. As Ralph Bunche put it:

> Both France and Britain will sooner or later have to face a day of reckoning with their Negro populations which are daily becoming more intelligent and articulate. The French may be able to postpone this day longer than will the British, because France finds it possible to mollify the native elite by giving them racial and social equality.[17]

Who will win this confrontation? Ralph Bunche was pessimistic about the chances of the subject peoples of Africa and Asia. "At the present their outlook is not bright: the international order and their race are both arraigned against them."[18] To Bunche's mind, not only was racism used to justify imperialism at its height, but the international order was unwilling to intervene on behalf of the subject peoples; for the same capitalist interests that caused imperialism also dominated the international establishment.

Ralph Bunche deplored the rapacious nature of the colonial empires, the racist ideologies that were used to justify and facilitate them, and the deleterious effect it had on the peoples of Africa. He disapproved of the determination of the colonial powers to maintain their hold on these colonies indefinitely. However, he did not advocate a precipitous dismantling of the colonial empires. What he proposed was an alternative project, based on a colonialism that could be morally justified and made to be a positive force in the development of Africa. This project was to be founded on two premises: (1) "the only sound objective of African colonial policies should be to prepare the African for membership in the community of the civilized world," and (2) "the social and political development of the native in the African colony must at least keep pace with the economic exploitation of his country and whatever economic development may be presumed to accompany that exploitation."[19] On the basis of these principles, Ralph Bunche believed that it would be possible to develop criteria for judging colonial policies and for creating a system of international accountability to oversee colonial policies, with a view toward the eventual termination of imperial rule.

Ralph Bunche's analysis of the causes and consequences of the situation in colonial Africa; his evaluation of colonial activities; and his recommendations for the development of Africa derive from three basic orientations: a normative commitment to egalitarianism, an affective commitment to African peoples, and a belief in the feasibility of the modernization of "backward" societies.

Ralph Bunche's commitment to the principles of "human equality" and "natural rights" is immediately apparent from a reading of the introductory chapter of *A World View of Race*. In this chapter, Bunche laments the fact "the ideal doctrine of the 'equality of man' . . . has fallen upon hard times."[20] It is on the basis of this commitment that Bunche rejected imperialism and colonialism in principle. Imperialism, he notes, is a negation of the principle of the equal rights of peoples, and his concern for the plight of Africans was partly based on the fact that Africans were the victims of imperialist and racist exploitation.

There was another reason for Bunche's concern for Africans. It developed from his sense of kinship with "our cousins."[21] This sense of kinship was based on an awareness of the origins of black Americans, and also on the fact that they faced the same kind of political and economic exploitation and discrimination because they were victimized by the same racist ideology. It was this sense of kinship with Africans that led him to an early scholarly interest in Africa and to the choice of a topic for his doctoral dissertation.

The recommendations that Bunche made in connection with the reform of colonial administration were based on his belief in the possibility of political and social development. This belief in the development of human civilizations is not explicitly stated. However, Bunche's work is full of references that strongly imply a belief in the possibility of societal improvement. One such reference is the statement that "a new and better civilization may be cultivated, through the deliberate application of human intelligence and understanding."[22] Also, in this context, he placed Africans squarely within a hierarchy of human development.

> There is nothing particularly unique about either the African or his problems. The African native today is comparable with the peasant and workman of England and France of a century ago and with other workers and peasants today in less advanced countries of the modern world.[23]

Again, the dynamic nature of this developmental process is not spelled out in any detail. However, Bunche suggests that this development can be achieved through apprenticeship over a period of time.

> Though the time when the West African will be able, in the words of the League Covenant, "to stand alone in the strenuous conditions of the modern world," is probably many generations removed from the present day, he should be serving an apprenticeship in the art of self-rule under the tutelage of his immediate rulers.[24]

In order to assess the impact of Ralph Bunche's thinking on Africa, it would be necessary to differentiate between his analysis of the conditions in Africa, and his recommendations regarding what ought to be done to improve that situation. Much of Bunche's analysis of colonial Africa was well within the mainstream of the contemporary analysis of the period. As such, his contribution to the literature on the subject was not particularly dramatic. For instance, his analysis of colonial administration is very much consistent with what was being offered by other writers of the period such as Padmore, Roberts, and Buell.[25] Similarly, his analysis of the causes and processes of imperialism is very much in the tradition of Hobson.[26] In particular, Bunche's analysis of the development of the native elites, the eventual antagonism between them and the European colonizers, and their role in the process of decolonization, has been borne out by subsequent research.[27]

To be sure, some of his conclusions regarding colonial society in Africa have had to be revised. For example, his contention that the French are free of race prejudice is inconsistent with the experience of the majority of Africans, in spite of the camaraderie that, as an American abroad, may have impressed him, between Frenchmen and évolué Africans, the westernized African natives who served as agents of French civilization for the masses.[28] Even today, many white Americans may enjoy a great deal of camaraderie with their black colleagues although they may have racist attitudes.

The aspects of Bunche's thinking that have had an important impact on Africa were his recommendations regarding colonial reform. First, these recommendations and their theoretical underpinnings were not entirely new at the time. However, they were controversial, and they were debated and criticized from all angles. Nevertheless, these recommendations have had a significant impact on United States and subsequent United Nations policy on trust territories and colonial territories in Africa and throughout the world.

As noted earlier, Ralph Bunche's approach to Africa was based on his uncompromising commitment to the ideals of human equality and natural human rights. It was reported that for him, the most important part of the Atlantic Charter was the part that stated:

> They respect the right of all people to choose the form of government under which they will live; and they wish to see sovereign rights and self-government restored to those who have been forcibly deprived of them.[29]

He was especially committed to the belief that these ideals be applied to Africa. In fact, as a member of the Committee on Africa, the War and Peace Aims he had urged the recommendation that "the 'Eight Points' of the Charter should be applied to Africa in keeping with the broad humanitarian and democratic principles enunciated."[30] For Bunche, the problem was how to give life to these ideals in light of the realities of the world as he saw them. In this regard, some of the recommendations that he proposed and helped to draft for the Committee include the following revealing sections:

> That the goal of ultimate self-government should be definitely accepted in every colony, and that controlling governments should show themselves both willing and eager to fit the African people for larger and larger participation in their own affairs. That the word "guardianship" is better than trusteeship as applied to an African territory under Mandate control as it rightly implies that the relationship is not permanent but has as its purpose the fitting of the ward for self-government as soon as his education and experience permit.[31]

Not surprisingly, when Bunche had an opportunity to do something about this issue as a leading member of the U.S. delegation to the United Nations Conference on International Organization, he is reported to have vowed that "When the United Nations Charter is signed, there will be a section on trusteeship. Not as a postcript. Not a parenthesis. Trusteeship will be as important as any other element in the Charter."[32]

Underlying this commitment to the idea of trusteeship was Ralph Bunche's view of the place of Africa in world civilization. He believed that Africans were as completely human as any other group of people. However, he considered African society to be primitive, that is, less advanced than European society. His view was somewhere between the view that Africans were "essentially inferior, sub-human, without soul and fit only for slavery" and the notion of the African as "a man and brother to whom should be extended the equalitarian principles of the French Revolution," both of which he considered unscientific.[36] For Bunche, the African, as a primitive, needed to be prepared before the principles of the French Revolution could be fully applied. Of course, he noted that not all Africans were primitive; some of them "are culturally in a transitional stage: in reality, they were neither primitive nor civilized in their present mode of living. . . . There are many of them who wear fine European clothing, speak polished French or English, construct beautiful homes and send their children to school. Yet they may worship fetishes, marry several wives, eat without cutlery and sleep on floors in bare bedrooms despite elaborately furnished parlors."[34]

According to Bunche, the backwardness of the African is not due to any biological or genetic deficiency, as some racist propagandists have tried to argue. He sides with those "unbiased social scientists" who assert that Africa's backwardness is due to adverse environmental factors, such as the relative isolation of the continent and the retarding influence of pernicious external contacts.[35] In this argument, Bunche seems to differentiate between primitiveness or backwardness and inferiority. That is to say, his position is that Africans may be backward, but they are not inferior. To him, the badge of inferiority is arbitrary, and in any case it is a specious pseudo-scientific judgment used to justify the subjugation of Africans.

Many writers have argued, and some continue to argue, that Africans are simply benighted, without any possibility of development. In contrast to this notion, Ralph Bunche's view was considered progressive. It was also shared by other progressives in the black American community like W. E. B. Du Bois, who insisted that Africans were capable of making the highest possible contribution to world civilization in due course.[36] Indeed, this was the viewpoint of most of the native elites referred to by Bunche as "Black Frenchmen" and their counterparts in British controlled West Africa. Because of their role as transmitters of European civilization to their African countrymen, most of them believed they were in the vanguard of a movement of modernization that would bring Africa more fully into world civilization.

Bunche did not completely approve of all aspects of European civilization. In fact, he deplored the immorality and greed in those societies that produced imperialism. However, he was unwilling to take the argument to its logical conclusion and deny the moral superiority of European civilization. That was the problem. Once Bunche had conceded the backwardness of African society, for whatever reasons, it was difficult to repudiate the imperial ideology of the civilizing mission. Indeed the principle of "trusteeship," "guardianship," or "wardship" that Bunche subscribed to represents an affirmation of the civilizing mission, even if it is a more humane and temporary version.

A few African intellectuals have rejected the notion of the backwardness of the African. Notable among these was Edward Wylmot Blyden, who insisted that if we take into consideration both the technologial and moral aspects of culture, it cannot easily be demonstrated that European culture is superior. According to Blyden, the fact that one culture is different from another does not make it superior or inferior. For that reason, he is against the idea that Africans can progress through tutelage. In fact, he believes the main problem with Africans is that their cultural self-confidence has been so shattered by the ideology of white superiority that they have been unable to develop their own society. As he puts it, "The evil, it is considered, lies in the system and method of European training to which Negroes are . . . subjected, and which everywhere affects them unfavorably."[37] As far as Blyden is concerned, the way for the African to progress is to minimize the influence of Europeans:

The African must advance by methods of his own. He must possess a power distinct from that of the European. It has been proved that he knows how to take advantage of European culture, and that he can be benefited by it. This proof was perhaps necessary, but it is not sufficient. We must know that we are able to go alone. To carve out our own way. We must not be satisfied that, in this nation, European influence shapes our polity, makes our laws, rules in our tribunals, and impregnates our social atmosphere. We must not suppose that the Anglo-Saxon methods are final, that there is nothing for us to find for our own guidance, and that we have nothing to teach the world.[38]

Events in Africa after independence seem to support Blyden's point. It is clear that the "institutional transfer" in which Apter and other sympathetic Africanists put so much stock has not taken.[39] It may be that the expectation that European institutions and norms could simply be imitated by Africans as a result of a period of tutelage, was naive. As any observer can attest, contemporary Africa is fraught with all manner of political and economic crises. A variety of explanations have been offered for this situation. The one explanation that I wish to recommend is Willie Abraham's suggestion that the root cause of Africa's problems is the great desire of the African elite to mimic European models and solutions. According to Abraham:

> Because the vast majority of our populations are still traditional, politicians and statesmen of Africa have a clear choice before them: whether to be as alien to their own people as the colonial government has been, to complete the deculturization which set in, and to substitute in Africa some new effective culture which has no roots in Africa, or whether to pose problems, to formulate ideals and national objectives meaningfully in terms of the cultures of Africa, which have in fact continued to be in force.[40]

Unfortunately, at the time Abraham posed this dilemma, the African leaders, the native elites, had already decided to continue the work of the colonial governments. It is this attempt of the African elites to impose on the African people what they consider to be "civilized" European institutions that lies at the root of Africa's problems.

If this analysis is correct, then the period of colonial tutelage was not only unnecessary but detrimental. For, why does a society need to be prepared for self-government when it was self-governing before it was conquered? It was this colonial tutelage that created the native elites who lack the cultural self-respect and self-confidence that are needed to be able to develop. I am not arguing that development requires cultural isolation. Indeed, it is clear that the way a society does things "may sometimes be modified to advantage by wise and judicious external agency." My argument is that it is only from a position of cultural confidence that we can find out what we need to borrow and consider the possibility of integrating it into our own cultures, indeed discover what we may wish to discard in our own culture.[42] Without this cultural confidence, a society loses the ability to choose; it is simply overwhelmed.

Ralph Bunche might have subscribed to this argument. In his early work, he had observed that "the employment of this racial elite class as a device for the control of the country is a condition viciously inimical to the best interests of the masses of the natives."[43] Bunche might have argued that the colonial subjugation of Africa should never have occurred. However, at the time of his writing, colonialism was a reality. He could not wish it away. His problem was how to ensure that the colonial condition would not be permanent. The colonial powers had already expressed their determination to keep their colonial territories indefinitely. How could he convince them that the progressive demise of the colonial state in favor of African autonomy of independence would be beneficial to all? The principle of trusteeship provided both a normatively defensible and a practical answer. He was right. It was on the basis of the United Nations program of decolonization that most of the African countries, and other dependent territories, gained their independence.

In concluding, Ralph Bunche is best known for his contribution as a United Nations mediator, which earned him the Nobel Prize for Peace. However, his work on Africa as a scholar was the most significant. First, this work was central to his intellectual and affective preoccupations. Second, and more important, it was responsible for the way his career developed. To be sure, his work on behalf of blacks in the United States was impressive. However, all that he did subsequently flowed from his knowledge, his experience, and his reputation as an expert on Africa.

The process began with Bunche's 1934 dissertation on "A Comparison of the Rule of a Mandated Area, French Togoland, with that of a Colony, Dahomey." By the time of the publication of his *A World View of Race* in 1936, he already had a reputation as a specialist on colonial administration in Africa as well as in other territories around the world. In 1941, he was appointed to the Committee on Africa, the War, and Peace Aims, which produced the influential book entitled *The Atlantic Charter and Africa from an American Standpoint.* Then followed a rapid succession of government positions, based on his reputation as a specialist. First, in 1941, Bunche was appointed to the Office of the Coordinator of Information (OCI) for the Armed Forces in the Africa and Far East Section. In 1942, he was appointed Chief of the Africa Section of the Research and Analysis Branch of the Office of Strategic Services (OSS). Bunche became a specialist on Africa and Dependent Areas in the Department of State in 1944. From this office, he participated as a member of both the U.S. delegation to the Dumbarton Oaks Conference and the United Nations Conference on International Organization, where he was the principal architect of the U.S. proposals on trusteeship that were adopted in the United Nations Charter.[45]

On the basis of his experience and commitment, he was loaned to the United Nations as Director of the Trusteeship Division, a position he later accepted on a permanent basis. From this position he rose to the office of Under Secretary-General, Special Representative of the Secretary-General, and Chief of United Nations Operations in the Congo.[46] In addition to his celebrated work on Palestine, and other areas like Kashmir and Yemen, Ralph Bunche always kept a close and special eye on issues involving the decolonization process, especially in Africa. Thus, by the time of his resignation he had come full circle. His early African scholarship shaped his career, and his career was used most significantly in the service of Africa. In the final analysis, there can be no more fitting comment about Ralph Bunche than this:

> It must be remembered that in his U.N. role as director of the Department of Trusteeship, Bunche did more than any other single man in setting out the guidelines which helped the nations of Africa reach independence.[47]

For that achievement, this African salutes Ralph Bunche.

Notes

1. See Samuel R. Spencer, *Booker T. Washington and the Negro Place in American Life* (New York: Little, Brown & Co., 1955).
2. The global scope of Du Bois's treatment of blacks is illustrated in the following partial listing of his scholarly works: *The Suppression of the African Slave Trade to the United States of America* (1896), *The Philadelphia Negro* (1899), *The Souls of Black Folk* (1903), *Black Reconstruction* (1935), and *Africa: An Outline of the History of the African Continent and Its Inhabitants* (1959).
3. Ralph Bunche, *A World View of Race* (New York: Associates in Negro Folk Education, 1936), p. 3.
4. Ralph Bunche, *The Political Status of the Negro in the Age of FDR.* (Chicago: University of Chicago Press, 1973).
5. Peggy Mann, *Ralph Bunche: U.N. Peacemaker* (New York: Coward, McCann & Geoghegan, 1975), p. 70.
6. Bunche, *World View of Race*, p. 41.
7. Ibid., p. 44.
8. Ibid., p. 38.
9. Ibid., p. 42.
10. Ibid., p. 41.
11. Ibid., pp. 38, 41.
12. Ibid.

13. Ibid., p. 47.
14. Ibid., p. 41.
15. Ralph Bunche, "French Administration in Togoland and Dahomey" (Ph.D. diss., Harvard University, 1934), p. 398.
16. Bunche, *World View of Race*, p. 44.
17. Ibid., p. 63.
18. Ibid., p. 65.
19. Ibid., pp. 46–47.
20. Ibid., p. 1.
21. Ibid., p. 90.
22. Ralph Bunche, "French Administration," p. 2.
23. Bunche, *World View*, p. 63.
24. Bunche, "French Administration," p. 388.
25. George Padmore, *How Britain Rules Africa*. (N.Y.: Lothrop, Lee & Shepherd, 1936); S. H. Roberts, *History of French Colonial Policy*, 2 vols. (London. P. S. King, 1929); *Raymond L. Buell, The Native Problem in Africa*, 2 vols. (New York: Macmillan, 1928).
26. J. A. Hobson, *Imperialism* (London: Allen and Unwin, 1905).
27. See I. Wallerstein, *Africa: The Politics of Independence* (New York: Vintage Books, 1961).
28. Bunche, *World View of Race*, 50, 53.
29. Mann, *Ralph Bunche*, p. 95.
30. Committee on Africa, the War, and Peace Aims, *The Atlantic Charter and Africa from an American Standpoint*, p. 105.
31. Ibid.
32. Mann, *Ralph Bunche*, p. 115.
33. Bunche, *World View of Race*, p. 46.
34. Ibid., p. 43.
35. Ibid., pp 45–46.
36. W. E. B. Du Bois, *On the Conservation of the Races* (1897), p. 64.
37. Edward Wylmot Blyden, *The African Problem and the Method of Its Solution* (Washington, D.C.: Gibson Bros., 1890), pp. 11–12. Another writer who strongly rejected the idea of the inferiority of black people was Paul Robeson; see Paul Robeson, *Tributes: Selected Writings*, compiled and edited by Roberta Yancy Dent, assisted by Marilyn Robeson and Paul Robeson, Jr. (New York: The Paul Robeson Archives, 1976).
38. Blyden, *African Problem*, p. 20.
39. David Apter, *Ghana in Transition* (Princeton: Princeton University Press, 1956).
40. W. E. Abraham, *The Mind of Africa* (Chicago: University of Chicago Press, 1962).
41. Edward Wylmot Blyden, *West Africa Before Europe* (London: C. M. Phillips, 1905), p. 140.
42. Abraham, *Mind of Africa*, p. 39.
43. Bunche, *World View of Race*, p. 51.
44. For analysis of the UN process of decolonization see W. Ofuatey-Kodjoe, *The Principle of Self-Determination in International Law* (New York: Nellen Publishers, 1975).
45. Mann, *Ralph Bunche:* pp. 124–130.

46. For accounts of Bunche's role in the solution of the Congo, see Gordon King, *U.N. in the Congo: A Quest for Peace* (New York: Carnegie Endowment for International Peace, 1962) and Ernest LeFever, *Crisis in the Congo* (Washington, D.C.: The Brookings Institution, 1965).
47. Mann, *Ralph Bunche:* p. 333.

· 7 ·

BUNCHE AND THE COLONIAL WORLD:
From Trusteeship to Decolonization

Lawrence S. Finkelstein

Schemes of international organization . . . these are all means and not ends. . . .The real objective must always be the good life for all of the people. . . . peace, bread, a house, adequate clothing, education, good health, and above all, the right to walk with dignity on the world's great boulevards.[1]

Ralph Bunche first made his mark as an official dealing with colonial and African affairs. It was here that his preparation and expertise lay. It was as a government officer dealing with these matters during World War II that Dr. Bunche established the reputation that paved his way for his recruitment to serve in the United Nations after the war. And it is often forgotten that the subsequent service that won him world renown, as mediator in Palestine and as United Nations peacemaker extraordinary, resulted from his appointment to the UN Secretariat (in the spring of 1946) as head of the UN Trusteeship Division.

Indeed, Dr. Bunche believed that what launched him on his international career was the attention attracted by his remarks extracted in the headnote above. They comprised the peroration of a speech he gave at the Institute of Pacific Relations Conference in Mont Tremblant,

109

Quebec, in December 1942.[2] At that time, he was a Senior Social Science Analyst on Colonial Affairs in the Office of Strategic Services (OSS), the wartime precursor of the Central Intelligence Agency.

Any appraisal of Ralph Bunche, therefore, would be incomplete without considering his beliefs and role in that extraordinary historical episode that may be thought of loosely as the ending of colonialism. This chapter will examine that aspect of the saga of Ralph Bunche and his turbulent time.

The enterprise is not without hazards, of which the reader is forewarned. The first is the probability of author's bias. The author served under Ralph Bunche, as a very junior professional officer, during the years 1944, 1945, and 1946, in the Department of State and the United Nations Secretariat. In both organizations, the service was in units having to do with non–self-governing territories, as colonies were quaintly called in those self-conscious times. Friendship, to put it conservatively, outlasted the employment and flourished until Ralph's death. The author thus shares with all who knew him an incapacity for objectivity on the subject of Ralph Bunche.

There are further hazards, beyond the presumption of bias in the author. It is intractably difficult to differentiate Dr. Bunche's role in the development of U.S. positions leading up to the San Francisco Conference in 1945 and the inauguration of the U.N. (in the following year) from the roles of his fellow workers in the Department of State, some of whom were his superiors in the hierarchy.[3] Dr. Bunche himself was too busy making history to record it. No memoirs by other relevant American participants have come to the attention of the author. Therefore, this chapter represents and invites an ongoing effort of interpretation.

Views on Colonialism and Its Remedies

Ralph Bunche wrote and spoke about colonialism quite a lot, and his views reflect the liberal, anticolonial sentiment of the times. His Ph.D. thesis was submitted at Harvard in January 1934, the fieldwork in Africa completed in the winter of 1932–1933. In the thesis are the main outlines and much of the content of his views about colonialism, which were embellished but fundamentally unaltered in later years.[4]

His outlook was naturally informed by the writings of those who had preceded him. He was familiar with the work of J. A. Hobson and the communist writings on imperialism, although, surprisingly, the thesis contains no direct reference to Lenin, not even a citation. Thus, a strong strain of economic determinism is explicit in denying that any "single motive" can sufficiently explain the motives behind European partition of Africa in the last quarter of the nineteenth century, and it is equally clear in saying that "the economic motive" was the dominating one in partitioning Africa. This analysis comes straight from Hobson, even though, strangely, Hobson is not cited at this point. Bunche, following Hobson, focused on specific factors as motives for imperialism: the rate of increase in production, leading to "surplus manufactures" and the need for expanded markets; the demand of industrialized nations for tropical and subtropical products, especially raw materials; the creation of surplus capital and the resultant demand for opportunities to invest overseas; and the communication and transportation revolution, the exact influence of which the thesis does not develop.[5]

The economic determinist theme appears in Dr. Bunche's monograph, *A World View of Race,* published in 1936. Arguing that race did not explain imperialism, but had rather been "a convenient device for the imperialist," he struck the chord again and again: "the directing motive in the process is human greed"; "the so-called backward peoples would hold no attraction for the advanced peoples if they possessed no human or material sources which are needed by the industrial nations"; "imperialism is an international expression of capitalism"; "back of this partition of Africa were the compelling economic forces of modern capitalism."[6]

Without doubt, he believed then that greed, pure and simple, was the predominant motive of imperialism. In addition to the explicit statements to that effect, such as those quoted above, there is the further evidence of Dr. Bunche's dissertation, which is suffused with analysis and examples of the French economic interests that both accounted for and shaped French West African colonialism. Although the economic determinism of Bunche's analysis is evident, the evidence also seems to be that he was no simple ideologue. For one thing, he always took pains to make clear that other motives were also present, for example, the growing spirit of nationalism, the desire to spread "superior" civilizations among other peoples, which he characterized more often as "sales talk" by imperialist propagandists than "missionary zeal," and religious mission.[7]

Half a century later, this seems dreary stuff. The economic determinism has been by and large discredited, at least in the macro-deterministic dimensions of Hobson's and Lenin's explanations of imperialism.[8] In truth, none of this was particularly original, or leading, even when it was written. On the whole, it seems probable that although Bunche said these things he did not hold them to be really important. Moreover, there is not much evidence, if any, that he was moved by economic determinism in his later career as a public servant.[9] Perhaps he was by then more focused on solving the problems of colonialism than on explaining them. He was, for example, much less enthusiastic about the "open door" as a specific remedy for economic monopoly by the colonial powers than was his colleague at the State Department Benjamin Gerig.[10]

It seems probable, and plausible, that he espoused the economic explanations not because he was deeply committed to them, but for two other reasons. The first is, simply, that the economic explanations were there and they were fashionable. He believed them and thus was not inspired to criticize them theoretically or discredit them empirically, as later scholars did. Indeed, it would have been stranger for him to have attempted a refutation, or even to have taken a different tack, than for him to have followed the then fashionable theory which he had no special reason to challenge. The second reason is more interesting and more relevant to Bunche's deep commitments. He used the economic arguments to refute what he thought to be the myth of racial difference as the explanation of imperialism. His thesis nowhere refers specifically to Social Darwinism; the bibliography contains no reference to Herbert Spencer. There is, however, a direct assault on the views of Jan Christian Smuts and others accepting Kipling's version of the colonized native as "half devil and half child."[11]

Here is a theme that mattered to Bunche and mattered deeply. As his work *A World View of Race* showed unmistakably, he saw colonialism and imperialism as manifestations of racism. And when he wrote his thesis at Harvard, he had every reason to understand how unusual was his own role as a Negro (a term he bore with pride) in white precincts. Later, he experienced African racism directly and personally when only an intervention by Cordell Hull himself, the American Secretary of State, unblocked the permission for Bunche to visit South Africa on scholarly business that had, until then, been denied him.[12]

More broadly, the predominant belief of the time was that races were more than different. They were hierarchically ranked. The concept of human equality, Bunche wrote, and the doctrine of natural rights "were cradled in the modern Western world." The " 'sacred' concept of the 'natural rights of man' and its international corollary, the 'rights of peoples' " were paid "lip service," however, and abused in the service of the economic and political interests of "the dominant peoples and powerful nations."[13] Moreover, scholarly efforts to refute the prevailing dogmas were in their early stages. Bunche was compelled to argue mainly by fervent assertion, for example: "Nature says boldly and undeniably that man is a single species." And quoting with approval from John Stuart Mill: "Of all the vulgar modes of escaping from the consideration of the effect of social and moral influences upon the human mind, the most vulgar is that of attributing the diversities of conduct and character to inherent natural differences."[14] Bunche fortified his claim by occasional references to such early pioneers of refutation as Lancelot Hogben.[15] And his thesis is peppered with references to African and other black leaders serving in high positions of authority within the French colonial system. The sparseness of scholarly support at the time for what Bunche knew to be true may be part of the explanation for his own determination to provide proof of human equality by his own example. It is certain that he saw his own career as a means of showing that blacks were not racially inferior.

If ideas in the preceding paragraph leave the impression that Dr. Bunche's interpretation of colonialism was too much influenced by personal grievance or a sense of personal inequity, that is not the intention; nor would it be the truth. At the heart of the matter was his deep and abiding commitment to the fundaments of Western democracy. The consent of the governed was for him the measure of good government, and this theme appears in his dissertation. He was clear, moreover, that for self-government to be complete it had to extend to the bases of government. Such a requirement would not be met by self-rule doled out, as it were, and subject to limitations fixed by a governing power.

Colonialism, in this view, could never meet the standard Bunche set for self-government, except in those cases when the people of a country chose a colonial regime in an act of self-determination. He put it this way: "The right of a people to govern themselves involves the right of those people to change the form which that government assumes."[16] This belief, however, was not simplistic; nor did it resolve for Bunche the issues concerning policies toward colonies. He recognized all too well that Africans were not, in the words of the mandates article of the League of Nations Covenant (Art. 22), "ready to stand by themselves in the strenuous conditions of the modern world."[17] His commitment to what was in fact "self-determination," a term he seems not to have employed in his thesis, did not resolve issues. It merely posed them.

Ralph Bunche recognized and grappled with complexity. Even so, his commitment to the fundamental requirement that colonial peoples be enabled to decide for themselves became more resolute and was amplified over the years. This author well remembers lengthy discussions with Bunche in the mid-1940s about the issue between conservatives and liberals over "good government versus self-government." Bunche was inclined to assume that this issue would be resolved in individual cases by the inevitable emergent will of a colonized people signifying their readiness to assume management of their own affairs. The evidence of that will would then be unmistakable. Indeed, when he wrote his thesis in the early 1930s, he already discerned signs that "the educated African is rapidly acquiring a zest for" decisions by majority vote in representative assemblies and government by debate, which he termed "political fetishes of the western world."[18] On the whole, he seemed impatient with, even scornful of, the idea that anyone's views of what good government required should, but perhaps even more, *would* obstruct self-government when people themselves were prepared to claim it.

He saw little merit in the argument as to whether "good" government or "self"-government should be the criterion of policy toward colonies. His impatience with that debate reflected his own unyielding belief in the principle of "consent of the governed" as well as his pragmatic expectation that pressures for self-government would prevail. His belief, though, in the principle of the "consent of the governed" did not necessarily mean applying the procedures of choice which had evolved in the various cultural settings of the Western democracies to the cultural milieux of Africa.

His characterization of Western democratic processes as "fetishes," referred to above, was no accident. He was deeply concerned about the disruptive effects of the wholesale implantation of alien Western ways in the native cultural soils of the colonies, and this concern is recurrent throughout his thesis. He was, for example, extremely critical of that "extreme of policy" which, basing itself on sentiment, regarded the African as man and brother, and which extended to him the humanitarian principles of the French Revolution and sought to Europeanize him overnight. He found this extreme no more satisfactory than its opposite—the policy based only on greed, which regarded Africans as essentially inferior and subhuman, without soul, and fit only for slavery.[19] This concern of Bunche's culminates in his forthright identification of the basic question whether European political institutions should be introduced in Africa and especially whether the method of electoral representation should be adopted.[20]

There were two reasons underlying his concern. One was his despair over the bastardization of indigenous culture and values (although he did not use that word) and his clear preference for preserving the cultural and social heritage and integrity of the native peoples. In this, he anticipated the principle of endogeneity that has of late played a large role in the philosophy of development guilding international organizations, mainly UNESCO. The second reason was his fear that the cooptation of native elites to serve as collaborators of the colonial rulers, especially in the French territories where race was not itself a barrier to status, would result in schismatic, or layered societies, riven between the évolués cooppted into the ruling class and the rest of the population from whom they would be divided by conflicts of role and interest. In this, Bunche foreshadowed more recent neo-imperialist theories of "structural imperialism" that emphasize the lateral connections between economic interests in rich countries and the rich people allied with them in poor countries. On the other hand, he saw weaknesses also in the British system of indirect rule. While the latter presumed to preserve native institutions of administration and governance, it in fact substituted the authority of the colonial power and, moreover, risked rigidifying the inherited role of tribal chiefs who were often authoritarian, backward-looking, and undereducated.[21]

Confronted with these complexities, not only does Bunche's analysis seem, on the whole, inconclusive, but he also seems to recognize that those changes he decries are inevitable and already under way. He repeatedly asserted the importance of clarifying the political objectives of colonial government. What was needed were definite programs that would lead natives toward ultimate political and social status. "The only sound objective, of African colonial policies," he said, "should be to prepare the Africans for membership in the community of the civilized world, not as individuals, *but as communities*."[22] In the language of the 1940s and 1950s, this was self-determination. He did struggle very hard with the well-nigh intractable problem of deciding what was a "community" to which membership in the world community should be given.[23]

Another problem he confronted more conclusively. How could he reconcile a commitment to the principle of self-determination (reaching to the bases of government) with the irresistible evidence that African colonies were far from ready to perform the function of self-government? His answer was tutelage. The automaticity he foresaw for self-determination was to develop over time. In the meantime, guidance was needed, as well as schooling, in the arts of government. The African, he wrote, "should be serving an apprenticeship in the art of self-rule under the tutelage of his immediate rulers."[24] This advice, of course, left unresolved the dilemma of how to reconcile European tutelage with the desire to preserve indigenous values, culture, and institutions as the bases for ultimate self-government.

What was clear was Bunche's definite preference for principles, which were to play an important part in his later public service. For instance, he was strongly committed to the necessity for external surveillance of colonial administration. He believed that colonial powers were, and should be held, accountable for their administration. He was clear-sighted about the limitations of the mandates system under the League of Nations. Yet, his detailed comparison of the administration of Togo, which was under a mandate, and Dahomey, which was not, led him to see real advantages in the system.[25] Bunche argued for strengthening the supervisory powers available to the mandates organization of the League of Nations. He advocated a right of direct appeal to the League about administration of mandated territory. Better yet would be domiciling a representative of the Permanent Mandates Commission in each mandated territory or, failing that, provision for periodic visits for inspection. He also exhibited interest in even more far-reaching schemes to internationalize the administration of colonies. His model was a plan, considered by the League of Nations Council to enable it to have a direct advisory role in Liberia, involving guaranteed rights of permanent League representation in the country. Although the plan never was given the Liberian approval it needed to be undertaken, Dr. Bunche advocated it as a model for African colonies at two different points in his dissertation.[26]

His faith in the reliability and good intentions of the administering powers was evidently not very great. Moreover, he saw in international involvement—the more the better—assurances of good behavior by the colonial powers. He seems also to have been attracted to international mechanisms as means to introduce broader experience, disinterested criticism, and a diversity of views as potential remedies to the defects he discerned in colonial administration, resulting at least in part from those economic motives that guided colonial policies.

Role in Planning the United Nations System for Non-Self-Governing Territories

Evaluating, or even describing, Ralph Bunche's role in the development and inauguration of postwar international institutions to deal with colonial issues is difficult and also problematic. As discussed at the beginning of this chapter, he was but one of many actors and a fairly junior one at that. Constraints were set by decisions reached before he even joined the Department of State in January 1944. Diplomatic exchanges, especially with the British, had already begun to outline the limits of what might be achieved in new arrangements for the period after World War II. His arrival on the scene more or less coincided with the activation of the fierce War and Navy Department resistance to trusteeship, which, because of the threat it posed to their interests in bases in the Pacific, was to preoccupy the planners for the next year and a half. In no sense was Bunche a free agent. Nor was there a blank slate on which to write.

Let us look first at the record of Bunche's service in the Department of State. It began before the Dumbarton Oaks Conversations in the summer of 1944, at which a draft of the UN Charter was agreed upon among the "Big Four": the United States, the Soviet Union, the United Kingdom, and (in a separate round, without the Russians present), China. His service continued through the period of the Yalta Conference among Roosevelt, Churchill and Stalin in February 1945; the death of Roosevelt in April 1945; and the United Nations Conference on International Organization (UNCIO) in San Francisco from April 25 to June 26, 1945, at which the UN Charter was adopted. His term also covered the period of the preparatory commission that was set up by UNCIO in San Francisco. This commission was to arrange the first meetings of the UN, which were to be held after enough states had ratified the Charter. The commission and its executive committee met in both the summer and fall of 1945. His service also included the first part of the first session of the

UN General Assembly, which met in London in January and February of 1946. The session had the job of trying to translate the provisions of the UN Charter into effective rules and procedures for carrying out the Charter mandates. Dr. Bunche attended most of these meetings as part of the American staff. When he did not, he was nevertheless a backup, monitoring the negotiations, providing support and instructing the delegation.

For some months, after he transferred from the Office of Strategic Services to the Department of State, Dr. Bunche served, nominally at least, in the Division of Territorial Studies. During that time, he served on the inter-divisional committee that dealt with dependent area affairs. Soon after he arrived at the State Department, Benjamin Gerig sought his transfer to the Division of International Security and Organization (ISO) to work under Gerig on postwar plans concerning dependent areas. By mid 1944, Bunche had moved to the basement corridor, near the State Department incinerator, in the old State-War-Navy Building to join the other UN planners.[27] His formal transfer to ISO occurred soon thereafter, in July 1944. As a result of a department reorganization late that year, he formally became part of the newly formed Division of Dependent Area Affairs (DA). In February 1945, he was named acting associate chief of the division, with Gerig as chief. Then, in April he was formally appointed associate chief, a position he retained for the duration of his service in the department.

Thus, although Ralph Bunche had an unusual opportunity to play a part in stirring events, especially for so relatively young a man, he was not positioned to exert a dominant influence on issues that remained open for decision. He was relatively low in the hierarchy, and Ben Gerig, his chief, was older, more experienced, and had been with the division longer. Although there is no reason to doubt Gerig's commitment to the same goals of progress for colonial peoples and a world at peace that motivated Dr. Bunche, Gerig's approach was more conciliatory and less obdurate on the central points of principle and on those, as will be seen, Bunche was likely to "hang tough." Besides, the record shows that, at least during the first months of Bunche's service at the State Department, Gerig, rather than Bunche, was the one to participate in those meetings involving policy-level officials of the government. Even Gerig reported through a hierarchy, comprised of a division chief, at the time Dr. Harley Notter, and later an office director, at first Ambassador Edwin C. Wilson and then Alger Hiss. The responsible officer in the Department of State was Dr. Leo Pasvolsky, who, as Special Assistant to the Secretary of State, had overall charge of postwar planning and also seemed to enjoy the special confidence of Secretary of State Cordell Hull. That was a wasting asset, however. Hull was aging, and by the time of the Dumbarton Oaks Conversations, he was increasingly handicapped by illness. In November

1944, poor health forced Hull to resign, and he was replaced as Secretary of State by Under-Secretary Edward R. Stettinius, Jr. Many interpreted this to mean that FDR intended to continue as the nation's primary foreign policy maker.

Thus, although Bunche was listed among the American technical staff at the Dumbarton Oaks Conversations, he did not participate in decision-making meetings of senior officials. Indeed, as an "assignment secretary," he appears to have served mainly as a note taker.[28] Trusteeship was not formally on the agenda of these meetings in any case, and there is no evidence that he was an important participant in the informal international exchanges that took place at higher levels. When decisions were needed from the White House, neither Gerig nor Bunche was present. Pasvolsky was the lowest ranking State Department officer in such meetings during that period. At the Yalta meeting of heads of government the following February, at which a critical decision was taken affecting trusteeship, the State Department brief was handled by Alger Hiss, then the Director of the Office of Special Political Affairs, with no direct participation from the Division of Dependent Area Affairs.

Later on, things changed. The pressures on a relatively small staff grew. Gerig's responsibilities had broadened for he was not only Chief of the Division of Dependent Area Affairs but also Associate Chief of another division. Thus his time and energies were spread more broadly than were those of Bunche, most of whose effect was focused on colonial issues. Bunche's competence was making its mark. Beginning with the negotiations between the State and Interior Departments, on the one hand, and the War and Navy Departments, on the other, over whether the United States would make a trusteeship proposal at the San Francisco Conference, Bunche became more deeply involved in high-level decisions. He is listed among the State Department officials who participated in the *ad hoc* group that prepared for the Interdepartmental Committee on Dependent Area Aspects of International Organization, which was set up to deal with cabinet-level disagreement. He is not, however, listed as having represented the department in the committee meetings themselves, although Gerig and colleague James Frederick Green were so listed.[29] In April 1945, he was one of a small group who drafted the final U.S. plan for trusteeship on the train going to San Francisco. And at UNCIO, his was an important role in supporting the U.S. representative dealing with the agenda concerning non-self-governing territories, Commander Harold Stassen. By the time of the first UN General Assembly session in London in January 1946, Dr. Bunche was even more visible as a principal backup for John Foster Dulles, who was the U.S. delegate in the relevant committee, Committee 4. When Dulles could not attend the sessions, Bunche frequently represented the United States.

Thus, toward the end of the period of creating and installing the UN's arrangements for non-self-governing territories Bunche had a growing importance and effect. All the same, it should not be surprising that Gerig, rather than Bunche, was seen as the more significant American official on colonial affairs in the standard postwar histories of the development of policies on postwar colonial administration. If any "working-level" American official is credited with a significant role in planning for postwar arrangements for the colonies it is Gerig's name, rather than Bunche's, that turns up.[30]

Bunche's impact was limited by the fact that he arrived late on the State Department scene and was hierarchically situated where little leverage was normally available to him. His potential influence was circumscribed also by the fact that, for the most part, the outlines of U.S. policy on postwar colonial arrangements had been fixed long before he turned up.[31] So, there was little opportunity for intellectual leadership. Most of the conceptualizing had already been done by others. What was tested during his years as an official dealing with non-self-governing territories was far less his ability to lead in setting major new directions of policy and far more his capacities to convert policy objectives into realized programs. In this respect, he was not found wanting.

By the time Bunche assumed his tasks at the State Department, a system of trusteeship had been well established as the official objective for the United States. It had early been decided that trusteeship should be designed to deal with territories that had been under League of Nations mandate and those that might be taken from the Axis powers because of the war. British resistance had made itself felt in the decision, reached as early as late 1942, that trusteeship should not be applied to all other colonies. However much Bunche, and others, might have preferred the broader concept of the scope of trusteeship (and he no doubt did prefer the broader scope), there was no room for change. The policy outline was firmly set. The American plan retained a small loophole, namely the provision that ended up in Article 76 of the Charter, allowing for the extension of the trusteeship system to other territories placed under it voluntarily by the powers administering them. This provision was always wishful thinking since no colonial power volunteered to place a territory under trusteeship under this clause.

Moreover, the opportunity to achieve another of Bunche's preferred solutions—more direct international involvement in supervising the administration of trust territories, perhaps even direct international administration—had also long since gone by the boards. The policy was that administration should be by the states, principally the mandatory powers in cases of territories that had been under mandate.[32] Trusteeship was to be essentially supervision by the international organization, employing specified powers. In this respect, the system, as it had been

designed before 1944, met those standards Bunche had derived from
the fieldwork he did in connection with his Harvard thesis. The contemplated powers of supervision were far more extensive than those
available under the mandates system. In fact, draft proposals of the U.S.
even planned on giving the international organization complete authority to set the terms under which trusteeship administration was to be
exercised in each territory and also to appoint the administering authorities, as well as to remove them for cause. These provisions remained
in U.S. drafts until the very eve of UNCIO, but then fell victim to the
War and Navy Departments' determination to be assured of full and
unchallengeable control over the Japanese-mandated territory in the
Pacific, which became the Trust Territory of the Pacific Islands. By this
time, Bunche was deeply involved in the negotiations. It seems reasonable to presume that he would have resisted the adulteration of the
powers of the organization. No record of the relevant argument has
been available to this author, and therefore it is not possible to know
what position Bunche took. If he defended extensive authority for the
UN, he lost the argument to the big guns of the U.S. Navy.

The political objectives to be established for trusteeship administration had also long since been fixed, by decision of Secretary Hull in
1942–1943. The goal was to be self-government, rather than independence, which stuck in the British craw. The available evidence does not
illuminate the position Bunche took on this question. The evidence of
his Ph.D. thesis suggests he might have thought a process of guidance in
self-government, leading to an act of choice by the population of a
colony, better than a bald assertion that independence was to be the goal
for all trust territories. On the other hand, it seems likely that in 1944
and 1945, he was among those favoring the more advanced statement. It
is certain that he advised Commander Stassen against his public resistance to including "independence" among the goals for trusteeship when
that issue arose during the San Francisco Conference.[33] Stassen did not
follow his advice, and "independence" got in the Charter over the initial
resistance of the United States. What is not certain is whether Bunche
advised Stassen as he did because he preferred "independence" over
weaker statements, which is probable, or because he thought it tactically
and perhaps politically unwise for the United States to oppose "independence," which is also possible. Certainly, he felt that the intervention by
Stassen was unnecessary, because the British delegate, Viscount Cranborne, had been prepared to take up the cudgel against "independence"
as the stated objective and was thus spared the necessity of taking so
exposed a position.

Two other components of the American outline of postwar colonial
arrangements were also well set by the time Bunche took up his State
Department duties. One was the idea of a general declaration of princi-

ples to govern administration of all colonies, especially the great majority that did not come under the trusteeship system. Bunche certainly favored this idea. His enthusiasm for it was invigorated by his experience as a member of the U.S. delegation to the conference of the International Labor Organization (ILO), held in Philadelphia in the autumn of 1944, to plan for the postwar period. Bunche played an active and important role in negotiations leading to the adoption of the ILO Recommendation on Minimum Standards of Social Policy in Dependent Territories. He was pleased by his involvement in that development, in large part, because the Recommendation was believed to be the first international instrument to establish standards for the administration of all colonies.[34] Bunche saw it as a precedent for a declaration, at the U N Conference, going beyond the social standards addressed by the ILO within the latter's narrower mandate.

As things developed, the tense struggle with both the War and Navy Departments in the winter of 1944–1945 and the spring thereafter overwhelmed the planners. The U.S. plan to propose a declaration was abandoned.[35] There is no evidence as to Bunche's part in this process, which came at a time of enormous stress in Washington. The number one item on the relevant agenda was the struggle to preserve the trusteeship position against the War and Navy Departments. That was an all-consuming preoccupation, especially in the hectic days of the presidential transition from Roosevelt to Truman, which coincided with the final frantic preparations for the San Francisco Conference.

The other component of U.S. policy, which was in place before Bunche's arrival in the State Department, was a plan for a worldwide network of regional commissions to deal with colonial problems in the regions on a non-compulsory basis. The model was the Anglo-American Caribbean Commission (AACC) that had been established early in the war to permit the two governments to collaborate, especially in coping with problems that had been accentuated by the war. The experiment was generally regarded as successful, and plans were underway to extend the AACC to encompass other colonial powers in the area—France and the Netherlands. More broadly, the idea of regional commissions was British in inspiration. It had been advanced by the British Colonial Secretary, Oliver Stanley, in 1942, as a less threatening alternative to the developing U.S. plans for trusteeship. At that time, the latter had not yet clearly been limited only to the mandated and ex-enemy territories.

The idea of introducing a plan for regional commissions at the San Francisco conference died at the same time that the idea of a declaration was dropped,[36] in the spring of 1945. Enthusiasm at the working level was probably minimal to begin with because it had been inspired by the British idea. It cooled even further because of the Latin American ambush Secretary Stettinius had encountered at the Pan American Conference he attended at Chapultepec on his way home from Yalta. The Latins had pressed hard for regional adaptations of the global security system the U.S. planners favored. Regionalism was thus not a favored idea in the State Department at the time. No general plan for regional commissions was introduced at San Francisco. Later, the AACC did evolve into the broader Caribbean Commission, and Dr. Bunche served as an American member of that body. A South Pacific Commission was also established after the war.

With so many avenues blocked for Dr. Bunche to potential policy influence, what possibilities remained? The answer is unmistakable. The one real colonialism "game in town" during his tenure in the State Department was the issue whether there could be a U.S. trusteeship policy at all.

On this point, there was no room for doubt about where he stood. He stood four square behind trusteeship. His scholarship had pointed him toward the greatest attainable internationalization of colonial administration as the remedy for the abuses colonialism inflicted on the peoples of the colonies. Not only had the mandated territories been administered a shade better than the pure colonies, but the power of example would be very great. He had written that it was ". . . certain that the mandates system will exert an influence far beyond that affecting those areas presently subjected to its provisions. The inexorable force of public opinion will compel, as it has to an extent already, the extension of identical principles to retarded peoples throughout the world, whether they dwell in areas held as colonies and possessions or not."[37] Trusteeship was clearly central for Bunche.

There is no reason to doubt that he advocated unwavering resistance to the demands of the armed services and their formidable civilian cabinet secretaries, Henry Stimson and James Forrestal, that trusteeship be scrapped. That is how this author recollects Dr. Bunche's role at the time.

Dr. Bunche was probably insufficiently established and too late on the scene to have had much to do with the first major battle in the campaign. That was a loss for trusteeship advocates because trusteeship had to be dropped from the proposals the United States introduced at Dumbarton Oaks in the face of the claim by the military chiefs that the topic might invite contentious debate over territorial issues and thus threaten allied unity in the war. The tale of the continuing struggle, thereafter, to ensure that the United States could take an initiative on trusteeship has been told too often to repeat it here.[38] The trusteeship advocates prevailed in the end when President Roosevelt, in Warm Springs just before he died, endorsed the State and Interior Departments' recommendation that the United States proceed with a proposal to establish the principles and machinery of a trusteeship system.

It has been argued elsewhere that the victory may have been a pyrrhic one.[39] The principle of trusteeship was preserved to be sure. But the system the United States was able to advance was a pale reflection of the design before it had fallen victim to the surgery of the service departments. As has been mentioned above, the declaration of principles to apply to all non-self-governing territories was abandoned as a project of the U.S.

An even greater cost may have been the loss of initiative that resulted. There was an embargo on all policy initiative on colonial issues, which ensued from the decision not to go ahead at Dumbarton Oaks. During crucial months, when civil administration was being restored in Pacific territories recaptured from the Japanese, the United States was without a policy.

There was also the handicap imposed on U.S. leadership at San Francisco by the necessity to defend at all costs the assured control the Navy had demanded over the Japanese mandated islands as its price for acquiescence in the trusteeship initiative. In the circumstances, Commander Stassen, supported by his working-level assistants, including Bunche, performed brilliantly. But, rather than being free to lay the base for confident relations with emergent nationalist forces in the colonial revolution soon to come, the Americans were shackled and essentially unable to capitalize on the opportunity at San Francisco.

These prices were paid because the trusteeship advocates persisted in demanding both that trusteeship be preserved as a U.S. objective and also that it be applied to those Pacific Islands that the Navy coveted. Elsewhere, this author has criticized this obduracy on two grounds. The first ground is that the resulting victory was hollow, as described in the preceding paragraphs. The second is that greater flexibility might have led to better solutions.[40] At the same time trusteeship partisans were concentrating on establishing the norm of trusteeship for some colonies, they were rejecting a British suggestion that might have led to some international surveillance of all colonies. They did so because they were mesmerized by trusteeship. To use a word from Bunche's doctoral thesis, trusteeship had become a "fetish" for them. They also strongly distrusted the British motives and were inclined to assume "if British, not acceptable," an attitude that permeated wartime Washington from FDR down.

The trusteeship advocates never clearly established why it was better to settle for a denatured trusteeship system for only a few territories than to try for a kind of mandates system for all colonies. Nor did they establish all that convincingly why it was essential to the interest of the United States, or to the improvement of colonial conditions worldwide, that the sparsely inhabited Pacific Islands be forced under the trusteeship scheme, rather than insulated against it as the Navy admirals sought to do.

On these matters, Bunche did not waver. He was thus allied with Leo

Pasvolsky in the Department of State and with Secretary of the Interior Harold Ickes and, especially, Under-Secretary Abe Fortas, without whose support trusteeship might well have succumbed to the assault of the services.[41] The trusteeship advocates were encouraged, of course, by the evidence right up to the end that FDR supported them. Although he would not deny the Navy its bases, he would insist that they be placed under trusteeship. In the State Department, views were not uniform. It is certain that Secretary of State Stettinius wavered. He was very uncomfortable defending the trusteeship views of his subordinates against Secretaries Stimson and Forrestal and almost killed the trusteeship plan at one tense moment.[42] It is probable that Gerig was less fixated on trusteeship for the Pacific Islands and more prone to find a workable compromise on that issue than was Bunche. There is no documentary evidence to support that surmise, which rests on the author's impressions, harbored for many years. What is reasonably clear, however, was that Bunche had long since concluded that trusteeship was desirable. He had no doubt that the principle had to be defended and that, moreover, it had to be applied to the islands the Navy wanted to govern. What cannot be known is how far the *expectation* of FDR's support on this issue deflected Bunche and the others from alternative solutions they might otherwise have considered. When FDR died, they lost that source of support. The trusteeship they preserved was a shell, deprived of much of the meat and juice that had attracted the devotion of the aficionados.

Bunche had different kinds of opportunities to influence events. He seized on them with great manipulative dexterity and a keen sense for what may be called situational leverage. He showed no more respect than was prudent to the rules of protocol thought to constrain a government civil servant, among them the documents classification system. The following three examples are documented nowhere but in the vivid recollection of this author.

It may be remembered that no decision had been reached in Washington to authorize the U.S. delegation to introduce at UNCIO the draft declaration of principles governing all dependent territories, which had been developed in the Washington committee structure during the war. Without authority, the delegation at San Francisco could not take an official initiative on the subject. Those familiar with the UN Charter, however, will be aware that it contains a whole chapter, Chapter XI, called Declaration Regarding Non-Self-Governing Territories. That chapter was built on an opening made by the British delegation, which had introduced a flimsy draft on trusteeship that was designed to counter the stronger American one. The draft included preambular language fashioned after the preamble to the mandates article of the League of Nations Covenant, Article 22. It became the basis for Chapter XI. The Australians had been working on colonial issues during the war, and their views were closer to those of the liberal Americans than to those of the conservative British. The opportunity was identified and exploited by Bunche. He passed, informally, to an Australian opposite number a copy of the U.S. draft declaration. The Australians drew on it in preparing the proposal they introduced to amend and greatly strengthen the British draft. The Australian proposal shared many characteristics with the U.S. draft and thus so does Article 73 of the Charter. If Bunche cannot claim paternity, he at least attended at the *accouchement.*

Labor Day weekend, 1945, saw the small DA staff scattered on various missions. Three officers were in Washington—Bunche, Thomas F. Power, and this author. It thus fell to them to respond to the request received from the new secretary of state, James F. Byrnes, at sea en route to the first Council of Foreign Ministers meeting in London, to equip him with drafts of trusteeship agreements suitable for the three Italian-administered territories in Africa. The future of the territories of Libya, Somaliland, and Eritrea was to be settled in the peace the foreign ministers were meeting to work out. What astonished the DA staff in Washington was their instruction to draft agreements on the assumption that Italy was to be named the administering authority for the three territories under the arrangements to be agreed. Until then, the rather loose assumption, consonant with planning during the war, had been that Italy would be deprived of the colonies as a penalty for having entered the war on the Axis side and because its administrative record was thought to be inadequate. The expectation was that they might well come under direct administration by the UN. Italian administration seemed the least probable solution.

Anyway, orders were orders. So, under Bunche's directions, the three set out to prepare the requested drafts. None was especially expert with respect to any of the territories, and little help was to be anticipated on the Labor Day weekend. So the allocation of responsibilities was effected by straw vote. Bunche drew Libya, Power drew Somaliland, and this author got Eritrea. The point of the story is that it was Bunche who conceived the notion that, since the Italians should be grateful to have their status in the territories confirmed, they would be in no position to bargain too hard over the terms. The trusteeship agreements, therefore, should be rigorous in establishing protections for the peoples of the territories and should go as far as possible in developing the supervisory powers of the UN organs. Bunche saw the instructions as a heaven-sent opportunity to design a model of what trusteeship should be.

In any event, U.S. policy changed before the Council of Foreign Ministers met. The United States advocated direct UN administration of the three territories. None of the three Labor Day drafts was used. Amusingly, however, the draft on Somaliland turned up years later, introduced by the Philippine delegation participating in a committee to draft terms of trusteeship for Somaliland after the UN General Assembly had decided it should be placed under Italian administration. It is not known how that unused U.S. draft found its way into Philippine hands, especially since Bunche had long since left government service.

The third incident occurred a few months later, during the first part of the First Session of the UN General Assembly. Bunche was a member of the U.S. delegation staff. An issue on which the U.S. was not prepared to act officially was whether something should be done to build on the limited obligation contained in Article 73(e) of the Charter, which required colonial powers "to transmit regularly to the Secretary-General for information purposes, subject to such limitations as security and constitutional considerations may require, statistical and other information of a technical nature relating to economic, social and education conditions in the territories for which they are respectively responsible." If no action were taken by the General Assembly, that provision would mean no more than that the information thus submitted would be filed. The Secretary-General would be no more than a clerk, or librarian. In the circumstances, Bunche found a way to work informally with the Chinese delegation, which introduced the proposal that led to the creation, at first, of the Ad Hoc Committee on Information for Non-Self-Governing Territories and, later, its more lasting replacement. He thus had a significant part in laying the bases for what proved to be an important United Nations function affecting all dependent territories in subsequent years. What he did was no doubt inspired by his deeply held belief that maximum international surveillance of colonial administration was essential to the well-being of colonial peoples.

Another example of Bunche's constructive dexterity can be documented from the record. He joined the UN Secretariat in April 1946 as Acting Director of the Trusteeship Division, on loan from the State Department. The first part of the First Session of the General Assembly had resolved that states administering mandated territories should submit draft trusteeship agreements to place them under the system in time for the second part of the General Assembly session to act on them at its meeting scheduled for September 1946. Late in the spring, no such agreements had yet been proposed. Nothing in the Charter authorized the Secretary-General to take any initiative in the matter. There was no precedent for Secretariat initiative in a matter of such delicacy and obvious importance to the mandatory states concerned. All the same, Bunche on 2 June 1946 proposed that the Secretary-General take the initiative by sending a letter, a proposed draft of which was attached, asking the mandatory powers to transmit trusteeship agreements to him by September 3rd.[43] The draft requested, in the meantime, information on the prospects for trusteeship agreements being submitted, a report on progress in any negotiations under way, and any other useful information. The Secretary-General, Trygve Lie, had inclinations toward activism himself and the proposed letter went out under his signature on June 29th.[44] While it was not too likely that the question of trusteeship agreements could have been swept under the rug, the Secretary-General's letter ensured that it could not be and thus set the precedent for activism and initiative by the Secretariat in trusteeship matters.

By and large, the position in the UN Secretariat, to which Dr. Bunche moved from the State Department, offered little opportunity for direct and open participation in making international policy affecting the colonies. Inherently, the Secretariat role is not officially a policy-setting one. That is a function for member governments, and Secretariat initiative can be risky and harmful both to the Secretariat and the cause its policy intends to serve. Bunche did, however, find opportunities to exercise his activist inclinations. Under his direction, for example, the staff of the Trusteeship Division took the initiative in preparing drafts of questionnaires, which it circulated before the Trusteeship Council to be considered for adoption by the council as the basis for the annual reports required of administering authorities under the UN Charter (Articles 87 and 88). Similarly, the Secretariat did not wait for member governments to take the initiative in working out rules for the handling of petitions that might be received in accordance with Article 87 of the Charter. Once again, the Secretariat took the initiative in proposing rules for consideration by the Trusteeship Council committee that was created for the purpose. Similarly, Dr. Bunche encouraged members of his staff to take active roles in preparing for and staffing the periodic visits that the Trusteeship Council was authorized to conduct in the trust territories.

Altogether, Bunche gave every indication that he intended to fill all the available crevices with staff leadership in making the trusteeship system the most effective possible advocate of the rights and interests of the peoples of the trust territories. His career as a scholar had acquainted him with people around the world who were involved in the affairs of the colonies. His recent experience in the government had introduced him to officials in other countries, adding to the list of those to whom he could have easy access. He made friends with ease and had no enemies known to this author. Moreover, his Secretariat post gave him opportunities for a kind of informal influence, and his lines to Washington remained open and useful.

His influence on the organization of trusteeship was thus considerable, although immeasurable. He did not stay at the job very long, however. Although he remained Director of the Trusteeship Division nominally until 1954, by some time in 1947 his energies were already focused on duties of peacekeeping in the Middle East. And, though he returned to the Trusteeship desk for periods of time thereafter, his foot was essentially set on the peacekeeping road. That may have been just as well because there is no way of knowing how well Ralph Bunche would have taken to the tedium of administering a system that had become routinized. Even so, his influence on the activism of the Secretariat staff outlasted his actual service in the Trusteeship Department.[45]

Measuring the achievement is difficult. Ralph Bunche had a considerable part in helping to shape the UN's principles affecting colonialism. He had a perhaps even greater role in ensuring that the principles were incorporated in the Charter. It is, however, difficult to know how significant it all was. The principles of Chapter XI and the trusteeship arrangements no doubt were part of the setting for the colonial revolution that speedily followed the inauguration of the UN. Bunche was early in discerning the restlessness beginning in the colonies, which came to full flood after the war. He sought to devise in the UN an apparatus able to channel those forces constructively and peacefully toward self-government.

What he did not see, however, what may have been visible only with hindsight, was how little relevant to the drive for decolonization would be his favored instruments of internationally institutionalized tutorship. The UN components of the colonial revolution were only part of the picture, perhaps the smaller part. There was the impact of the Japanese occupation during wartime, which unleashed aspirations for self-rule. There was the impact of the Cold War on colonial powers, reluctant to spare resources for colonial wars and concerned about the effect that trying to hold onto the colonies might have on the East-West balance. There was also the effect of the anticolonial philosophy and policy projected by the United States, of which the UN and its role were only one manifestation.

It may exaggerate, but it makes the point, to say that the colonial provisions of the Charter may not have been exceptionally relevant to the colonial revolutions. Acute cases of colonial conflict came before the UN, but under the general authority of the UN plenary bodies or the peace and security provisions of the Charter, rather than the specially designed colonial sections. Except for the possible influence of the trusteeship system on the trust territories themselves—and, even here, it pays to be cautious in attributing causality to the UN—the idea of trusteeship was too little and too late. It did not serve as the model for colonial administration its designers intended it to be. In concluding that the UN trusteeship system had been outflanked, I. L. Claude may have come as close to the truth as any.

In summary, it might be said that Ralph Bunche tried to reconcile self-determination with tutorship. They proved irreconcilable. The learned works about decolonization rarely mention the United Nations as having had a significant role in the rush to decolonization and independence.

Trusteeship is virtually never mentioned. What trusteeship unmistakably did was to launch Ralph Bunche on his unique career of public service thereafter. In itself, that was no small achievement.

Notes

1. Unattributed remarks of Dr. Bunche's, delivered during the Institute of Pacific Relations Conference at Mt. Tremblant, Quebec, December 1942, as recorded in Institute of Pacific Affairs, *War and Peace in the Pacific: A Preliminary Report of the Eighth Conference of the Institute of Pacific Relations on Wartime and Post-war Cooperation of the United Nations in the Pacific and the Far East, Mont Tremblant, Quebec, December 4–14, 1942* (New York: Institute of Pacific Relations, 1943), p. 113.
2. Author's recollection of a conversation with Dr. Bunche, probably in 1945 or 1946.
3. The point was made recently about Leo Pasvolsky in the paper presented by Ruth Russell to the panel "The United Nations and Peace: Perspectives of Some Forty-Fivers" at the Annual Meeting of the International Studies Association, Anaheim, California, 27 March 1986.
4. Ralph J. Bunche, "French Administration in Togoland and Dahomey," (Ph.D. diss., Harvard University, 1934). Cited hereafter as "French Administration."
5. Pp. 75–76.
6. Ralph J. Bunche, *A World View of Race* (Port Washington, N.Y.: Kennikat Press, 1968; reprint), pp. 23, 28, 39, 40, 42.
7. Bunche, "French Administration," p. 76.
8. For a good and convenient presentation of theoretical and empirical criticisms of Hobson's, Lenin's and other Marxists' economic interpretation of imperialism, based on the works of Schumpeter, Morgenthau, Langer, Viner and Aron, see James E. Dougherty and Robert L. Pfaltzgraff, Jr., *Contending Theories of International Relations: A Comprehensive Survey*, 2nd ed. (New York: Harper & Row, 1981), pp. 218–30.
9. Author's recollection, confirmed by two other State Department colleagues of Dr. Bunche.
10. Gerig had written on the subject, drawing on his experience in the Mandates Section of the League of Nations Secretariat. See his *The Open Door and the Mandates System* (London: Allen and Unwin, 1930).
11. Bunche, "French Administration," pp. 76–77. See also the reference to the Aristotelian idea "some men are born to serve and some to rule" in *A World View of Race*, p. 2, and Chap. 3, "Race and Imperialism."
12. Author's recollection of a conversation with Dr. Bunche, probably in 1944 or 1945.
13. *A World View of Race*, p. 1.
14. Ibid., frontispiece and p. 14.
15. Bunche, "French Administration," p. 78.
16. Ibid., p. 161.

17. That day, he said, was "probably many generations removed from the present day." Ibid., p. 388.
18. Ibid., p. 392.
19. Ibid., p. 80.
20. Ibid., p. 391.
21. Ibid., pp. 123–25, 148–61.
22. Ibid., pp. 81–82, and *A World View of Race,* pp. 46–47.
23. For illuminating treatments of the difficulties of the idea of self-determination, see Benjamin Rivlin, "Self-Determination and Colonial Areas," *International Conciliation,* no. 501 (January 1955), and Rupert Emerson, "The Principle of Self-Determination," in Rupert Emerson, *From Empire to Nation: The Rise to Self-Assertion of Asian and African Peoples* (Boston: Beacon Press, 1960).
24. Bunche, "French Administration," pp. 81, 388.
25. Interestingly, among the first chores Dr. Bunche assigned the author, then (1944) an intern in the Department of State, was a comparative examination of administration in Western Samoa, which was administered by New Zealand under a League of Nations mandate, and American Samoa, which the United States administered directly as a colony (as it does to this day.)
26. Bunche, "French Administration," pp. 142–42, 427–28.
27. Author's recollection. A bare outline of Dr. Bunche's service in the State Department can be deduced from the detailed record of wartime planning in Department of State by Harley Notter, *Postwar Foreign Policy Preparation, 1939–1945* (Washington, D.C.: Department of State, 1949; Department of State Publication 3580; General Foreign Policy Series 15); cited hereafter as "Notter." The author is grateful for notes provided by Barbara H. Nelson, now of the Ford Foundation.
28. Notter, p. 303.
29. Ibid., pp. 387–88.
30. For example, Rudolf von Albertini, *Decolonization: The Administration and Future of the Colonies, 1919–1960* (Garden City: Doubleday & Company, 1971); Wm. Roger Louis, *Imperialism at Bay: The United States and the Decolonization of the British Empire, 1941–1945* (New York: Oxford University Press, 1978); and Prosser Gifford and William Roger Louis, eds., *The Transfer of Power in Africa: Decolonization 1940–1960* (New Haven: Yale University Press, 1982).
31. For guidance as to the development of U.S. postwar policy on colonial issues, two works are indispensable: Louis, *Imperialism at Bay,* cited above; and Ruth B. Russell (assisted by Jeanette Muther), *A History of the United Nations Charter: The Role of the United States 1940–1945* (Washington, D.C.: The Brookings Institution, 1958). See also Lawrence S. Finkelstein, "Castles in Spain: United States Plans for Trusteeship in the United Nations Charter," paper presented to the panel "The United Nations and Peace: Reflections of Some Forty Fivers," Annual Meeting, International Studies Association, Anaheim, California, March 27, 1986. (This paper drew on the author's Ph.D. dissertation *Castles in Spain: US Trusteeship Plans in World War II,* Columbia University, 1970.)
32. The Charter contains a clause in Article 81 leaving open the possibility of direct administration of a territory by the UN itself. That results from a Chinese proposal at the San Francisco conference. It is hard to see how such

an arrangement could have come to pass, however, given the procedures for placing territories under trusteeship that left full control in the hands of each administering state. A colonial power would have had to want to "unload" a territory pretty badly before the provision could be applied.

33. Author's recollection of a conversation with Dr. Bunche at the time.

34. Dr. Bunche believed this, to the author's knowledge, and it was generally believed that the ILO Recommendation was the first international instrument with such general application to colonies. Article 23 of the League of Nations Covenant, however, bound all League members "to secure just treatment of the native inhabitants of territories under their control." Enthusiasts for the ILO recommendation (which included this author at the time) seem to have lost sight of the Covenant provision that antedated the ILO recommendation, was no less broad in its coverage, and, unlike the ILO action, presumed to have binding effect on League members.

35. See Finkelstein, "Castles in Spain," cited above; Russell, *A History of the United Nations Charter,* p. 808; and Notter, *Postwar Foreign Policy Preparation,* pp. 428–29.

36. Notter, *Postwar Foreign Policy Preparation.*

37. "French Administration," p. 143.

38. See Works by Louis, Russell, and Finkelstein, cited above.

39. Finkelstein, "Castles in Spain."

40. Ibid.

41. See Louis, *Imperialism at Bay,* esp. p. 490.

42. Ibid., pp. 489–94.

43. TR/ASG/2, 13 June 1946. The letter memorandum is signed by Ping-chia Kuo, who had been director of the division and may perhaps have still been formally. It was unmistakably drafted by Bunche, however, and initialed by him. In the margin is a note: "I agree. TL"

44. TR/Dir/ASG/6a, 29, June 1946.

45. The author is grateful to William Mashler for making the point during the Ralph Bunche Conference at which this essay was first presented.

· 8 ·

THE CONTRIBUTION OF RALPH BUNCHE TO TRUSTEESHIP AND DECOLONIZATION

Herschelle S. Challenor

Forty years after the establishment of the United Nations, all but one of the UN Trust Territories and virtually all of the former colonies have gained their independence. Dr. Ralph Johnson Bunche made a valuable contribution to this transfiguration of the world, bringing a unique perspective to the process of decolonization. Bunche's perspective was influenced by the sensitivity gained from being a black in America and the knowledge gained from his academic, government, and international service.

It was not uncommon for observers of Dr. Bunche's career at the United Nations to speculate whether his position as an international civil servant had enabled him to transcend the parochial race consciousness of American society. Yet, perhaps there is a correlation between his activities regarding colonial problems abroad and racial problems in the United States. Moreover, his work at the United Nations on decolonization and peacekeeping issues served to underscore the pervasiveness of racial and ethnic prejudice in human affairs.

Race and Decolonization

Racial and ethnic problems were central not only to the issues of decolonization that preoccupied Bunche during his service in the State Department and in his early days at the United Nations, but also to his later responsibilities for United Nations peacekeeping activities. Every peacekeeping operation—Palestine, Congo, Kashmir, Cyprus, Bahrain—in which he became involved had its genesis in a colonial situation. Bunche's rich background in racial and ethnic tensions undoubtedly not only affected his work on trusteeship, but also his special political responsibilities with respect to United Nations peacekeeping in formerly colonial territories.

Any appraisal of Bunche's efforts on trusteeship and decolonization must seek to understand the beliefs and values that shaped his world view. Bunche revealed a basic commitment to humanism early in his life in the valedictory address, entitled "The Fourth Dimension of Personality," delivered when he graduated from the University of California at Los Angeles in 1927.

Humanity's problem today is how to be saved from itself. . . . It did not require the Great War to convince us of this sobering fact. . . . Prejudice, antipathies, hatreds still disrupt with their sinister influences the equilibrium of the world. The war has, however, contributed its "jot of good"—it set mankind in a universal quest of a panacea for its suffering . . .

. . .This fourth dimension—call it "bigness," soulfulness, spirituality, imagination, altruism, vision, or what you will—it is that quality which gives full meaning and true reality to others . . .

If the mission of this education be filled, there is planted in each of us those seeds from which fourth-dimensional personality will spring. We shall have become more altruistic and less selfish. We shall *love* more, and hate less. We shall have succeeded in "slipping into the skins of others." We need not be less intellectual, we need be more spiritual. We need not think less, we need only *feel* more. We shall not only have developed the intellect—we shall have educated the *heart*.[1]

Fundamental to Bunche's world outlook is his perception of race and, earlier in his career, of class and its relationship to race. In his monograph *A World View of Race* (1936), he stated inter alia, "The world race war will never be fought. . . . Race issues tend to appear but tend to merge into class issues. Throughout the world, the issue between working and owning class is sharpening. The Titanic conflicts of the future will be between those who have and those who have not."[2] In later pronouncements, without referring to class, Bunche still maintained that race was an unsettling force in the world that pitted white and black peoples against each other.

Ralph Bunche was unequivocal about his own racial identity. In a speech entitled, "The World the UN Seeks," delivered at Howard University on 14 May 1964, he addressed the issue of nationality and racial identity. He said, "I am a Negro and an American and I am proud to be both. I am neither a racialist nor a chauvinist, but I have great contempt for any Negro who, for whatever reason is reluctant to identify himself with his ethnic group and its epic struggle for justice in this society."[3]

Most importantly, in his last address entitled "On Race: The Alienation of Modern Man," given at the University of Hawaii in 1969, two years before his death, Bunche considered racism the salient factor of division among the peoples of the world.

> I have chosen tonight to consider race and color as a major, possibly a preponderant fact in alienation. . . . First off, may I explain that I have made this choice not because of my own racial identity, but primarily because I come from mainland United States, where the growing alienation of the black American is the outstanding domestic problem and becomes ever more serious and dangerous. . . . Secondly, I come from the United Nations, where it is apparent that on the international side, race is all-pervasive and often decisive, and presents a formidable obstacle to that harmony amongst peoples that is essential to a world at peace, which is the main objective of the United Nations. . . . Racism, certainly, is the foremost obstacle to the harmonization of peoples . . . being alienation at its emotional worst. . . . There are no more abrasive issues at the United Nations than those involving racial injustice. . . .

> [In the United States,] there are 22 million black Americans—whose constitutional rights are being violated flagrantly and persistently. . . . There are only two solutions, separation or integration. . . . As I see it, separatism is based on a philosophy of defeat, or surrender to bigotry. . . . It seems painfully clear to me that there is no possibility in the affluent, industrialized white-majority American society for anyone to be at once black, separate, and equal. It follows that only the politics of integration makes practical sense. . . . White men, whether in the majority as in the United States and the United Kingdom, or the minority as in South Africa, Southern Rhodesia, and the world at large, must find a way, if such there is, to purge themselves completely of racism, or face an ultimate fateful confrontation of the races which will shake the very foundations of civilization, and indeed threaten its continued existence and that of most of mankind as well.[4]

I contend that Bunche's views of 1936 and 1969, which see class and race, respectively, as divisive, are not only both correct but suggest that the problem of the twenty-first century will be the *convergence* of the poverty line with the color line.

The Principle of Trusteeship

Early in 1944, Ralph Bunche transferred from the Office of Strategic Services, where he was head of the Africa Section of the Research and Analysis Branch, to the State Department. There he joined the postwar planning unit that Secretary of State Cordell Hull established, under the direction of Dr. Leo Pasvolsky. A focus of the Pasvolsky unit was to develop proposals for a postwar international organization to ensure world peace. Within the purview of this unit was the future of the colonial world. Bunche became a member of the unit's subcommittee on dependent areas, which was engaged in developing proposals for the future of non-self-governing territories once the war was over.

Long before Bunche joined this subcommittee, many discussions had already taken place in the White House on the subject of colonial development and change. Even before the United States formally entered World War II, there were strong indications that it did not favor a return to the status quo ante, insofar as colonies were concerned. The joint statement of war aims, the Atlantic Charter, issued by President Franklin D. Roosevelt and Prime Minister Winston Churchill on 14 August 1941, enunciated the principle of self-determination: ". . . the right of all peoples to choose the form of government under which they will live." Churchill asserted that this passage applied only to the Nazi-occupied countries of Europe and not to colonial peoples, contending that "I have not become the King's First Minister in order to preside over the liquidation of the British Empire." Roosevelt categorically rejected this view, insisting that the Atlantic Charter had universal application, not merely in Europe.[5] Within a month of the Japanese bombing of Pearl Harbor on 7 December 1941, twenty-six nations signed a declaration endorsing the Atlantic Charter that became known, at the suggestion of Roosevelt, as a Declaration by the United Nations.

Both Roosevelt and Hull condemned colonialism as morally wrong and as contrary to the aims of the United Nations. On 23 July 1942, Hull declared:

> We have always believed—and we believe today—that all peoples, without distinction of race, color, religion, who are prepared and willing to accept the responsibilities of liberty, are entitled to its enjoyment. . . . It has been our purpose in the past—and will remain our purpose in the future—to use the full measure of our influence to support attainment of freedom by all peoples, who by their acts, show themselves worthy of it and ready for it.[6]

In fact, the first official policy recommendations on trusteeship, submitted by Secretary Hull to President Roosevelt, reflected these views.

It is the duty and purpose of those of the United Nations which have, owing to past events, become charged with responsibilities for the future of colonial areas to cooperate fully with the peoples of such areas toward their becoming qualified for independent national status.[7]

Although Roosevelt believed world peace was neither attainable nor sustainable if nationalism in the colonial territories were not defused, it was for less altruistic reasons that he and Hull were motivated to end the imperial preference systems. Indeed, there were economic and political objectives related to the interests of the United States. They sought status for Indochina as a trust territory, mainly to prevent future French governments from according military privileges to Japan, as the Vichy regime had done with Germany after 1940. They wanted Hong Kong to be a free port in order to satisfy both Chinese claims and British interests. There was also talk of internationalizing the Kurile Islands, Dakar, Roberts Field in Monrovia, and the Netherlands Indies because of their strategic importance. It has even been suggested that the United States saw trusteeship as a convenient means for acquiring control over such strategically important areas as the Pacific islands without appearing to violate the spirit of the Atlantic Charter.

The British were noticeably cool toward the first American provisions for trusteeship. Prior to the Yalta Conference of 4–11 February 1945, they had suggested that the international supervision of colonial territories be undertaken by regional commissions, composed only of the colonial powers. The State Department rejected this proposal. It is quite clear that after July 1943, as a result of British concern as well as U.S. War and Navy Department pressure, State Department colonial policy shifted from emphasizing the welfare of peoples to the maintenance of international security. U.S. policy modified its original position, which advocated the incorporation of all dependent territories under the trusteeship provisions and viewed independence as the ultimate goal, adopting a more restrictive one that merely called for self-government. The revised position would encompass under the trusteeship system only those territories detached from enemy states and those voluntarily placed under the system by the allied powers. Thus, when Bunche joined the State Department to work on American proposals regarding trusteeship and dependent areas, less than six months before the start of the Dumbarton Oaks Conference in August 1944, it was at a time when the humanitarian impulse underlying United States postwar plans for colonial territories was eroding within the government under the pressure of security and economic considerations.

When the Dumbarton Oaks Conference convened in August 1944 to prepare proposals for a new international organization to replace the League of Nations, Bunche was part of the American delegation as an adviser on colonial affairs. Although the State Department had prepared proposals on dependent areas for inclusion in the projected new world organization, they were never discussed at Dumbarton Oaks primarily because of opposition by the Joint Chiefs of Staff. At issue were the islands that had been wrested away from Japan during the bloody war in the Pacific. These islands, which Japan had administered under a Mandate from the League of Nations since the end of World War I, were among the small number of colonies that the State Department plan for international supervision would apply *a priori*. The Joint Chiefs adamantly refused to consider anything but total American control over the Pacific islands for strategic reasons. Meanwhile, Bunche and Benjamin Gerig strove to have the Dumbarton Oaks proposals include provisions for freedom and self-government for *all* dependent territories in the future charter of the United Nations.

One month before the Dumbarton Oaks Conference of 1944, President Roosevelt wrote the Joint Chiefs of Staff. "I am working on the idea that the United Nations will ask the United States to act as trustee for the Japanese mandated islands."[8] Yet, this did not assuage the American military leaders. As commander-in-chief, President Roosevelt felt obliged to consider the importance of these islands for American security, particularly as this discussion was taking place during the final stages of the war with Japan. It was decided that colonial matters would not be taken up at Dumbarton Oaks. Upon being informed by Gerig of the president's decision, Bunche said to him:

> When the charter is signed, there must be a section on trusteeship. Not a postscript. Not a parenthesis. Trusteeship must be as important as any other element in the world organization. It must be that way, Ben, if we are to have a future world—that works: We've lost the first battle, but not the war.[9]

Forming Policy on Trusteeship

In the months after the Dumbarton Oaks conference, the State Department team on dependent areas, Gerig, Bunche, James Green, Lawrence Finkelstein and others, worked incessantly on proposals and working papers in the hope that the president would approve, including the colonial issue on the agenda of the upcoming United Nations Conference on International Organization, to be held in San Francisco. When it was announced that trusteeship would be discussed at Yalta by Roosevelt, Stalin, and Churchill, Bunche's staff prepared a draft proposal that Roosevelt took with him. Bunche was one of the few officials who were kept informed about the progress of the discussions at Yalta. The trusteeship issue, particularly as it applied to the future of Italy's African colonies, gave rise to some heated discussions among the three

Allied leaders. Since no final decisions were reached on the issue, it was decided that the three powers would consult prior to the June 1945 United Nations Conference on International Organization, to be held in San Francisco, on the trusteeship provisions of the Charter. As things turned out, because of Roosevelt's death in April, these prior consultations never took place. Instead, they were carried out at San Francisco itself while the full conference was taking place.

Between the Yalta Conference in February 1945 and the San Francisco Conference, Bunche and Benjamin Gerig, chief of the subcommittee on dependent areas, worked diligently on the trusteeship proposals to be presented by the United States at San Francisco. Their proposals encountered considerable opposition from the War and Navy Departments who were anxious to retain full control over the islands in the Pacific ruled by Japan under terms of the League of Nations Mandate System. On 15 March the Interdepartmental Committee on Dependent Areas, including representatives of the departments of State, War, Navy, and Interior, met under Dr. Pasvolsky's chairmanship to consider the proposals drafted by Gerig and Bunche. This meeting resulted in what became the ninth draft of the proposal for trusteeship provisions in the Charter, which reconciled the positions of the civilian and military departments by establishing two categories of trust territories, strategic and nonstrategic, their major distinction being that the former would be accountable to the Security Council where the major powers would have a veto whereas the latter would be reporting to the veto-free Trusteeship Council.

Despite the military's participation in the interdepartmental committee, some officials in the War and Navy departments still advocated outright annexation of the Japanese mandated islands. This became apparent at a meeting of the secretaries of state, war, and the navy, where they reviewed this ninth draft prior to sending it to President Roosevelt. Unable to reach agreement on 2 April 1945, Secretaries Edward Stettinius, Henry Stimson, and James Forrestal decided that further consideration of the matter required the President's participation. Consequently on April 9th, Stettinius sent a memorandum to President Roosevelt, then resting at his vacation home in Warm Springs, Georgia, which summarized the committee's views on trusteeship and recommended that the government make public its decision within the next few days. On April 10, Roosevelt informed Secretary of State Stettinius that, "your message on international trusteeship is approved in principle,"[10] and he agreed to see the representatives from the three departments on April 19. However, when President Roosevelt died on April 12th, and was succeeded by Vice President Harry S. Truman, the timetable for dealing with the trusteeship provisions of the Charter was upset.

Following extensive interdepartmental consultations and briefings, President Truman adopted the broad outlines of Roosevelt's provisions on trusteeship. As there was wide interest in the U.S. position on trusteeship, the secretaries of state, war and the navy agreed to a draft text for a possible press statement on this question. Although this statement was never released, the text below provides important insights into the watering down of the U.S. position.

> The United States Government considers that it would be entirely practicable to devise a trusteeship system which would provide, by agreements, for (1) the maintenance of United States military and strategic rights, (2) such control as will be necessary to assure general peace and security in the Pacific Ocean area as well as elsewhere in the world, and (3) the advancement of the social, economic, and political welfare of the inhabitants of the dependent territories.

> It is not proposed at San Francisco to determine the placing of any particular territory under a trusteeship system. All that will be discussed there will be the possible machinery of such a system. It would be a matter for subsequent agreement as to which territories would be brought under a trusteeship system and upon what terms.[11]

Bunche and Lawrence Finkelstein shared a sleeper on the train to the United Nations Conference on International Organization in San Francisco. During the four-day cross-country trip, they completed the sixteenth draft of the trusteeship proposals.

At San Francisco, the United States introduced its novel notion of strategic trusts which represents a considerable weakening of the concept of internationalizing responsibility for trust territories, so designated. Nevertheless, it should be noted that even in their less progressive form, the American proposals on trusteeship, presented at San Francisco, were more advanced than those of France and the United Kingdom. The French plan merely called for a "progressive development of political institutions." The British plan proposed a much more limited notion of trusteeship, that is, "self-government" rather than "independence," as the goal of the trusteeship process; colonies would become trust territories only by voluntary submission of the colonial power; no provision for visiting missions or petitions; and making the Trusteeship Council a subsidiary body of the Economic and Social Council rather than establishing it as a principal organ of the United Nations.[12]

Drafting the Charter Provisions

At the San Francisco conference, Bunche was at the center of the negotiations over the sections of the Charter dealing with colonialism. His work earned him a reputation as a skilled negotiator and expert draftsman. According to a Chinese delegate to the conference, Dr.

Victor Hoo, Bunche "was the fastest draftsman I'd ever seen. He would listen to a discussion, no matter how complicated, and right away he would make a draft of it, adding his own ideas, which were always very good."[13] Many delegates said that more than any other single person Ralph Bunche was responsible for the adoption of the trusteeship section in the United Nations Charter, drafted at San Francisco.

Bunche had long been concerned about the reduced scope of the trusteeship provisions that no longer included all of the colonies. Only ten areas, with approximately 17 million people, would be covered by the trusteeship provisions, leaving the nearly 200 million persons in sixty-five colonies and dependencies devoid of international supervision. Bunche advocated an earlier proposal considered by American planners for inclusion in the UN Charter as an international standard for the administration of all non-self-governing peoples. When, however, Bunche failed to convince the U.S. to insist on including this proposal at San Francisco, he reportedly passed the draft language on to the Australian delegation. They introduced it, and the declaration became Chapter XI of the Charter. With this act, Bunche finally won the war, as he had promised Gerig in August 1944.

Many would argue that Chapter XI, rather than the international trusteeship system outlined in Chapter XII of the Charter, was the most significant in propelling the majority of dependent territories toward independence. The compromise on trusteeship that emerged at the San Francisco conference was weaker and less inclusive than the original U.S. proposal in 1942. Instead of one category of dependent peoples, for whom independence was the ultimate expectation, three categories emerged: strategic trusts under the supervision of the Security Council; ordinary trusts for which the UN had full supervisory responsibility; and the remaining colonial territories, by far the majority protected only by the Chapter XI general declaration of administrative principles.

Writing about this period later, Bunche said that it was recognized at San Francisco that the well-being of dependent peoples "is a matter of proper international concern." The mandate system, he argued, introduced the notion of a "formal and direct international responsibility for the well being of peoples in territories administered by mandate" . . . and was based on the high moral principle that "weak and defenseless peoples and territories are not to be bartered and distributed among the victors of war."[14] This latter statement is important for those who have suggested that Bunche had paternalistic attitudes toward dependent peoples. It clearly suggests that his concern about their welfare was not based upon any notions of their inherent inferiority, but rather upon an understanding of the vulnerability of their situation.

Bunche frequently criticized what he called the "Kiplingesque" view most Europeans had of third world peoples. He pointed out several differences between trusteeship and the mandate system, not the least of which was the "principle of the third party, or international responsibility." The international authority under trusteeship was greater than under the mandate system. For instance, annual reports based upon a questionnaire prepared by the Trusteeship Council had to be submitted by the administering authorities. Moreover, any person in a trust territory could petition the UN for grievances, and the UN had the authority to undertake periodic visits to trust territories and submit reports on their findings.[15]

Bunche's role in bringing into being the UN Charter chapters on trusteeship and non-self-governing territories was completed with his service on the American delegation to the United Nations Preparatory Commission, which met in London in the fall of 1945. John Foster Dulles was the member of the U.S. delegation responsible, among other matters, for trusteeship and non–self-governing territories, and Bunche was his deputy in this area. This meant that most of the work dealing with implementing the charter provisions on colonies fell to Ralph Bunche. As he had in San Francisco, Bunche greatly impressed the members of other delegations with whom he dealt. It was during this meeting that Dr. Victor Hoo, who was the new head of the UN Department of Trusteeship and Non-Self-Governing Territories and who had praised Bunche's work at San Francisco, asked the United Nations to approach the State Separtment to request that Ralph Bunche serve as the Director of the UN Trusteeship Division.[16]

Shortly after the First Session of the UN General Assembly, which was held in London in January 1946 and at which Bunche was a member of the American delegation, Bunche assumed his position as Director of the Trusteeship Department of the UN Secretariat. Having played so central a role in the process of drafting the UN Charter provisions dealing with colonial matters, it was not surprising that Bunche was asked to assume this post.

In light of this record, it is quite clear that Ralph Bunche had more than a marginal influence on American policies regarding the treatment of colonial questions in the drafting of the United Nations Charter. It is true that the paternity of an idea can be difficult to trace in a bureaucracy, where the anonymity of ideas of those at the working level is legion. What is needed, therefore, is meticulous research to trace the flow of memoranda during this period, in order to ascertain not only their contents, but the identity of the drafters. It may never be known which ideas, put forward in high-level staff meetings by Leo Pasvolsky or Benjamin Gerig, may have been initially implanted by Bunche. It should be noted that when Pasvolsky first spoke to Bunche about working in the

Dependent Areas (DA) subcommittee, planning for the future of dependent territories, at the State Department, he reportedly said, "You know more about colonies and the dependent areas than the rest of us put together."[17]

Trusteeship and Decolonization

Some have suggested that the UN Charter's trusteeship provisions had only a minor impact on the decolonization process since, as things turned out, independence was achieved first by colonies not under trusteeship. The rapidly moving events in the postwar period, triggered by the rise and spread of assertive nationalist movements that challenged the old colonial order throughout the world, seemed unwilling to wait for the slow trusteeship machinery to respond to their demands and needs. As originally conceived, the trusteeship system was considered more conducive to bring about political change in the colonial world. Article 76 spoke of "development towards self-government or independence" as a goal of the system, while Article 73 of Chapter XI applicable to the bulk of the colonial world referred only to developing "self-government" and "free political institutions" and omitting any reference to independence. Bunche himself said that the "trusteeship machinery is not self-propelling. It must depend for its success upon the good faith and constructive action as expressed through the policies of governments."[18] He also stated that, "the true measurement of the effectiveness of the principles and mechanisms will be found in the extent to which they become over the years self-liquidating."[19]

It is a fact that implementing the elaborate provisions of the trusteeship system, which applied only to ten territories, was cumbersome. The trust territory of the Pacific Islands is not yet independent. However, these provisions had a synergistic effect. There is no question but that the news of the petitioners' appearances before the Trusteeship Council and the visiting missions to the trust territories created rising expectations among the peoples in the dependent areas. Nor can it be contested that the promise of independence to the trust territories of Cameroon and Togo in 1960 stimulated French colonies in Africa to seek, and win, approval for their own independence that same year.

In addition, while technically not a part of the trusteeship system outlined in Chapters XII and XIII of the UN Charter, Chapter XI, the Declaration on Non-Self-Governing Territories, must be seen as part of the compromise over trusteeship at San Francisco. In due course, Chapter XI became a legal point of reference for United Nations General Assembly Resolution 1514 (XV), the Declaration on the Granting of Independence to Colonial Countries and Peoples. As more countries gained independence between 1946 and 1960, there was a clear shift of active concern about decolonization away from the Trusteeship Council to the General Assembly. By 1960, the newly independent states had become the driving force in the General Assembly for the liberation of the other colonies.

Ironically, the United States, the first "new nation" to fight a war of independence (as it had) and win, abstained on General Assembly Resolution 1514. Prime Minister Harold Macmillan made a direct appeal to President Eisenhower not to support the resolution in order to avoid placing the United Kingdom in an awkward position. Eisenhower's position was opposed by the entire U.S. delegation. Resolution 1514 was approved on 14 December 1960, by a vote of 89 for, 0 against, and 9 abstentions. Zelma Watson George, the only black member in the U.S. delegation, reportedly stood up and applauded.[20]

Conclusion

The achievement of independence by practically all the colonial territories of the world in the two decades after the end of the second World War can be attributable, in part, to the efforts and influence of Dr. Ralph Bunche. It is no exaggeration to say that Bunche worked indefatigably throughout his professional life—as scholar, U.S. government official, and as international civil servant—for basic change in the colonial world.

Bunche was one of the prime movers within the American government for the formulation of an enlightened postwar policy that recognized the rights and aspirations of colonial peoples. The essence of his thinking was that the United States, in keeping with its democratic heritage and as a world leader, must "come to think of people in the Near East, the Far East, the Caribbean, and Africa—with regard to their abilities and potentialities—as equals, really as equals, and to be able to treat them as much in our policies and actions in a convincing way."[21] Even after he left U.S. government service, Bunche felt it incumbent upon him to call attention to his fellow citizens of their need to adopt a new attitude toward colonial peoples. Thus, at a tribute to him by the Phelps-Stokes Fund, after he had been awarded the Nobel Peace Prize, he upbraided the western world for its "apathy and complacency . . . its lack of understanding of these [Asian and African colonial] peoples and its unwillingness to put forth much effort to do so, and its reluctance to cast off its outmoded, obsolete, and dangerous prewar attitudes toward the so called 'backward peoples.' "[22]

Bunche's most direct contribution to the decolonization process is embodied in his involvement in the shaping of the United Nations organization into an instrument for change in the colonial world. As perceptive thinker, accomplished technician, and superb negotiator, he was a catalyst for change. He was both a source of knowledge about the colonial condition and of know-how about what should be done to ameliorate its inequities. In his person, he was a symbol of the struggle against anticolonialism and an inspiration for all striving for human betterment. After Bunche achieved world renown for his role in Palestine, he used his newfound position to call attention to the aspirations of colonial peoples for freedom and emancipation. Thus, ten years before the United Nations General Assembly adopted its momentous *Declaration on Granting Independence to Colonial Countries and Peoples* (1960), Bunche anticipated this resolution, in his Nobel Peace Prize acceptance speech, by calling for "an acceleration in the liquidation of colonialism."[23]

Bunche's contributions to decolonization were not achieved single-handedly. Bunche was part of a network of scholars, freedom fighters from throughout the colonial world, and civil servants, national and international, who pulled together to place the issue of colonialism in the forefront of world consciousness. In many ways, he was the linchpin of this network and his contribution was of lasting significance.

Notes

1. See Appendix B for full text of valedictory address.
2. Ralph J. Bunche, *A World View of Race* (Washington, D.C.: The Associates in Negro Folk Education, 1936), p. 96.
3. Unpublished speech by Ralph J. Bunche, "The World the UN Seeks," Sidney Hillman Lectures, Howard University, 14 May 1964, p. 16.
4. See Appendix F for full text of this address.
5. See *Complete Presidential Press Conference of Franklin D. Roosevelt* (New York, 1973), vol. 19: 3–3; vol. 20, 178–79, and *Memoirs of Cordell Hull* (New York, 1948), vol. II, pp. 1478, 1484.
6. Ernst Haas, "The Attempt to Terminate Colonialism: Acceptance of the UN Trusteeship System," in Robert S. Wood (ed.), *The Process of International Organization* (New York: Random House, 1971), p. 382.
7. Ibid., p. 383.
8. Harvey A. Notter, *Postwar Foreign Policy Preparations, 1934–1945* (Washington, D.C.: U.S. Department of State, Division of Studies, 1950), p. 387.
9. Peggy Mann, *Ralph Bunche: UN Peacemaker* (New York: Coward, McCann & Geoghegan, 1975), pp. 99–100.
10. Notter, *Postwar Foreign Policy,* p. 431; see also Ruth B. Russell (assisted by Jeannette E. Muther), *A History of the United Nations Charter* (Washington: Brookings Institution, 1958), chap. 23.
11. Notter, p. 433.
12. See discussion in Russell, *A History of the United Nations Charter,* chap. 31.
13. Mann, p. 126.
14. Ralph J. Bunche, "International Trusteeship and Accountability: The Prob-

lem of the Colonies," in Martyn Estall, ed., *Rights and Liberties in Our Time* (The Canadian Institute on Public Affairs: The Ryerson Press, 1946), p. 25.

15. Ibid., pp. 26–27.
16. Mann, p. 136.
17. Ibid., p. 141.
18. Ralph J. Bunche, "The International Trusteeship System," in Trygve Lie, ed. *Peace on Earth* (New York: Hermitage House, 1949), p. 124.
19. Bunche, in Estall, *Rights and Liberties in Our Time*, p. 30.
20. David Kay, "The Politics of Decolonization: The New Nations and the United Nations Political Process," in Wood, *Process of International Organization*, p. 382.
21. Bunche, in Richard Frye, ed., *The Near East and the Great Powers* (Cambridge: Harvard University Press, 1951), p. 3–5.
22. Cited in *Ralph Bunche: Peacemaker, Addresses at dinner in honor of Ralph J. Bunche* (New York: Phelps Stokes Fund, January 18, 1951), p. 21.
23. See Appendix C for text of speech and see UN General Assembly Resolution 1514 (XV), 14 December 1960.

As a child in Detroit circa 1910

Ralph Bunche with members of his staff of the Africa Research Section of OSS (1944). Benjamin Rivlin, the editor of this book, is on the left in the front row.

Examining a copy of the
Carnegie-Myrdal Study,
An American Dilemma
(1944), to which he made
significant contributions

Greeting Secretary of
State Edward Stettinius at
the Dumbarton Oaks
Conference in the
summer of 1944 as Dr.
Leo Pasvolsky looks on

Boarding the UN
Mediator's plane with
Count Folke Bernadotte
in 1948

Addressing the UN Security Council as Acting UN Mediator for Palestine in Paris,
10 October 1948 (Official United Nations Photo, Department of Public Information)

Shooting "snookers" during the Israeli-Arab Armistice talks at Rhodes in January 1949 (Courtesy of William Mashler)

Chairing the signing of the Egyptian-Israeli Armistice Agreement on the island of Rhodes on 24 February 1949. Facing camera, from left to right, are: Constantine Stravropoulos; U.S. Brig. General William O. Riley; Dr. Bunche; Henry Vigier; and UN Palestine Military Observers Col. Millett and Col. Langlois. At the left side of the table is the Egyptian delegation and at the right is the Israeli delegation. (Courtesy of UNATIONS)

Holding the Nobel Peace
Prize Medal, 1950

With Israeli Prime Minister
David Ben-Gurion and UN
Secretary-General Trygve Lie
in 1951 (Courtesy of
UNATIONS)

With Secretary-General Dag Hammarskjöld in 1955 (Courtesy of United Nations)

With Chief Albert J. Luthuli, President of the African National Congress of South Africa and recipient of the Nobel Peace Prize in 1960 (Courtesy Ralph Bunche Papers, UCLA)

With President
Lyndon B. Johnson
and
Secretary-General
U Thant

With members of the Domestic Peace Corps in 1963

In the front line at the start of the long march to Montgomery, with Rev. Ralph Abernathy, Dr. Martin Luther King, Jr., and Rabbi Abraham Joshua Heschel on 21 March 1965 (The Bettmann Archive)

Meeting at the UN in April 1967 with leaders of a massive anti–Vietnam War march. From left are David Dellinger, Rev. James Bevel, Dr. Benjamin Spock, Cleveland Robinson, Dr. Martin Luther King, Jr., Dagmar Wilson, and Dr. Bunche. (The Bettmann Archive)

PART III

WORLD STATESMAN

· 9 ·

RALPH BUNCHE AS UN ACTING MEDIATOR: The Opening Phase

J. C. Hurewitz

I

The line between success and failure is as a rule thin and at times invisible. Admittedly, skill is almost always an essential ingredient in success. So, too, are luck and timing. If Ralph Bunche were around today, he would doubtless have agreed. Consider, for example, his statement to the First Committee of the UN General Assembly on 25 November 1948, when he warned that "the truce was precarious and might not be maintained for long. There was no guarantee that it would bring about an armistice." He therefore "expressed his full support for the establishment of a conciliation commission" to replace the Mediator's office, as originally recommended in Count Bernadotte's Progress Report to the General Assembly, released after his murder in mid-September.[1] This was hardly a forecast of an impending break in the Arab-Israeli impasse just six weeks before the Egyptian government notified Bunche that it would accept his good offices to open armistice talks with

© J. C. Hurewitz. This paper draws upon the forthcoming volume 3 of *The Middle East and North Africa in World Politics*, to be published by the Yale University Press with research support from the Ford Foundation.

the Provisional Government of Israel (PGI). Even then, at the time of the initial signals of such an opening, the Palestine Conciliation Commission for which the General Assembly had provided a month earlier had not yet come into being.

The evidence suggests that in the late fall of 1948, the Acting Mediator seemed to despair of his ability to help the belligerents stop fighting and start talking. Yet when the stalemate suddenly lifted, he wasted no time to exercise his mediatory powers in the knowledge that such an opportunity for which Bunche, and before him Bernadotte, had waited so long might slip away.

Bunche fully understood the uniqueness of his role. He was the first member of the UN Secretariat other than the Secretary-General in whom the Security Council vested such high executive responsibility. By the accident of a political murder, Bunche had been catapulted from a middle-level managerial post in the UN bureaucracy into that of a top-level executive diplomat. His new responsibilities and the positive use to which he put them must have exceeded his wildest dreams. Yet he lost none of his devotion to the Secretariat. "What is most significant about this entire operation since 17 September last," he told his colleagues in the Secretariat in an informal lecture on 16 June 1949, "is the fact that since that date it has been exclusively a Secretariat operation in so far as the mediation and truce supervision work is concerned. . . . [W]e have been very proud out there of the fact that there was sufficient confidence in the Secretariat, on the part of the Members of the United Nations, to leave a task as responsible and difficult as this one entirely in the hands of the Secretariat."[2]

While appreciating the uniqueness of his holding so high an office, Bunche did not overlook the realities. Following Bernadotte's murder on 17 September 1948 the Security Council, in acquiescing in the UN Secretary-General's prompt appointment of Bunche as Acting Mediator, had seen the action as a temporary expedient. In his progress report, as it was styled, Bernadotte implied that he had gone as far as possible to implement his instructions. In the closing days of the first truce, the Arab League on behalf of its warring members and the PGI had both rejected Bernadotte's preliminary territorial proposals for a formal set-tlement. The substance of the proposals—except on Jerusalem, which at first had been assigned to the Arab area and later was to be "placed under effective United Nations control"—remained unchanged in his final report. Bernadotte counseled the General Assembly to replace the office of Mediator by a conciliation commission. He was thus implying that his usefulness as Mediator had been spent once he had created the oversight machinery for truce compliance, shaped a framework for a possible formal settlement, and urged the assembly to take needed action for the relief of the Palestine Arab refugees. The choice of an experienced member of the UN Secretariat rather than a political appointee enabled the Security Council, on the motion of its president, to avoid the inescapable delay in trying to find a qualified candidate who would be willing to accept an interim assignment that offered almost no attractions and underlined the memory of the first incumbent's political assassination.

Ralph Bunche spent most of the fall of 1948 in Paris, the temporary UN headquarters at the time. There he found ready cooperation in the Security Council to deal with frequent breaches of the truce and complaints of the parties that could not be settled on the spot by the elaborate UN Truce Supervision Organization (UNTSO) that Bernadotte had bequeathed to Bunche. At the Third Session of the General Assembly, the Acting Mediator made himself available to the delegations and the assembly's political committee for consultation on the report. In that activity he had to parry the diplomatic thrusts of Britain and the U.S. for and of the regional parties against Bernadotte's proposed framework for a mediated settlement. It was widely suspected that the murder of the Mediator was attributable to the deep hostility that his territorial replanning had aroused in Israel. "There is no doubt," reported Foreign Minister Moshe Shertok [later Sharett] to the PGI State Council on 27 September 1948, "that Bernadotte's report was prepared by its author jointly with very important elements on the international scene. The full and immediate approval of the report by the American and British governments testifies to this fact."[13] At the same meeting, Prime Minister David-Ben Gurion flung down the gauntlet:

> No matter how successful our information program, is there any chance that we can convince the UN to give us the Negev, a corridor to New Jerusalem. Ramle and Jaffa, central and western Galilee, at least the new section of Jerusalem, the port of Eilat, a continuous land area running up to the Dead Sea, and not impose external control on Haifa? And if, by some miracle, such a resolution is adopted by a two-thirds majority, won't we still have to fight to implement it just as we had to fight this year for the November resolution?[4]

An article in *The Nation,* almost certainly planted by the PGI, singled out Ralph Bunche as the "medium for the betrayal of the original United Nations decision of November 29. . . ."[5]

Reactions among the Arab warring states were hardly less hostile, but the impact was blunted by a lack of common purpose. They failed even to coordinate their military effort. The Arab League members, it is true, still refused to accept the existence of Israel. But they did virtually nothing about setting up the unitary (Arab) state which they insisted was the only legal heir of the sovereignty once exercised by the defunct League of Nations mandate. As a riposte to Bernadotte's provisional plan, it might be argued, the Arab League published on 10 July 1948 a provisional constitution for such a government. But it remained a dead letter. So, too, a few days after Bernadotte's murder did the Palestine

Arab Higher Committee's proclamation, with Egypt's blessing, of a Government of All Palestine. By November it was becoming evident that Transjordan, as a potential beneficiary, was starting to break ranks and to reveal an interest in the slain Mediator's proposals. In explaining the basis for not advocating the creation of a Palestine Arab state, Bernadotte had observed that "The Partition Plan [of the General Assembly had] presumed that effective organs of state government could be more or less immediately set up in the Arab part of Palestine. This does not seem possible today, in view of the lack of organized authority springing from Arab Palestine itself, and the administrative disintegration following the termination of the mandate."[6]

In the field Bunche had delegated authority to his staff and colleagues fanned out among Israel and each of its four adjacent Arab states. Soon after succeeding Bernadotte, Bunche appointed, as replacement for the Swedish chief of the military truce observers, a retired brigadier-general of the United States Marine Corps, William E. Riley. As chief of staff of UNTSO, Riley supervised an international military observer organization that acquired professional skills and experience on the job and relieved the Acting Mediator of the distractions of reviewing every infraction of the multiple cease-fires. Similarly, under Bunche's direction, Henri Vigier, an international lawyer and senior Secretariat colleague, served as the Acting Mediator's spokesman in Beirut and Damascus. Representing Bunche in Cairo was Dr. Pablo de Azcarate, whose diplomatic career reached back to 1922, when he first joined the League of Nations Secretariat, rising to the rank of its Deputy Secretary General from 1933 to 1936. Perhaps busiest of all the Acting Mediator's personal civilian aides in the belligerent zone was Dr. Paul Mohn in Tel-Aviv, who was at the center of most of the action.

To return to the substance of the mediatory effort, what changed Egypt's mind early in January 1949 or, for that matter, Bunche's? For the answer to that question, and it is essentially only one question, we must probe deeply into the opening months of Bunche's career as UN Acting Mediator. That phase, from the murder of Count Bernadotte to the start of the armistice talks on Rhodes (17 September 1948–13 January 1949), was one of almost unrelieved frustration and has not been closely analyzed. Yet Bunche's experience and the reputation that he had built for fearless integrity at that time proved indispensable to his later success. The second phase, from the formal start of the Egyptian-Israeli talks to the Security Council's termination of the office of Mediator (13 January–11 August 1949), embraced the framing of the four agreements that constituted the armistice regime. It has understandably received most attention.

This discussion examines the less-advertised near denial to Bunche, for reasons beyond his control, of the opportunity to mediate the Arab-

Israeli armistice that in mid-November 1948 he persuaded the Security Council to sponsor. Ralph Bunche, the record shows, came within a hair of not making it. The short answer for the near denial is this: given Britain's relentless pursuit of "the Bernadotte plan," Israel's adamant resistance to it, and the mounting confusion of the Arab belligerents' collective and individual efforts, there was a recurrent need to restore cease-fires and to investigate their violations. But there was no scope for meaningful political mediation. In London, Washington, and at UN headquarters in New York, a three-man Palestine Conciliation Commission was being formed to replace the Mediator.

II

As a loyal UN official, Bunche sought guidance and support from the Security Council. But in the fall of 1948 the Security Council was measurably weakened by the ambivalence of the United States, on which Britain and the PGI heavily leaned and to which the two governments had made contradictory appeals. The Department of State failed to find a harmonizing formula. Meanwhile, "the Bernadotte plan" bore diminishing relevance to the rising realities in the Middle East.

Bernadotte had advocated a dramatic rearrangement of the UN General Assembly's 1947 terms for the division of Palestine. He suggested that the Negev (the relatively large and thinly populated southern district of the former Palestine mandate) be lifted from the area allocated to the Jewish state and be given along with east-central Palestine (later known as the West Bank) not to a Palestine Arab state, as foreseen by the assembly resolution, but to Transjordan; that Israel be compensated by receiving western Galilee, which the General Assembly had earmarked for the Palestine Arab state; and that Haifa be declared a free port and Lydda a free airport, both under international administration. Although the proposed redrawing of the map was not Bernadotte's invention, there is nothing inherently wrong, in principle, with a mediator appropriating someone else's ideas. Sound mediation calls not necessarily for originality, but for feasibility.

The plan had been framed incrementally in Whitehall by the collegial effort of the senior resident staff of the Eastern Department of the Foreign Office with important input by their colleagues serving the Chiefs of Staff Committee and the Ministry of Defense. It centered on assuring continued British access to the Negev for imperial defense and had begun to be put together even before the mandate's formal expiration in mid-May. Foreign Office spokesmen promoted the scheme as an improvement upon the General Assembly's design of November 1947. They claimed that it would endow the Jewish state with "sensible frontiers," making it more "compact and homogeneous" and thus also more readily defensible. The Jewish state, they continued, would not miss the Negev, which was largely desert with very few Jewish residents. Far more fertile, the western Galilee would offer larger opportunity for economic development and growth. On the other hand, noted the Eastern Department's brief, the grant of the Negev to Transjordan with a fragment possibly also going to Egypt would assure the contiguity of the Arab states of Africa with those of Asia without a break by an alien country. Such cartographic reshuffling, the British promoters contended, might make the Jewish state more acceptable to the Arab belligerents and thereby create a practical base for a formal and durable settlement of the dispute. The Foreign Office "officials feel it important," Ambassador Lewis Douglas reported to Secretary of State George C. Marshall, "that from [the] moment [the] proposals become known they should carry as [their] label 'Mediator—made in Sweden'."[7]

The Foreign Ofice in mid-June instructed Sir Oliver Franks, the British ambassador in Washington, that it would "like to try and agree with the Americans . . . [that] any advice to the Mediator or to the parties should as far as possible either be joint advice or advice on lines we have agreed on between ourselves beforehand . . . [and] we should jointly exchange and pool all our information about developments. We were already keeping the State Department fully informed through the United States Embassy in London. We hoped the State Department would make sure that the [American] Embassy [in London] received for communication to us all information available to them also. . . ."[8] This was the rationale of the British appeal to the State Department for cooperation to persuade the Mediator to adopt the plan and to win UN endorsement. If the project accurately reflected the prevailing judgments in Whitehall's foreign-policy establishment, one would have to question how seasoned diplomats could have come so wide of the mark.

In the General Assembly's 1947 partition resolution, the truncated Negev comprised nearly half the land area set aside for the Jewish state. At no time were the Israelis willing to acquiesce in a contraction of what they already viewed as a minuscule state. The importance of the Negev to Israel, Prime Minister Ben-Gurion reported to the PGI on 17 June 1948, derives precisely from its being "an empty and desolate area . . . because we can turn it into a flourishing center of Jewish settlement." It also provides access, he went on, to the minerals of the Dead Sea and to a Red Sea outlet.[9] Nor were the Arab belligerents, other than Transjordan, in a mood to acquiesce in the permanent presence in their neighborhood of an intrusive and unwanted country, even if Israel were voluntarily to surrender the Negev. After all, they had entered the war so as to wipe the nascent Jewish state out before it could take hold and thereby "redeem" Palestine "for its rightful owners."[10]

What needs explaining is not the Foreign Office pursuit of national and imperial interests, which is its function, but the obsession—and, at times, the desperation—of the project's promoters at the UN and in their dealings with American diplomats in the final quarter of 1948 and the first half of January 1949. For perhaps a year after leaving Palestine in May 1948, Great Britain had not fully adjusted to the restraints of its changed role. As mandatory power, it had doubled as arbiter and as interested party in all deliberations on Palestine. After mid-May 1948 the UN became the forum for arbitration. Reduced to the position of an interested party only, the UK had lost its decisive edge of influence in competing with the regional contestants. The cartographic suggestions, in a word, had less to do with claimed post-mandate realities in the Middle East than with the evolving postwar realities in Britain's Middle East empire. The suggestions had been put together in Whitehall to uphold the perceived strategic imperative of preserving Britain's primacy there. Ernest Bevin, from his early days as foreign secretary of the Labor government (1945–1951), held that without continued access to Middle East bases, oil, and communications, Britain could not remain a world power.[11]

After 1945 Britain could no longer afford to hold its wards on a tight leash. Neither in Whitehall's book could it afford to cut them loose. Britain's imperial position in the Middle East was thus entering an involuntary process of diminution. Surrendering an empire is never easy and rarely graceful. At the outset, Bevin experimented with slowing the process down by trying to change preferential alliances into "equal partnerships." But primacy and equality are conflictual concepts. Arab nationalists received Bevin's démarche as purely cosmetic, as a device for replacing visible by invisible preferential imperial practices. Nationalist skepticism informed the stillborn treaties with Egypt (October 1946) and Iraq (January 1948).

Whitehall's insistence on a permanent presence in the Negev rested on the felt need for strategic depth in defense of the Suez Canal. It traced back to World War I and Britain's diplomatic bargaining with its allies and with the Zionists, and culminated in its obtaining the Palestine mandate in the peace settlement. Every British proposal to resolve the Arab-Zionist conflict over Palestine set the Negev aside for direct British rule—the Royal Commission plan in July 1937, the secret recommendations of a cabinet committee in September 1944 on long-term policy in Palestine, and the Morrison-Grady project of July 1946.

The belief of the British Chiefs of Staff in the need for unquestioned access to the Negev persisted throughout the period between the UN General Assembly's preparation and adoption of the Palestine partition resolution (September to November 1947) and the start of the armistice negotiations in January 1949.[12] Indeed, early in 1948 the Eastern Department had already put preliminary measures in place. Article 7 of the annex of Transjordan's "equal" alliance, signed on 15 March and ratified six weeks later, permitted "ships of His Britannic Majesty's Navy to visit the *ports* of the Hashemite Kingdom . . . at any time upon giving written notification" [underline added]. Yet note this: "Aqabah was the only port of the kingdom, then as now. Early in June 1948, Bevin's adviser on Palestine told the director of the Office of Near Eastern and African Affairs in the State Department that cession of the Negev to Transjordan "would be of definite stategic value, because of the possible port development at Gaza. As things stood at present, the British had no land connection from the sea to Transjordan."[13]

With the entry into Palestine of the Arab armies at the mandate's end on 15 May 1948, the appointment on May 20th of Count Bernadotte as the UN Mediator and Ralph Bunche as his chief of staff, and the adoption on the 29th by the Security Council of a resolution threatening sanctions for noncompliance by the Arab states and Israel with the Mediator's efforts to negotiate a truce, the Foreign Office gave top priority to putting the finishing touches on the design for establishing a legally tenable British military access to the Negev. Major responsibility was entrusted to the Eastern Department.

The British felt that unconditional American co-sponsorship of the envisaged territorial exchange was indispensable for its acceptance by the Mediator as well as by the Security Council and the General Assembly. Unwavering United States help would also be required to secure—by coaxing, persuasion, or coercion—Israel's consent to the suggested abridgement of what it held to be its territory. Britain itself would undertake the task of convincing the Arab belligerents that it was in their interest to recognize a diminutive Jewish state. If it worked—and, to make it work, the Eastern Department appeared ready to pull out most of the stops—the strategy would have enabled Britain indirectly to regain access to the Negev through its alliance with Transjordan without bearing the onus of the Arab-Zionist dispute that had plagued the last dozen years of the mandate. It would also have measurably improved the prospects, the strategy framers contended, for revising the alliance with Egypt.

On the eve of the first Arab-Israeli truce (11 June–8 July 1948), the Foreign Office approved guidelines that would "ruthlessly" seek to modify the General Assembly's recommended boundaries so as "to ensure that the Jewish state was compact and defensible and that the Arab areas could easily be incorporated in the neighbouring Arab states. The Negev would clearly have to be Arab," with most of western Galilee going to Israel in compensation. In this regard, the Assistant Under-Secretary for Foreign Affairs pointed out that, as Count Bernadotte conducted his talks with Jews and Arabs, "We must be prepared for the fact that . . . we shall probably have to play a considerable role at least in the back-ground." Another author of the strategy went on to advise that "So far as procedure is concerned . . . the best course would probably be to let Bernadotte take the intitiative in submitting proposals."[14] By the month's close, the UN Mediator became the route for communicating to the Arab governments and to the PGI the recommended cartographic surgery. If the parties failed to reach an accord on frontiers, Britain's Bernadotte plan laid down that a UN technical commission should undertake the demarcation.

The British authors of the diplomatic strategy were clearly convinced that its full realization depended on American cooperation, and this in turn on Whitehall's approval of the partition formula, which up to then it had withheld. "If we get a breathing space of four weeks," the Palestine watcher on the British delegation to the UN advised the Eastern Department several days before the first truce, "the chances of extending that and arriving at a negotiated settlement without a resumption of hostilities will . . . depend primarily on the extent to which the United States Government is ready to exert pressure on the Jews. . . . I doubt whether we should have any chance of arriving at an agreed policy and ensuring the using of . . . [American] influence on the basis of any federal plan. I think it might be wiser, particularly in view of the short time we may have at our disposal, to aim at doing the best we can on the basis of accepting partition in principle."[15]

They accordingly confided in their trans-Atlantic ally the minutest details of the unfolding scheme. Almost from the outset U.S. Ambassador Lewis Douglas, in whom Secretary Marshall placed deep trust, served as the primary communicator in both directions. The British government late in June tried to convince the Department of State to make a single transmittal of the plan to Bernadotte. While Marshall consented to common sponsorship, he declined united action. He pointed out to Douglas that "there is a very large measure of agreement between outselves and [the] British Foreign Office as to the most sensible arrangement of the Palestine issue, keeping always in mind the requirements on this govt to maintain its recognition of the State of Israel."[16] Preferring to retain flexibility, Marshall insisted on handing the American endorsement to Bernadotte separately through the UN Truce Commission in Jerusalem, consisting of the American, French, and Belgian consuls in that city, whereas the Foreign Office dealt directly with the Mediator through its resident consul on Rhodes. Bernadotte received the desired message and incorporated the essentials of the plan into his recommendations to the Arab belligerents and the PGI.

By September the Negev transfer project had matured. The Foreign Office sought yet again to bring the Department of State into full alignment in anticipation of Bernadotte's schedule for completing his progress report to the General Assembly. This time, the Eastern Department declared that it did not favor "handing [the] Mediator an agreed Anglo-American statement." Instead it proposed that each side appoint a representative to confer with the Mediator as an Anglo-American team and to "say substantially [the] same things." The department concurred. Marshall sent to Rhodes as his spokesman Robert M. McClintock, the special assistant to the director of UN Affairs, with instructions that his "conversations with Count Bernadotte will be concurrent with, but not necessarily a joint representation of, similar conversations to be had with the Mediator by representatives of the United Kingdom."[17] The Foreign Office named as its spokesman Ambassador John M. Troutbeck, the director of the British Middle East Office in Cairo, which served in part as a center for evaluating British diplomacy in the Arab East. On 13 September, Troutbeck coming from Cairo and McClintock from Athens via London and a briefing visit to the Eastern Department, talked with the Mediator "more . . . [on the] perfection of . . . [his] first draft of the conclusions than . . . [on] matters of substance in which all three were in agreement."[18]

III

At the start of his career as Acting Mediator, Bunche almost became entrapped in the cross fire between Whitehall's attempted use of the UN system to help Britain procure easy and durable access to the Negev for imperial defense and the PGI's determined measures to occupy the barren district that the General Assembly resolution had originally placed in the Jewish sphere, while consolidating Israel's grip on the remaining districts that Ben-Gurion had listed in September. In the end, Britain's strategy broke down step by step, and Israel's worked steadily more smoothly. The contest first brought Bunche's career to almost total frustration and then to undreamed success.

For nearly a month after inheriting Bernadotte's mantle Bunche was spared unusual crises in the field as he settled into his new duties. The reciprocal complaints of the PGI and the Arab belligerents about truce violations seemed minor and susceptible to adjustment by UNTSO without a demand for the services of the Acting Mediator, who nonetheless kept fully informed from his base in Paris at the UN temporary headquarters. The breathing spell turned out to be the calm before the storm.

Israel was not on the verge of surrendering its claim to the Negev. The space was needed for the absorption of immigrants, it was stated, and the PGI was wholly prepared to accept the challenge of developing the economy of a large desert patch. Besides, the Negev would be valuable for international trade and for defense. Its southern apex fronted the

Gulf of 'Aqabah, thereby adding to Israel's established Mediterranean presence the promise of free access through the Red Sea to the Indian Ocean as an alternative to the Suez Canal.

Meanwhile in Paris, the British and the Israeli delegations to the UN had been engaged in relatively low-key rival efforts in Paris to line up support for their colliding positions on the the Bernadotte plan among the delegations to the General Assembly. The pace abruptly quickened and passions rose on scale in mid-October. British steps to line up support for the Bernadotte plan prompted Israel to mount a preemptive military strike in the Negev and a diplomatic offensive in the United States. In neither case was Britain able to neutralize the Israeli moves.

On 15 October, units of the Israel Defense Force (IDF), as the fighting components of its military establishment were called, thrust through the Egyptian lines in the Negev's northwest. By the time the military action ran its course a week later, Israeli troops had immobilized Egypt's two brigades deployed there. The brigade at al-Majdal was allowed to "trickle southward through [a] loophole [on the] coast." The PGI decided, however, to keep the second one at al-Falujah "hermetically sealed"; with its shortage of food and arms, an early surrender was expected.[19] Israel insisted on clinging to the new lines, giving it an incontrovertible presence to sustain its claim to at least the northwestern central sections of the Negev, for the IDF had driven to a line just south of Beersheba. Still, it did not intend to stop there. Plans were already afoot for clearing the Egyptians out of the rest of the bases in the western half of the Negev.

In the theater of battle, Egyptian and Israeli units had given ample scope to both sides for protest to UNTSO. In mid-September the Central Truce Supervision Board, as Bernadotte called the senior echelon of his military observers, had ruled that supply convoys of each side should be allowed to use a short section of the one all-weather road in the neighborhood at specified times each day and that Israel should stop supplying by air its collective villages south of the Egyptian lines, with the exception of those villages inaccessible by surface transport. The recurrent Egyptian breach of the ruling gave Israel an arguable case for military action. In the opening days of the weeklong battle, the Acting Mediator did not suspect Israel's ulterior motive of undercutting Britain's thinly concealed scheme to pry the Negev loose so as to attach it to the Arab sphere.

In this light, Bunche's modulation in coping with the first major truce violation in his service as Acting Mediator is understandable. His conferring in Paris on 17 October with Moshe Shertok elicited from the Israeli foreign minister a plausible evasion. Bunche presented a mild formal report to the Security Council two days later; the operational paragraph noted the basis of the complaints of both parties and the obstacles to demarcating truce lines, given "the fluid nature of military dispositions." In the combat zone, Britain's hands were tied. Its 1936 preferential treaty with Egypt, though disputed by the latter, was nonetheless still in effect. But Britain could not go to the aid of its ally, even if Egypt were willing, since it was bound by the Security Council resolution of 29 May "not [to] introduce fighting personnel into Palestine" or any of the Arab League states nor even to export arms to those countries. It therefore had to rely upon the Acting Mediator through Security Council instructions to compel Israel to withdraw its troops to the cease-fire lines of 14 October. Once the outcome of Israel's military offensive and the Acting Mediator's refusal to bend to the pressure of the Negev transfer planners in Whitehall became known, the British delegation nervously stepped up the schedule for transforming the Bernadotte plan into a UN plan in the form of a proposed enabling resolution for adoption by the General Asembly. At the same time it sought to bind the Acting Mediator, under Security Council instructions, to restore and stabilize the former cease-fire lines in the Negev.

Even more serious in Britain's view at the time was the PGI's plea for American political and diplomatic support. It had appeared that Britain and the United States were still pulling in harness in the early fall when Marshall as well as Bevin urged the plenary session of the UN General Assembly to accept the Bernadotte territorial recommendations "in their entirety." A few weeks later the Foreign Office sensed serious slippage in the Department of State's commitment to the Bernadotte plan, when the American delegation counseled caution and a fortnight's delay in seeking any kind of action either in the Security Council or in the General Assembly. The Labor government had made similar mistaken assumptions in 1945–46, when it attempted to tie the United States to a common purpose on Palestine through a shared inquiry into the Arab-Zionist controversy. On both occasions, American opponents of British policy, bypassing the State Department, won assistance from the White House. It seems hard to believe that the Negev transfer promoters were so inured to their parliamentary system that by 1948 they still did not fully comprehend that, in the American system, all federal agencies are advisory bodies of the president, with no larger formal power than policy implementation. Admittedly, in practice, more often than not, the policy recommendations of the federal agencies receive White House approval with little or no change. Yet, in the making of postwar foreign policy in particular, presidential intervention has occurred—often unexpectedly—whenever the president has felt such action politically desirable.

The timing of the latest battle favored Israel's petition for White House support. It took place at the climax of an American presidential election. The Democrats and the Republicans had nailed into their platforms strongly worded pro-Israel planks—these, both candidates reaffirmed more than once, because the party pundits in key states were reporting wide public sympathy for Israel and for its declared policy of resettling the Jewish survivors of Nazi bestiality. Pro-Israel politicians of both parties rallied to the cause. Even Secretary Marshall could not deflect the president from directing the United States delegation in Paris to delete a reference to the avoidance of "partisan political pressure from outside the UN" in the American statement urging the General Assembly to defer consideration of Palestine until after the election returns became known. Security Council action was also comparably delayed. Thus, nearly two weeks elapsed after the latest cease-fire was put in place before the Security Council finally approved a resolution that had been drafted by Britain and presented jointly, not with the United States, but with China.

By 4 November the draft had undergone three revisions, resulting in the removal of some of its teeth, especially a clause that would have imposed sanctions for noncompliance. Israel nevertheless dismissed the latest resolution as punitive, finding little satisfaction in assurances that its "rights, claims or positions with regard to a peaceful adjustment of the future situation in Palestine" would not be prejudiced. The resolution was also intended to diminish Bunche's freedom of action by providing for an advisory committee of the five permanent, along with two non-permanent, members of the Security Council to shore up the perform-ance of the Acting Mediator. By this means, the British delegation had secured a voice in the upcoming mediatory process before its results were reported to the council. The resolution "authorized" Bunche "to establish provisional lines beyond which no movement of troops shall take place," presumably if Israel, not mentioned by name, did not "withdraw those . . . forces which have advanced beyond the positions held on 14 October." This was a prescription for unavoidable failure, given the widening division between the British and the American posi-tions.

It was Bunche's practice to consult the parties in advance of any basic moves by him or the Security Council, so as to learn their reactions in advance. This helped shape his judgments of the evolving situation in the field. On 2 November, for example, Bunche met with Ambassador Aubrey Eban, the chief of Israel's delegation to the UN, to discuss the British sponsored—and American attenuated—draft that the council approved two days later. Eban in an outspoken letter warned Bunche that its adoption "would open up a dark horizon of continual conflict between yourself and Israel . . . and the destruction of that confidence which you must surely restore if you wish to play a constructive role with Israel in the task of mediation."

Bunche's reply of 4 November conveys a calm yet vigorous statement of where he stood as Mediator. He was fully aware of the difficulties raised by Eban, labeling them "an occupational hazard," largely attributable to combining in one office the duties of truce supervision and mediation. The resolution, in the form adopted or in any other form, was not his handiwork; it was "exclusively Security Council business." As standard procedure, he referred "to the Council any situation which our Truce Supervision Organization was unable to contain." Eban had contended that the PGI "viewed its positions in the Negev as . . . on its own territory, rightfully gained in response to an Egyptian invasion [on 15 May], followed by a sustained truce violation." With this stand Bunche took issue, asserting "that the truce resulting from the 15 July resolution of the Security Council applies to the Negev on exactly the same basis as to the rest of Palestine and, indeed, to the seven Arab States." Bunche pointed out that he was "but an agent" of the Security Council and the UN. Whenever he was called upon to implement the council's resolutions, he ran the risk of affecting the attitudes of either party toward him and his effort. "The most that I can do with that unpleasant situation is to be as fair and as sensible as possible." He had "been pressing strongly, as Count Bernadotte did, for bold steps toward settlement and an end to the truce," which, "if unduly prolonged," would inexorably yield "critical situations."[20]

While proceeding, under the watchful eye of the British delegation, with the predictably fruitless effort to persuade Israel to withdraw behind his suggested provisional lines, Bunche on his own initiative as early as 6 November proposed for consideration by the Security Council a draft resolution calling upon the parties to start negotiations "either directly or through the Acting Mediator" for "the attainment of an armistice." Ten days later the council endorsed an alternate version presented by Belgium, Canada, and France. It retained the option of direct or mediated talks but called for "the immediate establishment" of an armistice "in all sectors of Palestine." This was to include the demarcation of permanent armistice lines, "beyond which the armed forces of the respective parties shall not move," and such force reductions and withdrawals "as will ensure the maintenance of the armistice during the transition to permanent peace in Palestine." In a reply of 19 November to Bunche and the Security Council, the PGI reserved its position on the resolution of 4 November but applauded the call for an armistice, to which Egypt also subscribed on 6 December.

After Israel's military penetration into the Negev's northwest and central sectors in the third week of October and its later refusal to pull out even after the Security Council resolution of 4 November, Britain's dispute with Israel was superimposed on the Arab-Israeli conflict. The two governments appealed for American cooperation. Each found partial support, Whitehall from the Department of State, the PGI from the White House. From mid-October on, besieged by these contrary requests from friendly governments, the United States delegation to the UN engaged in the unrewarding exercise of striving to reconcile the polar positions. The British delegation saw in the delaying tactics late in October toward the draft resolution on [Israeli] force withdrawal from the Negev under consideration by the Security Council an American drift away from what it had earlier perceived as a full commitment to the Bernadotte plan. Britain's resolve, however, had not diminished.

Once welded to the scheme for preventing Israel from assimilating the Negev, Britain had become a disguised party to the post-mandate conflict. Israel, moreover, perceived Britain as a privileged party with strong influence at the UN: in the Security Council, as the holder of a permanent seat and, after 4 November, also as a member of the council's oversight committee on Palestine; and in the General Assembly, as the metropole of a Commonwealth with multiple members. Despite the conflicting pressures of these stubborn adversaries in the quarrel over Palestine, the American delegation kept firmly to its middle position.

After President Truman's intervention on 24 October, at the height of the election campaign, and his reaffirmation of that stance after his victory, the American delegation in Paris had no choice but to continue seeking a formula that might accommodate the British and the Israeli contradictions. This was the thrust of the doctrine that Professor Philip C. Jessup, the delegation spokesman in the General Assembly's First Committee, announced on 20 November. Israel was entitled to all the land allotted to it by the General Assembly, and no changes in that allotment might be made without its approval. If, however, it insisted on retaining any districts (for example, the western Galilee, forcibly seized late in October along with a rural patch of southeastern Lebanon, which the PGI later used for diplomatic bargaining), it would have to compensate the Arabs by relinquishing part of its entitlement (for example, the Negev).

The Jessup doctrine pleased neither the British nor the Israelis. But the United States did not budge from its midpoint. The British delegation introduced a draft resolution in the First Committee that upheld the essence of the Bernadotte plan. The United States went its own way, and its amendments reshaped the resolution, again softening the tone and the substance.

On one point the American and the British positions intersected. The office of the Mediator would give way to a Conciliation Commission of three, casting the United States—which agreed to sit on it—as leader to guide the warring parties to an armistice and then, it was hoped, to formal peace. Once the First Committee reached that decision, its adoption by the plenary assembly was assured. In committee, Bunche had given unconditional blessings in his accustomed style to a proposal that was about to receive approval by a principal UN organ. Still, as a UN official he continued executing his duties faithfully in what he believed was the windup of a paralyzed mediatory career in the transition to the creation of the Conciliation Commission.

The General Assembly on 11 December adopted resolution 181 (III/1), the commission's enabling instrument. Eleven days later Israel mounted a second preemptive military strike into the Negev southwest for the express purpose of clearing the Egyptian troops out of their last strongholds in the area of the former Palestine mandate. Egypt's permanent delegate to the UN on 24 December requested the president of the Security Council urgently to place on its agenda Israel's violation of the truce. On the same day the PGI in a note to the United States asserted that the military engagement could be ascribed to the "widening feeling [in Israel] that perhaps [the] only solution is for Israel to secure by its own efforts the territory in [the] Negev allotted [to it] under partition."[21]

The council on 29 December adopted, with three abstentions (the United States, the USSR, and the Ukraine), a British draft resolution calling for an immediate cease-fire and instructing the council's Palestine Committee to convene on 7 January 1949 "to report . . . on the extent to which the Governments concerned have . . . complied with the present resolution." The council also expressed the hope that the Conciliation Commission would be established "with as little delay as possible." In transmitting to the Acting Secretary of State on 30 December a *note verbale* from London to reiterate Whitehall's growing alarm, Sir Oliver Franks, the British ambassador, intimated that his government might invoke the 1936 treaty with Egypt. When asked whether that action would be taken on British or Egyptian initiative, he "could give no straight answer." Franks also warned that the British government might "find themselves in a position in which they are no longer able to refuse to carry out British [arms] contracts to the Arab countries." The ambassador was advised that Whitehall was applying a double standard, condemning Israel for "flouting" the UN while announcing its own intention of doing the same.[22]

This time, the uncertain policies of the envisaged Conciliation Commission probably no less than Britain's refusal to loosen its embrace of the Bernadotte plan accounted for Israel's infringement of the cease-fire. The Israeli units made a large sweep around the remaining Egyptian forces that had regrouped essentially in what later came to be called the Gaza Strip and south along part of the Negev-Sinai frontier. In the enveloping action, Israeli soldiers crossed the international border into Sinai. The British Middle East Command in Cairo pressed the panic button. On 7 January 1949, Air Marshal Lord Tedder authorized RAF reconnaissance aircraft to overfly the front. The Israel Defense Force shot down two low-flying and three high-flying RAF planes. The British government, in accounting for its action, stated that it had invoked the

1936 treaty with Egypt. That was the last thing that the government and the nationalist press and public in Egypt wanted to hear. If that were the price of British help against Israel, Egypt preferred to negotiate an armistice.

Indeed, as far back as mid-November 1948, Egyptian diplomats had begun tentatively to explore the possibility of negotiating with the PGI. That demarche did not last long and produced no solid results. Finally, on 4 January 1949, three days before the RAF episode, Egypt let Bunche's aide in Cairo know that it was ready to open talks with Israel on all outstanding questions. Bunche wasted no time in shifting his mediatory machine into high gear and, characteristically, he immediately alerted his resident team in Tel-Aviv to start negotiating the terms of a cease-fire. Simultaneously he shared the firm signal with UN Secretary General Trygve Lie to prepare for summoning the Security Council to supportive action at an appropriate moment. Through Lie's administrative assistant, Andrew Cordier, Bunche also informed the American delegation to the UN for added backup in the Security Council.

At this point Bunche nearly tripped over a formal obstacle. Into the American plans for attempting to settle the Arab-Israeli dispute, the Department of State had already factored the transfer to the projected Conciliation Commission of full responsibility for the expected armistice and peace-seeking process. Consequently, the department treated with great skepticism the Acting Mediator's estimate of the Egyptian initiative on 4 January. He described it "as [the] most encouraging [development] in [a] long time for there apparently are no strings attached. . . . Bunche feels strongly that Israel should grab this opportunity at once if they want a peaceful settlement. He feels certain that it is a bona fide offer." Instead of moving promptly on the Acting Mediator's plan, the department proposed that he approach the PGI directly.[23] By 6 January, Bunche was able to report to the president of the Security Council the "unconditional acceptance" by the two governments "of a proposal for a cease-fire . . . immediately followed by direct negotiations . . . under United Nations chairmanship on the implementation of the Security Council resolutions of 4 and 16 November 1948."[24] The department on that day was still preoccupied with how to dissuade Britain from yet again recommending to the Security Council's Palestine Committee sanctions against Israel at its meeting on 7 January and thus in its view impairing the effectiveness of the upcoming Conciliation Commission.[25]

The Conciliation Commission, however, had not yet come into being. France and Turkey named their representatives well before the turn of the year, while the United States acted slowly. Joseph Keenan, whom the president appointed on 28 December, was given an initial briefing at the Department of State on 3 January 1949. Five days later, on the eve of departure for the Egyptian-Israel armistice negotiations on Rhodes,

Bunche called on Keenan at his hotel in New York and found him unprepared for useful discussion. Keenan resigned on the 15th before taking office. Mark Ethridge, his successor, received the department's instructions on 19 January. By then, Bunche had already launched the Egyptian-Israeli talks on Rhodes, for he knew that junctures for positive action in the Arab-Israeli sphere, if not attended without delay, speedily vanish.

Once more, the accident of Washington politics influenced the direction of the Arab-Israeli mediatory saga. Truman's nearly full first term had been an inherited one. In 1948 he earned the office and thus won his own mandate. A genuine transition therefore followed from Truman I to Truman II. Dean Acheson did not replace George Marshall as Secretary of State until the inauguration on 20 January 1949, when he accepted a new assignment as ambassador to China. Ever since Marshall went to Paris in the early days of the meetings in the temporary UN headquarters, Robert A. Lovett had served as Acting Secretary of State. With the new table of cabinet and subcabinet organization still only on paper, the wheels in all federal departments, especially State, turned slowly. Once the department gave up, as it did within a few days, its original insistence that the Conciliation Commission should chair the armistice talks, it lent Bunche full support. Ironically, Britain, which had so singlemindedly refused to abandon its effort to replace the Acting Mediator, became, by its double blunder of angering the Egyptians and "flouting" the UN, an unwitting contributor to his continuing in office.

Britain finally cut its losses on 20 January, when Foreign Secretary Bevin ended a rambling apology in Parliament for his Palestine policy with friendly gestures to Israel. He announced that Britain would soon accord the new state *de facto* recognition and allow the displaced European Jews imprisoned on Cyprus to proceed to Israel, as initial gestures in an earnest search for the normalization of British-Israeli relations. From that moment on, although the devotees of the abandoned scheme in the Eastern Department and among the parallel bureaucrats serving the Chiefs of Staff required further time to readjust to the new realities, the Negev transfer plan, for all intents and purposes, was relegated to deep archival storage, awaiting exhumation decades later by inquisitive scholars. At the time of writing, the British, American, and Israeli governments have declassified most, but not all, the relevant papers. The Arab League and its member states have still not followed suit.

In the armistice negotiations that followed, Bunche brought to bear his cumulative wisdom on Arab and Israeli affairs. As chief of the Secretariat assigned to the UN Special Committee on Palestine (May–September 1947) and to the UN Palestine Commission (December 1947–April 1948) and as Trygve Lie's personal representative to the UN Mediator (May–September 1948), Bunche had undergone a unique apprenticeship for dealing with Arabs and Jews and, later, Israelis. Bunche thus took over the responsibilities of the Acting Mediator naturally and with a highly attuned sense of its challenge and opportunity. By the start of the armistice talks in January 1949, he had become by far the best informed international expert on the Palestine problem and the emergent Arab-Israeli dispute. The Acting Mediator put to consummate use the experience and skills he had acquired. Between 13 January and 21 July 1949, Bunche led Israel and its immediate neighbors to the conclusion of four separate agreements that interlocked into a relatively durable armistice system. Indeed, it proved to be the only comprehensive arrangement—built, it should be noted, of bilateral blocks—that the hostile neighbors have so far been able to agree upon.

Notes

1. United Nations General Assembly, First Committee, *Official Records* (III/1), pp. 770–71.
2. Typescript of lecture, p. 1.
3. Meron Medzini, editor, *Israel's Foreign Relations: Selected Documents, 1947–1974*, vol. 1 (Jerusalem: Ministry of Foreign Affairs, 1976), p. 156.
4. Ibid., p. 158.
5. Lillie Shultz, "Who Wrote the 'Bernadotte Plan'?," *The Nation*, 23 October 1948, pp. 453–54.
6. UN General Assembly, *Official Records* (III/1), suppl. no. 11, pt. I, chap. 6, para. 6.
7. See, for example, Michael R. Wright (Assistant Under-Secretary for Foreign Affairs) to Douglas, 23 June 1948, *Foreign Relations of the United States (FRUS), 1948*, vol. 5, pt. 2, p. 1144; and Douglas to Marshall, reporting on talk with Sir Orme Sargent (the Permanent Secretary), Burrows (Eastern Department head), and Wright, 3 September 1948, pp. 1373–75.
8. Great Britain (GB), Public Record Office (PRO), FO 371/68650/E8326, 18 June 1948.
9. Medzini, ed., *Israel's Foreign Relations*, pp. 148–49.
10. See, for example, the assessment of the Arab belligerent governments' predicament in the report of Ambassador John Troutbeck, the director of the British Middle East Office in Cairo, GB, PRO, FO 371/68650/E8409, 11 June 1948.
11. See Wm. Roger Louis, *The British Empire in the Middle East 1945–1951* (Oxford: Clarendon Press, 1984), pp. 1–50.
12. See GB, PRO, CAB 129/21, CP(47)262, 18 September 1947.
13. *FRUS, 1948*, vol. 5, pt. 2, p. 1100.
14. GB, PRO, FO 371/68566/E8524 and E8526, dated 9, 10, and 7 June 1948, respectively, in minutes by Burrows and Wright and in a letter from Beeley in New York; see also more detail on territory and rationalization in Beeley's minute of 17 June, FO 371/68567/E8764.
15. GB, PRO, FO 371/68566/E8524, Beeley to Burrows, 7 June 1948.

16. Marshall to Douglas, 25 June 1948, *FRUS, 1948,* vol. 5, pt. 2. p. 1148.
17. Douglas to Marshall, *FRUS, 1948,* p. 1390; Marshall to McClintock, p. 1387, both dated 10 September 1948.
18. McClintock to Lovett and Rusk, 15 September 1948, *FRUS, 1948,* p. 1398.
19. Doc. 81, Israel State Archives (ISA), *Documents on the Foreign Policy of Israel (DFPI),* vol. 2, doc. 81, p. 115.
20. Texts of the Eban-Bunche exchange in *DFPI,* vol. 2, pp. 120–21, 130–32.
21. Cited in *FRUS, 1948,* vol. 5, pt. 2, p. 1689.
22. Ibid., pp. 1701–03.
23. Ibid., pp. 609–10.
24. Ibid., p. 621.
25. Ibid., pp. 622–23.

· 10 ·

BUNCHE AT RHODES:
Diplomatic Negotiator

Shabtai Rosenne

In the Israeli delegation to the Rhodes armistice talks, we used to refer to Bunche by the Hebrew word of *egged* (which means "bunch"), hoping he wouldn't catch on that we were talking about him. My most vivid recollection of this physically huge man—handsome and attractive in his own way, a soupçon of a smile on his lips, a bubbling sense of humor that never seemed to leave him, a healthy touch of cynicism—is with a half-smoked cigarette dangling from his lips, after dinner bent over the billiard table in the games room of the Hôtel des Roses, vigorously playing a form of three-sided snooker with teams from the UN, Egypt, and Israel (possibly carefully choosing the winner for that night or at least ensuring that it would not be the UN). There were drinks around the table and the atmosphere became relaxed and human. At around 10 P.M. he would call a halt and summon members of one delegation or of both to meet in his room, where he would patiently, firmly, and sometimes roughly give his analysis or hear reports from the delegations, probe reactions to this or that suggestion, first from one side and then from the other. These meetings would sometimes last until morning, such was Bunche's physical and mental stamina. The physical demands he made on himself and on his staff, and on each delegation, were staggering.

Those games of snooker, never mentioned in the contemporary or subsequent literature, were, I often think, one of the keys to Bunche's success. Certainly they were the catalyst. They broke the ice. They showed us that the Egyptians were human like us, with similar emotions of pleasure when they were winning and of dismay when they were losing—Bunche insisted all the time on true sportsmanship in these games—and I hope and believe that the Egyptians observed the same human qualities in us.

When Bunche took over as Acting Mediator, he was by no means new to the problems of Palestine, the Middle East, and of the now forgotten Jewish displaced persons. In 1944 he had entered the State Department as a specialist on African affairs and together with Leo Pasvolsky had worked in the planning group for the new postwar international organization. At the San Francisco Conference he had been a technical adviser to the U.S. delegation on the commission, dealing particularly with trusteeship and colonial problems. He had played a major role in the drafting of the trusteeship provision of the Charter and early in 1946 he moved to the newly formed UN Secretariat as director of the Trusteeship Department. Bunche's primary interest in that period was Africa, and he must be regarded as one of the intellectual fathers of the decolonization process.

Although still young, Bunche had developed in the State Department and in the UN Secretariat a prodigious reputation for sheer hard work, self-sacrifice, a nimble mind, skillful and quick draftsmanship, a penetrating power of political analysis and an inborn diplomatic skill. When the United Nations Special Commission on Palestine (UNSCOP) was set up in the spring of 1947, he was appointed to its Secretariat, and it has been stated that "he himself drafted with an even hand both the minority and majority reports" of that Committee.[1]

Research into that stormy period in the history of the world and of the Middle East, and of Israel in particular, is now made easier by the three volumes of diplomatic documents recently published by the Israel State Archives, especially volume 3.[2] Alongside diplomatic documents proper, that volume contains quite a large number of personal letters from members of our various delegations at Rhodes, Rosh Haniqra and Mahanayim, and they give almost an hour-by-hour account of the negotiations. These letters were certainly never intended for publication. In very frank and undiplomatic terms, they sometimes describe not only what happened as it happened, but also the innermost feelings of their authors regarding various members of the Mediator's Staff (including Bunche himself), the other side, and their own superiors. I myself indeed am on record in some of those private letters as criticizing instructions I had received, hardly something to be included in an official collection of diplomatic documents, though doubtless of some interest to the researcher.[3]

As Acting Mediator, Bunche inherited a virtually impossible burden, stemming from three interconnected factors. The first was the unconcealed hostility—to which Bunche himself sometimes cautiously reacted (for example in doc. 114)—of the United Kingdom to any solution of the Palestine problem involving the establishment of a Jewish state, and, if that was unavoidable, to that state's acquiring the Negev. As a permanent member of the Security Council with the right of veto, the United Kingdom was able to influence very directly not only the decisions of the Security Council, then a much more potent body than it has since become, but also their implementation. The second and third factors, themselves directly related to the first, consist of two sets of incompatible resolutions. The two sets are incompatible with each other, and each resolution within each set is incompatible with the other.

The first set was composed of General Assembly resolutions 181 (II) of 29 November 1947 on the future government of Palestine, setting forth the detailed plan or partition with economic union, together with resolution 186 (S.2) of 14 May 1948, establishing the office of the United Nations Mediator on Palestine. That resolution made no reference to the previous one, but empowered the Mediator to use his good offices inter alia to "promote a peaceful adjustment of the future situation in Palestine." That language had led to a deep difference of opinion between the government of Israel and Count Bernadotte, especially concerning the nature of the Mediator's role and his interpretation of the exercise of third-party good offices. It cannot be overlooked that Bernadotte's assassination was the outcome of a widely held view that, whether or not he was correctly interpreting his terms of reference, his activities were inimical to Jewish interests. Bunche was certainly aware of this, and it is indeed noticeable that he carefully avoided some of Bernadotte's more obvious errors, such as premature and tendentious publicity for his ideas and excessive reporting of details to the Security Council. (Bernadotte once even asked the president of the Security Council for an interpretation of his instructions, apparently overlooking the fact that the president at that time was the representative of Syria.)

The second set of incompatible resolutions was, in fact, of Bunche's own making, though perhaps understandable when we look back to the pressures of the time. Those were the two key Security Council resolutions of 4 and 16 November 1948. Both related to the Negev, where tensions were high and the two armies inextricably mixed, and which had been partly divided in the partition resolution of 1947. The first resolution called for Israel's withdrawal to earlier lines because of an alleged breach of an arbitrary cease-fire ordered by the Security Council, with the aim of implementing negotiations to replace the cease-fire with something more solid. The second, on the other hand, called for negotiations for an armistice to facilitate the transition from the then existing but precarious truce to permanent peace in Palestine, however without prejudice to the resolution of 4 November. The existence side by side of these two resolutions and the underlying political issue of the freedom of the Negev caused great confusion at Rhodes. The Egyptian delegation naturally took its stand in support of the 4 November resolution, while Israel's position was based more on the second; and in negotiating the armistice agreement between Israel and Egypt, Bunche had to tread warily between the two positions.

Criticism of Bunche's handling of the negotiations does not always give due weight to these inherent contradictions, their political implications, and the quite enormous amount of ill will and mutual suspicions that they generated. Together with the games of snooker and the (deliberately conceived) attendant socializing, Bunche had another basic political rule to which he adhered quite firmly throughout all the negotiations. As far as he was concerned, the delegations met on a footing of complete equality, and he would not tolerate any idea that one was "victor" and the other "vanquished," quite a novel concept for armistices three years after the unconditional surrenders of all the Axis powers in the years 1944–1945. This basic political rule did not mean that Bunche was oblivious to the military and political, internal and external, situations of the parties. Very much to the contrary, he was well informed about all that, and skillful in putting his knowledge to full use.

Bunche's great success, of course, was in the principal Rhodes negotiations with Egypt, which lasted from 13 January to 24 February 1949. This was the Egypt of King Farouk and of Nokrashy Pasha, not the Egypt we know today. Here Bunche was acting virtually without any precedents to guide him. Everything had to be improvised from scratch. True, the UN had already started acquiring some experience in peacemaking, especially in Indonesia and in Kashmir, but the conditions there were entirely different, and that experience was of no assistance to anyone at Rhodes. There was no comparable inheritance from the League of Nations. Bunche therefore really had two main tasks to perform. In one of these tasks, Major-General William Riley, USMC, Chief of Staff of UNTSO after Bunche had taken over and the Swedish General Lundstrom had resigned, was the key figure; and in the other, Constantine Stavropolous, legal adviser of the Mediator's mission, a former member of the Greek government in exile in Egypt during the war and later legal adviser of the UN. Their first task was to work out, in viable terms that would withstand professional scrutiny, the actual armistice demarcation lines. This was treated in the negotiations as a military matter, and was handled in military subcommittees chaired by Riley. This procedure was wise, since it reduced political pressure fixing of the

Armistice Demarcation Lines (ADLs) and other purely military aspects while isolating for separate treatment those combined political and military factors of overriding importance, such as the Egyptian demand, maintained until the end, for an Egyptian civil governor in Beersheba, the center and capital of the Negev and key to its future.

The second task, with which the military delegations did not have to be directly burdened, was to establish an acceptable legal framework for the armistice agreement. While Bunche certainly had much to do with this, the details devolved essentially on Stavropoulos and the legal advisers, again leaving the most important and intractable issues to Bunche himself, with his unrivaled skill as a draftsman and his inventiveness producing many a solution. I'll give one example, ostensibly a technical one, on the question of the duration of the agreement. Historically, all previous armistice agreements had been established for a fixed period of time, that concept underlying Article 36 of the regulations respecting the laws and customs of war on land annexed to the Hague Convention No. IV of 1907, the only international rule on the subject. When the question of the duration of the Rhodes agreement first came up, it was Bunche who insisted on its unlimited duration, on the ground that the United Nations could not countenance any agreement that, even by implication, envisaged a renewal of hostilities in violation of the Charter. The logic is there, but looking back I have often asked myself whether the absence of a time limit in the long run did not do harm to the underlying concept of the 16 November resolution, that the armistice agreements were to be a transition to permanent peace. For by failing to include any such provision, there was no incentive for the parties to continue negotiating toward permanent peace as part of the armistice agreement; and the reference in the agreements to transition to permanent peace became a mere platitude.

A sense of Bunche's approach to this issue can be gleaned from his opening remarks at Rhodes on 13 January 1949: "I trust that there will be no tendency to be rigidly legalistic, picayunish about details or recriminations" (doc. 5). From a short-term perspective, the desire not to be "rigidly legalistic" might have been justified, especially given the tortuous and abortive efforts of the Palestine Conciliation Commission (which removed Bunche as the intermediary between Israel and the Arab states in the spring of 1949) to replace the temporary armistice agreements with a more positive and permanent peace. But taking a long-term view, the patchwork of compromised texts of which the Egyptian and Syrian agreements were composed carried the seeds of their own destruction; the Egyptian agreement collapsed by 1956, and the Syrian lasted until 1967.

It may come as a surprise to know that Bunche had little to do with the real negotiations with Jordan. Here the principal details were negotiated secretly at Shunneh directly with King Abdullah and embodied in agree-

ments of 23 and 31 March 1949 (docs. 248, 265), subsequently incorporated almost verbatim in the armistice agreement of 3 April. The
negotiations at Rhodes lasted from 4 March to 3 April, but the Jordanian
delegation was not plenipotentiary, and Bunche's task accordingly was to
keep the formal negotations going, while the real negotiations were
being conducted elsewhere. There is no doubt that Bunche was fully
aware of his limited role, and he played his part loyally.

The situation in the north was quite different: Israel was in occupation
of fourteen villages in southern Lebanon, while Syria was in occupation
of some Israeli territory. The fighting between Israel and Lebanon, or
more accurately an Arab League army operating from Lebanese territory, had gone badly for the Arab side, whereas there was no fighting
between Israel and Syria after the initial bouts in May 1948. This situation presented delicate military and political problems, especially as the
international frontier between Syria and Palestine had been drawn by
the British and the French in 1923 partly to ensure that one of the
sources of the Jordan and all the water line as far as the Dead Sea would
be in Palestine, which was vital for Israel's future and something that
Syria wished to see changed.

As for Lebanon, there had been some preliminary explorations as far
back as January, but the formal negotiations at Rosh Haniqra lasted from
1 to 23 March 1949. So as to ensure complete withdrawal of Syrian
forces to their side of the frontier and thereby regain possession of the
water line, Israel, which saw the whole of the Northern Front as one,
wished to connect the two sets of negotiations (with Syria and Lebanon)
and make its withdrawal from Lebanon conditional upon Syrian withdrawal. Bunche would have none of this, and in his inimitable way was
able to persuade Israel to renounce its starting point for the negotiations, and conclude an agreement with Lebanon unconditionally.

The actual negotiations were conducted by Bunche's deputy Henri
Vigier and by Major General Riley. Unlike the Rhodes talks, these negotiations took place alternately in Israel and in Lebanon, with each side
acting as host in turn, something that greatly eased the relations between
the two delegations. In fact, once the major political obstacle was cleared,
the military details were quickly settled in direct talks between Arabic-
speaking members of the Israeli delegation and their opposite numbers,
and the results simply incorporated in the agreement.

The negotiations with Syria were again difficult, in fact probably the
most difficult of all. They lasted from 5 April until 20 July 1949, and
took place in physically harsh conditions, in tents pitched between the
frontlines in the Mahanayim area (near where Jacob is reputed to have
had his dream), the approach to which involved precarious crawling
through minefields. I don't think even the Germans experienced that,
neither in 1918 nor in 1945.

In these negotiations Bunche's hand was missing, and there were several appeals for him to come back and take over from Vigier, but apparently his health would not permit that. Bunche conducted his part of the negotiations from the permanent missions in New York and through written communications with the political leaders, not a really satisfactory way of mediating the delicate matter of the location of the Jordan River boundary line. The negotiations at Mahanayim were deadlocked several times, and Bunche, in his usual way, was able to produce ingenious but ambitious compromises—again, I believe, on the assumption that they would not have to last for long. However, they involved the demilitarization of populated areas and did not deal adequately with the administrative problems that inevitably arose. Furthermore, the frontier itself was an artificial one, which left the Jordan Valley undefended and virtually indefensible from artillery attacks launched from the Syrian peaks, which were not in the delimitarized zone. It is a wonder to me that this agreement lasted until 1967, when the occupation of the Golan Heights put an end to the nightmare of the inhabitants of the Jordan Valley. Bunche's solution to *immediate* obstacles encountered in the negotiations did not take into account the underlying causes of those obstacles, and assumed that the compromise agreement would be maintained in good faith until replaced by the hoped-for peace as the outcome of Lausanne. I am not sure he would have put his compromises forward, at least in such an open-ended and ambiguous form, had he been reconciled to the fact that the agreement was to last indefinitely (doc. 341).

My praise of Bunche should not be mistaken. I do regard his services to the UN, to the world, and to us all in producing the armistice regime as one of the greatest diplomatic feats since the end of World War II, and I personally regard the award to him of the Nobel Peace Prize in 1950 as one of the most highly deserved awards of that prize since 1945. But that does not blind me to what I feel are legitimate criticisms of the whole mediation effort as it developed in the Middle East.

Bunche's determination to succeed at all costs before the Palestine Conciliation Commission could really get underway (docs. 7, 32, for example) distracted his attention from fundamentals; his use of the word "picayunish" in opening the Egyptian negotiations (doc. 5) is revealing. In this I think one can find some of the reasons for the breakdown of the armistice regime in 1956, despite Hammarskjöld's strenuous efforts to shore it up when its teetering became evident. I am on record as expressing dissatisfaction with the Egyptian agreement as a legal document (doc. 151), and I remain of that opinion. Its inherent weaknesses were never successfully overcome—weaknesses caused by deliberately ambiguous drafting to satisfy some immediate obstacle and its failure to look ahead and anticipate what would be likely to happen when both sides had recovered from their exhaustion of 1948. The same criticism can be made of the Syrian agreement.

One major weakness relates to the very nature of the armistice regime.

Israel took the view that the existence of the UN Charter had changed fundamentally the political and legal status of war as an instrument of national policy, in effect outlawing it; and that an armistice concluded within a Charter framework had to be read in the context of the new international law established by the Charter. Egypt, if I understood correctly conversations I had with their representatives at the time, took the view that whatever the Charter might be, armistice was and remained an incident of war, with a state of war existing between the two countries until replaced by a peace (as it now, happily, is). The practical manifestation of this apparently academic argument, as far as Egypt was concerned, was the maintenance of the blockade of the Suez Canal and the Strait of Tiran, positions regarded by many, including the Security Council in its resolution of 1 September 1951, as violations of the armistice, and which were to lead to the wars of 1956 and 1967. There was no meeting of minds on the nature of the armistice regime, and in fact little real effort to produce an agreement; and Bunche's famous statement to the Security Council in August 1949 that the establishment of the armistice regime would sweep away all vestiges of the war seems to have been wishful thinking on his part.

A second major criticism of the armistice agreement, running through the collection of Israeli documents, is a repeated contemporary assessment that in *all* the negotiations, both Bunche and Vigier made cardinal errors in submitting fully detailed proposals for the demarcation lines too early, before the real issues had been properly examined. Some of these internal documents that, as I have said, were never intended for publication, go further, suggesting that the entire mediation effort was structured in such a way as to keep the parties at arms' length concerning their cardinal issues and always threw one or the other on the defensive vis à vis Bunche himself, Trygve Lie, the Secretary-General of the United Nations, and through him the Security Council and the Great Powers. Despite the socializing, which was intended to remove some of the personal difficulties and shyness that were inevitable under these circumstances, the documents convey a contemporary impression that the mediation effort deliberately tried to prevent the parties from negotiating substantive issues directly, leaving them to be imposed by the Mediator; this attitude greatly complicated all the negotiations and in fact could only be remedied by direct talks between the parties. This criticism is too prevalent in the Israeli documents to be dismissed merely as examples of their authors' personal frustrations. And, in the end, it is a fact that the crucial issues of the Armistice Demarcation Line between Israel and Egypt, between Israel and Jordan, and between Israel and Lebanon—although less true of Israel and Syria—were produced by direct talks (partly in the military subcommittees) and simply incorporated in the armistice agreements.

The record shows that the conception of the armistice in lieu of the truce, as a transition to permanent peace, was Bunche's. In assessing his work, we must not forget the enormous pressures weighing upon him, as a man who, as his subsequent career in the United Nations was to show, was to place at the head of his priorities the maintenance of international peace in more than one trouble spot as well as the liberation of colonized peoples and areas. It is sometimes alleged that he had pro-Arab sympathies.[4] It is sometimes asserted that he was unduly influenced by the Arabists of the British Foreign Office and their American counterparts in the State Department, although the United States has always had a Middle East policy and a will of its own. But I personally never encountered anything of that kind, neither at Rhodes where I first came into contact with Ralph Bunche, nor in the period 1967–1971 (and beyond) when I was Deputy Permanent Representative of the Israel's UN delegation in New York and was in direct contact with him almost every day.

Bunche was tough; he could be harsh; he cajoled, he threatened, and he charmed. If he twisted your arm, it hurt, and was meant to. But he was fair and open to argument and persuasion and to me was the incarnation of belief in the UN—not the United Nations as viewed through the rose-tinted spectacles of a wishy-washy ideology but the UN as a necessity for the preservation of mankind in the nuclear age. From perhaps an opposing point of departure I personally could meet him halfway, and I regard him as one of the greatest men I have ever had the honor to meet and to work with, and against. On a personal note, shortly after the election of President Eisenhower, when the Korean armistice negotiations were being prepared, I received two virtually identical letters from the Israeli embassies in Washington and Moscow: Would I please send urgently half a dozen copies each of the small book I published in 1951 entitled *Israel's Armistice Agreements with the Arab States*. It is good to see that notice was taken of Bunche's creative work at Rhodes, and that if *he* had to work without precedents to guide him, he did supply important precedents to others.

Notes

1. Wm. Roger Louis, *The British Empire in the Middle East 1945–1951* (Oxford: Oxford University Press, 1986), p. 551.
2. *Documents on the Foreign Policy of Israel: Armistice Negotiations with the Arab States, December 1948–July 1949*, 3 vols. (Jerusalem: Israel State Archives, 1983).
3. Ibid., letter of 10 February 1949, doc. 111, note 6; companion vol. p. 136, letter of 6 March 1949, doc. 164.
4. Louis, *British Empire in the Middle East*, p. 551.

· 11 ·

RALPH BUNCHE AND THE DEVELOPMENT OF UN PEACEKEEPING

Brian Urquhart

In the foreword to a recent publication on United Nations peacekeeping, Secretary-General Pérez de Cuellar wrote as follows:

> Like many political institutions, the United Nations has been faced, virtually throughout its existence, with a deep gulf between theory and practice, between the principle and objectives of the Charter and the political realities of our time. The effort to bridge this gulf has been the main theme of the first forty years of the United Nations.
>
> Nowhere has the gulf between theory and practice been so evident as in the primary function of the United Nations, the maintenance of international peace and security. The Charter's provisions for this purpose, based primarily on the activity of the Security Council and the unanimity of its permanent members, have never yet been permitted to function fully. Being unable to exercise the magisterial but relatively simple powers prescribed in the Charter, the Council has had, time and again, to fall back on less well-defined measures—good offices, conciliation, mediation and delegation of responsibility to the Secretary-General.
>
> Of these less well-defined measures, the form of conflict control which is now known as peace-keeping is perhaps the most original and most ambitious. Peace-keeping is a technique not mentioned, let alone described, in the Charter. In fact it is in many ways a reversal of the use of military personnel

186

foreseen in the Charter. It has been developed for situations where there is no formal determination of aggression. Its practitioners have no enemies, are not there to win, and can use force only in self-defence. Its effectiveness depends on voluntary co-operation.

It may seem strange that the United Nations has turned to various forms of this technique no less than 13 times and that peace-keeping is widely regarded as one of the Organization's most successful innovations. The reason presumably lies in the nature of international relations in our time. There are now many conflicts which neither side can hope to win but in which peaceful settlement remains elusive. Peace-keeping offers a dignified and inexpensive escape from such situations. In the present relationship of the most powerful nations, it is usually impossible for the Security Council to reach more drastic decisions for putting an end to threats to or breaches of the peace.

In a time of nuclear armament, it is more than ever important that regional conflicts in sensitive areas should be kept out of the sphere of possible great-power nuclear confrontation. In this context, peace-keeping operations are one important means of conflict control, working, as they usually do, in partnership with the efforts of the Security Council and the Secretary-General to gain time and to promote just and peaceful settlements of international disputes. It is worth noting that peace-keeping operations tend to be established for conflict control in particularly sensitive areas of the world where the danger of escalation is high.

I believe that this novel but still fragile creation is an important addition to the armory of peace in the nuclear age . . . . [1]

Ralph Bunche was unquestionably the original practical architect of "this novel but still fragile creation" that is now called "peacekeeping," and he probably did more to develop the technique than any other person. He started in this function by accident when it became clear that the Mediator in Palestine would have to have an operational team to supervise the truces or cease-fires in the Arab-Israeli war if he was to be able to tackle his basic function of mediation. In 1948, this turn of events came as a considerable surprise to the United Nations, which had been set up as a primarily diplomatic organization with little provision for operational effort. Thus Ralph Bunche, as the right-hand man of Count Bernadotte and, after Bernadotte's murder, himself as the Mediator, found himself setting up the first peacekeeping operation of the United Nations.

"We started from scratch," he said in an informal talk in June 1949 on his experiences as Mediator in Palestine. "We did not know what we were going to have to do. We had to improvise as we went along. We made many mistakes. But if we produced results—and we did produce results—it was because of the fact that we had intelligent, adaptable, devoted members of this Secretariat who were even willing to risk their lives in order to carry on their mission."[2]

When Bunche came back to New York in 1949 he relinquished responsibilities both as Mediator and as the principal director of the Truce

Supervision Organization. He reverted to his original function in the Trusteeship Department and was supposed to take up a professorship at Harvard within a year. The pressure of events at the United Nations progressively deferred his development, and Bunche finally gave up all hope of an academic career for good.

When Dag Hammarskjöld became Secretary-General, he made a thorough study and reform of the Secretariat. One of his reforms was to appoint two assistant secretaries-general without portfolio attached to his own office to undertake specific political assignments which did not fall under the authority of other assistant secretaries-general. These two officials were to be American and Soviet in the touching belief that such a Secretariat arrangement would serve to bridge the East-West gulf in the Security Council. Ralph Bunche was appointed as the American Assistant Secretary-General without Portfolio and remained in that position, subsequently renamed Under Secretary-General for Special Political Affairs, until his death in 1971.

Ralph Bunche had little or nothing to do with the Palestine question, with the Truce Supervision Organization in the Middle East, which he had set up, or the armistice agreements that he had negotiated, until the Suez Crisis of 1956. To cope with this unique crisis, Hammarskjold co-opted Bunche as the organizer of the first United Nations peacekeeping force, UNEF I, and he remained the principal architect, coordinator, and director of United Nations peacekeeping operations from that time until the end of his career at the UN.

The First Peacekeeping Operation—UNTSO

In developing the organization, technique, and political and military theory of peacekeeping, Bunche's practical experience in Palestine in 1948 stood him in very good stead in later years, and many of the lessons that he drew from that experience can be seen as the basis for his later activities in developing peacekeeping. In the 1949 talk cited above, Bunche outlined in simple but vivid terms those experiences. I shall therefore quote from the lecture extensively.

"What is most significant," Bunche noted, "about this entire operation since 17 September last, is the fact that since that date it has been exclusively a Secretariat operation in so far as the mediation and truce supervision work is concerned. Of course, on 11 December of last year, the General Assembly adopted a resolution which set up the Palestine Conciliation Commission to deal with the problem of permanent settlement. But the mediation and the truce supervision work, since the assassination of Count Bernadotte, has been entirely in the hands of the Secretariat."

Bernadotte had arrived in the Middle East on 28 May 1948 with a very small staff that included Bunche, a personal staff of four, and eight members of the Secretariat from New York. Bunche continued:

When we went out to Palestine we did not know anything about supervising the truce and we had nothing at that time to supervise the truce with. As a matter of fact it was not a truce anyway, because when Count Bernadotte began to talk with the representatives of the Arab States and of Israel he found that they had accepted a truce in principle but that they had much to say about the conditions on which a truce might be adopted. Therefore, he had to negotiate a truce. And he set about to do this in eight days of the most intensive diplomatic negotiation, I think, that has ever been undertaken in the history of diplomacy, and finally persuaded the Arab States and Israel to accept a four weeks truce on conditions laid down by him. That truce went into effect on 11 June 1948. But then the truce had to be supervised. This was a basic condition of the truce, that it should be applied in such a way as to give no military advantage to either side. And we had, as I say, less than ten members of the Secretariat at hand at that time. The truce applied not only to Palestine but to seven Arab States, and it meant that the shipment of war materials had to be checked and controlled; the influx of immigrants had to be checked and controlled; the movement of war supplies had to be checked; it also meant checking airfields, ports, military lines, and it meant defining the military lines in order that it might later be decided whether either side had advanced beyond the positions held at the time the Truce went into effect.

Bunche's small staff had to improvise as best they could in supervising a truce in seven states. Their duties were various in the extreme. One found himself guarding a British supply depot at Suez, another took a taxi to the frontlines outside Tel Aviv and brought the Israeli and Arab commanders together in no-man's land. The United Nations staff were frequently shot at, either by mistake or on purpose.
Bunche continued:

Of course, we gradually had a full staff built up. We obtained military observ-ers which were recruited from the States members of the Security Council's Truce Commission. We obtained Belgian observers, French observers, Amer-ican observers—officers and enlisted men. We put United Nations armbands on them and we put United Nations flags on their cars and jeeps. In some areas we had to supplement the United Nations flag with a plain white flag because the United Nations flag was not always safe. As you know, its colors are blue and white. Those also happen to be the colors of the flag of Israel, and from a distance it was not always possible for the Arabs to be sure that the Secretariat members in the car were not the enemy. And so the cars started carrying plain white flags on one side and United Nations flags on the other. These United Nations flags tended to fade pretty rapidly anyway, and it was not always certain just what colors we were flying under.
We had to set up a full-fledged governmental organization. We diffused the observers all over the area; we maintained Secretariat representatives, who were similar to diplomatic officials, in all of the capitals, and they had some

very rare diplomatic experience, because they were constantly delivering threats and ultimata and deadlines to the Governments, and sometimes, in return, they received very unkind replies. But they stuck by their guns and they were objective. They served the interests of the United Nations very well indeed.

From Bunche's account it can be seen that total improvisation was the order of the day. One of the major problems was transport and communication, since commercial channels for either were impossibly unreliable and it was a matter of life or death that some communications go through, communications announcing the arrival of United Nations aircraft, for example. Nor was it possible to cross the various frontiers except in a United Nations aircraft or vehicle.

Bunche decided early on that the military members of the mission should be integrated into the Secretariat and should not be armed. This was partly because it was decided that arms would only be a provocation and a danger to the personnel concerned and also because at that time the observers were untried and could not be depended upon not to shoot at the wrong time at the wrong people. The only protection for the military observers was, and remains, the name and identification of the United Nations and the good faith that the parties would exercise their obligations to the United Nations. This was hazardous, and in less than a year, ten members of the team, including Count Bernadotte himself, had been killed and twice as many wounded.

There were immense practical problems since there was no administrative structure and the operation was spread over an enormous area. Money was also a problem since each member had to have enough money to carry out his mission and keep his staff supplied and paid. This required a mobile paymaster traveling by whatever transport seemed necessary.

The United Nations had a variety of aircraft, but the conditions were hazardous, not only for military reasons but also because of the lack of weather reports and radio contact and the fact that some airstrips had been damaged by the war and others mined.

In looking back at this operation, Bunche found it particularly encouraging that it was possible to bring together a completely heterogeneous group of the Secretariat who had had little or no experience of Palestine and to make the operation work under very unpromising conditions. The United Nations military observers were not particularly popular with either side, and there was no prior experience to guide them in the task of supervising and enforcing a truce and getting the local commanders to cooperate. It was indeed a triumph of leadership and *esprit de corps,* and the results were the shoring up of the cease-fire and finally the

armistice machinery that produced relative peace on the borders between Israel and her Arab neighbors for many years.

Bunche concluded with the following words:

> What has been accomplished is this: The truces checked the war. The first
> truce, the four weeks truce, which went into effect on 11 June 1948, stopped
> the fighting and it remained stopped pretty well throughout that four weeks.
> The second truce was imposed by the Security Council on 15 July 1948, and
> that truce also worked fairly well for the first few months. But we had warned
> the United Nations that no truce could go on indefinitely, and that some
> further step would have to be taken or that fighting would be inevitable.
>
> There was not quick enough action in taking that further step, demanding
> that further step, and fighting did occur last October and last December. That
> was a setback, as the assassination of Count Bernadotte was a setback. . . .
>
> After the Truces came the Armistice Agreements. These have been a big
> step forward. They have pledged the states involved in this conflict not to
> resort to force. Each of the Armistice Agreements incorporates an article
> which is, in effect, a non-aggression pact. They were difficult negotiations, but
> they were possible only because the delegations on both sides, Arab and
> Israeli, showed the statesmanship, the reason and the intelligence necessary to
> bring agreement out of disagreement. If that had not been present, the
> United Nations and no individual could have produced Armistice Agreements
> at Rhodes and at Rasen Naqura. . . .
>
> The questions of final settlement, questions involving permanent frontiers,
> the future status of Jerusalem, the status of those tragic victims of the fighting,
> the eight to nine hundred thousand Arab refugees—these are the problems
> which the Palestine Conciliation Commission served by a Secretariat staff,
> headed by Pablo Azcarate, is grappling with at Lausanne, in its meetings with
> the Arab and Israeli representatives now.

In those days it was confidently believed that a final settlement in
Palestine could and would be reached. Now, nearly forty years later, we
know better. We know that sometimes conflict control or limitation is the
best we can hope for. Bunche's efforts in Palestine laid the basis for
future conflict control operations by the United Nations using military
personnel. Bunche established the necessity of integrity and impartiality,
the importance of cooperation by the parties, the central role of the
Secretariat in running these operations, and the principle of the non-use
of force by UN military personnel. He wrote into the armistice agreements the functions of the military observers and the chief of staff of
UNTSO, who was the chairman of each of the four Mixed Armistice
Commissions. On the practical side, the communications and transport
system set up for the UNTSO survives to this day and has served as an
unofficial depot for other United Nations peacekeeping operations as
well as for developing the procedures and standards that have come to
be adopted throughout the system.

The First United Nations Emergency Force (UNEF I)

At the end of October 1956, an unusually severe and complex crisis arose over the joint invasion of Egypt by Israel, France, and the United Kingdom. Coinciding as it did with the Hungarian uprising and producing a situation in which Britain and France found themselves opposed by the United States and most of the Commonwealth, there was unusually heavy pressure to find a means to secure the peaceful exit of the invading forces and thus to resolve the crisis.

It was clear that the truce supervision machinery (UNTSO) that had previously supervised the armistice on the Israeli-Egyptian frontier and in the Gaza Strip would not be enough to secure the withdrawal of the British, French, and Israeli forces, and that something more substantial was required. Lester Pearson of Canada had abstained from the vote on the assembly's cease-fire resolution on 2 November on the grounds that it was "inadequate to achieve the purposes we had in mind at this session." The next day he introduced the idea of a United Nations force, initially with the idea of including the British and French forces in Egypt in the force, although it soon became apparent that this was politically impossible. In presenting his idea to the assembly, Pearson suggested that the Secretary-General be authorized "to begin to make arrangements with member states for a United Nations force large enough to keep these borders at peace while a political settlement is being worked out . . . a truly international peace and police force." The assembly in the early hours of November 4th voted on Pearson's proposal and requested the Secretary-General to submit within forty-eight hours a plan for the setting up, with the consent of the nations concerned, an emergency international United Nations Force to secure and supervise the cessation of hostilities.

Peacekeeping forces are now an accepted part of the international system, but in 1956 this was a revolutionary proposal. Many people did not believe it could possibly work, and even Hammarskjöld himself was initially skeptical of the practicability of Pearson's idea. In any case this was an entirely new enterprise that had to be set up with the maximum urgency.

Immediately the assembly had made its decision, Hammarskjöld called in Ralph Bunche to supervise the preparations for the emergency force, at the same time asking Lieutenant General E. L. M. Burns, the chief of staff of UNTSO who was to be commander of the new force, to submit suggestions and proposals from the field. Thus began a task which was to be the main part of Bunche's work for the rest of his life.

Hammarskjold had himself written the main report on the establishment of the United Nations Emergency Force (UNEF) in between other engagements on November 5th. This document both laid the foundations for a new kind of international activity and set out the principles and ideas that were to become the basis for future peacekeeping forces. Bunche's first association with this enterprise occurred at 10:30 P.M. on November 5th, when Hammarskjold went over his draft report with him, Andrew Cordier, and Constantin Stavropoulos, the legal counsel.

The basis of the cease-fire was the withdrawal of the invading armies; the condition for that withdrawal was the deployment of UNEF. It was imperative that the force should get to Egypt as soon as possible so that the British, French, and Israeli forces might start their withdrawal. There were two urgent problems in deploying the force. The first was to negotiate with Nasser the entry of the force into Egypt and to agree on the elements of the Status of Forces Agreement that would define the status and functioning of the force on Egyptian soil. This task was entrusted to Stavropoulos and was later taken on by Hammarskjöld himself. The second task was to bring the force into being—mobilize, equip, and transport it to Egypt with at least the essential rudiments of a directive, communications, logistics, accommodation, and supplies. In this completely novel task, every step was a step in the dark. Bunche summoned to New York the military attachés of the countries that were going to provide troops and set them up as a round-the-clock working group to deal with the organization, planning, and mobilization of the force, dealing with problems as they arose and improvising solutions to them. All practical matters were considered and decided in this working group, including transportation arrangements, identification insignia, levels of armament, logistical arrangements and supplies. Since there had recently been fighting between four armies in Egypt, identification was essential, and it was in this working group that the Blue Helmet originated. Initially the group was in favor of equipping the force with blue berets, but when it was found that they would take weeks to procure, it was decided to use helmet liners from U.S. stocks in Europe sprayed with United Nations blue paint. Another major problem was the feeding of a force that had no logistical pipeline. We solved this temporarily in the working group by deciding to requisition supplies from the seventeen ships that had been stuck in the Canal when the Egyptians blocked it. The guidelines and *modus operandi* of the force were also worked out in this working group on the basis of recommendations from General Burns. The decisions of the group were relayed back to the capitals from which troops were coming for the necessary action.

Bunche had the exceptional advantage of previously having organized a United Nations operation with military personnel in the Middle East, and he was very much the guiding spirit of the discussions. His practical common sense was matched by a masterly grasp of the political situation, of principle, and of Hammarskjöld's thinking about the nature and conduct of the new peacekeeping force.

Bunche was Hammarskjöld's principal adviser in the meeting of the UNEF Advisory Committee, consisting of representatives of the countries providing troops, which Hammarskjöld had set up to help in the extremely delicate questions of international politics and national sovereignty that arise when an international force is deployed on the territory of a sovereign state. The situation was particularly difficult in Egypt, which had just been invaded by three foreign armies and was extremely sensitive about the presence and activities of yet another group of foreign soldiers of a completely novel kind.

These problems became so acute that Hammarskjöld felt obliged to go to Egypt himself on November 14th to deal with the conditions for the arrival of the force, which had been raised by President Nasser. At the first meeting of the Advisory Committee just before Hammarskjöld's departure, Bunche was able to report that 650 officers and men were already in Naples awaiting the signal to go to Egypt and that in all there had been 21 offers of troops for the Force, "an army which everyone fights to get into."

Hammarskjöld flew into Egypt with the advance elements of the United Nations Force and spent three days intensively negotiating on the various problems of its presence, composition, and staffing. He came away from Cairo with the so-called "Good Faith" agreement that recognized Egypt's undisputed right to request the withdrawal of UNEF, but also got from Egypt an agreement by which the government would, in good faith, limit its freedom of action by making any request for withdrawal dependent upon the completion of the force's task, a question that should be submitted for interpretation to the General Assembly. This agreement did not save Hammarskjöld's successor from a disastrous responsibility in 1967. During Hammarskjöld's absence, Bunche held the fort in New York.

After the initial difficulties, the installation of UNEF went surprisingly well. The main problem then became to secure the withdrawal of the Israeli troops from Sinai. None of Hammarskjöld's efforts produced progress on this front, and the question was eventually resolved by the intervention of President Eisenhower. When Israel finally withdrew from Sinai in early March 1957, Hammarskjöld sent Bunche to the Middle East to coordinate the UNEF takeover in the Gaza Strip and along the international frontier and to hold things down until Hammarskjöld himself arrived on March 21st.

This was an extremely sensitive stage in the history of UNEF since the positions of both Egypt and Israel regarding the Gaza Strip were complicated, and it was essential that the presence of UNEF be used for solutions to these problems. Great political sensitivity and imagination were required. The Israelis reacted strongly to any notion that Egypt would be coming back in force into the Gaza Strip. The Egyptians were equally sensitive to any suggestion that their rightful position in the Gaza Strip was being challenged by the presence of UNEF. The actual take-over by UNEF troops and the way that was handled were thus of critical importance, and Bunche's presence to support General Burns at this time was crucial. It was essential to avoid the return of Egyptian troops to Gaza and to stop the resumption of the *fedayeen* raids that had been a main reason for the Israeli invasion of Sinai. It was also essential to keep the goodwill of Egypt. Bunche shuttled between Gaza and Cairo where he talked with Nasser in an effort to keep this critical situation under control. An unpublished agreement was eventually reached whereby Egyptian forces would stay 2,000 yards back from the international border. UNEF's presence would also make it unnecessary for Egyptian forces to return to the coastal gun positions at the entrance to the Gulf of Aqaba.

After initial uncertainties, UNEF settled down surprisingly easily to its highly successful ten-year presence as a buffer between Israel and Egypt. Its presence came to be welcomed by both Egypt and Israel. During this time Bunche was in direct charge of the day-to-day direction of UNEF and made a number of visits to the Force to deal with political, military, and administrative problems.

Hammarskjöld, assisted mainly by Bunche, had brought UNEF to maturity with extraordinary success in the face of great difficulties. In fact, this success became something of a hazard, leading to demands, from John Foster Dulles and both Houses of the U.S. Congress among others, for the establishment of a permanent United Nations peacekeep-ing force. Hammarskjöld and Bunche reacted with extreme caution to this enthusiasm, knowing better than anyone the sensitivities and diffi-culties involved in running a peacekeeping operation as well as the particular circumstances that would make it almost impossible to create a permanent institution to respond effectively to unknown future situa-tions. They were acutely aware of the sensitive balance between national sovereignty and international responsibility that had to be maintained if a force like UNEF was to function effectively, and both believed that any attempt to generalize such establishments or the solutions to such prob-lems would only serve to set back the very promising progress that had been made during the Suez Crisis. UNEF I was one of the most ac-claimed and successful achievements of the United Nations up to that time and was perceived as a pioneering action of great significance for the future. It was characteristic of the political wisdom of the two friends that Bunche and Hammarskjöld were wary of the praise that was show-ered on them.

Their caution was amply justified by the disastrous ending of UNEF I in 1967. Hammarskjöld had always been aware of the fact that the success of UNEF in maintaining peace on the border between Israel and

Egypt could have well become an embarrassment for Nasser. He had on several occasions urged the Jordanians not to attack Nasser on this score. Six years after Hammarskjöld's death, the situation could no longer be contained. Stung by Syrian comments about his comfortable arrangement of confronting Israel through UNEF, Nasser made a series of disastrous moves, requesting the withdrawal of UNEF and the cessation of its overall function. The arrangements that Hammarskjöld had made in 1956 proved of no avail under these pressures and landed his successor, U Thant, in an impossible and cruel situation. The UN could not accept a change in the arrangements for UNEF that had been agreed to by Egypt in 1957, but it had no right to object to Nasser invoking Egyptian sovereignty to call for the withdrawal of the force. Indeed, ten years before, Israel had insisted on its own sovereign right with regard to UNEF in refusing to have UNEF stationed in Israel. As a purely practical matter, there was no way in which UNEF, a very small and lightly armed force, could function on Egyptian soil without the cooperation of the Egyptian government and army. There was no doubt, therefore, in Bunche's mind when he advised U Thant that if it was impossible to dissuade Nasser from his demands on the grounds that they would certainly trigger a disaster, there would be no option but the withdrawal of UNEF. Bunche felt that if this happened, the withdrawal should be orderly, dignified, deliberate, and lengthy enough to make it possible to renegotiate UNEF's presence with Nasser.

Due to the complications arising from the British and French veto in the Security Council in 1956, UNEF had been set up by the General Assembly and negotiated into Egypt by the Secretary-General. Thus, the only body that could make decisions about UNEF was the General Assembly, in which a large majority was known to be in favor of meeting Nasser's demands. The responsibility for decision, therefore, fell squarely on U Thant, advised by Ralph Bunche. U Thant declined to take the only escape from this responsibility open to him, namely to invoke Article 99 of the Charter and throw the whole matter, as a threat to peace, into the lap of the Security Council. Although such a move would not have altered the outcome, it would have shifted the responsibility for the decision and for the disaster that followed.

I shall not repeat the dismal course of events of June 1967. The decision to withdraw UNEF, Nasser's announcement of the blockade of the Straits of Tiran, the only access to the Israeli Port of Eilat, and the devastating war that very soon followed were a bitter blow to Bunche, one of the main architects of the force, although ironically the disaster proved in a negative way the enormous, and widely forgotten, value of UNEF. Bunche himself received much of the blame for the advice he gave U Thant on this occasion, and U Thant became the principal scapegoat for what had happened, although he was the only world figure who actually went to Cairo to argue with Nasser. It is very easy to make scapegoats; it is extremely difficult, in analyzing the situation in 1967, to see how the disaster could in any practical way have been avoided, given the divisions of the Security Council and the intransigence of those involved. If, of course, the Soviet Union, the United States, and the Arab countries had all been united in persuading Nasser that he was embarked on a course that was certain to lead to disaster, something might have been done. There was never any hope of that.

Bunche was already in failing health in 1967, and I believe that the 1967 war was an important factor in accelerating his decline. I think this was also true of U Thant.

Other Observer Operations

Bunche was the main director of other observer operations over the years. The principal ones were the United Nations Observer Group in Lebanon in 1958, the United Nations Yemen Observer Mission from 1962 to 1964, and the United Nations India-Pakistan Observer Mission in 1965.

THE UNITED NATIONS OBSERVER GROUP IN LEBANON (UNOGIL)

The United Nations Observer Group in Lebanon (UNOGIL) was, in the complex circumstances of the summer of 1958, an extremely successful instrument in de-escalating a potentially very dangerous situation. It stabilized the situation in Lebanon and provided the pretext for the withdrawal of the United States forces that landed South of Beirut in mid-July following the overthrow of the Hashemite Kingdom of Iraq and the resulting request of President Chamoun of Lebanon to the United States to protect Lebanon's political independence and territorial integrity. UNOGIL was run personally by Hammarskjöld, who engaged in a complex exercise of personal diplomacy in the Middle East in order to set the stage for UNOGIL and to support its activities.

Ralph Bunche remained at United Nations Headquarters and supervised the recruiting, equipping, and dispatch of military observers, of whom there were at one time 591, and the procurement of transport, communications, and light aircraft for the group. Bunche's experience both in organization and in the diplomacy of peacekeeping proved invaluable in keeping under control this volatile situation, where there was a strong tendency by the parties to misstate the case. He also dealt with other governments concerned with the matter, with the press, and with those governments who were providing observers. Bunche and Hammarskjöld had by now become a well-attuned team, each man understanding the other's approach and foreseeing the other's reactions to problems which arose. UNOGIL was one of the few United Nations peacekeeping operations that was terminated and withdrawn in good order on the completion of its task. The withdrawal of UNOGIL was completed by 9 December 1958.

THE UNITED NATIONS YEMEN OBSERVER MISSION (UNYOM)

Far less satisfactory than UNOGIL was the United Nations Yemen Observer Mission. The situation arose from a rebellion against the Imam in September 1962. Egypt (then the United Arab Republic) and the USSR recognized the new insurgent government whereas other major powers, including the United States and the United Kingdom as well as Saudi Arabia, did not recognize it. The Imam escaped from the capital and, rallying the northern tribes, fought a fierce guerrilla campaign against the Republican forces. Saudi Arabia was involved in supporting the Royalists; a large Egyptian expeditionary force supported the Republicans. In view of the relations of the Soviet Union and Egypt, and the United States and Saudi Arabia, this was a civil war with major potential for external complications.

From the beginning Secretary-General U Thant had been concerned with this potentially explosive situation, consulting with the representatives of the Arab Republic of Yemen, Saudi Arabia, and the United Arab Republic and offering to make his good offices available to the parties "for such assistance as might be desired towards insuring against new developments in that situation which might threaten the peace of the area."

U Thant sent Bunche to the United Arab Republic and to Yemen to undertake a fact-finding mission regarding the volatile situation there. Bunche had an extraordinarily lively time, having at one point to take off across country in a jeep to escape an emotional mob. As a result of his activities—and a mission by Ellsworth Bunker for the United States government—U Thant was able to inform the Security Council that he had received from each of the three governments—United Arab Republic, Saudi Arabia, and Yemen—formal confirmation of their acceptance of identical terms of disengagement in Yemen. Under these terms, Saudi Arabia would terminate support and aid to the Royalists and prohibit the use of its territory to Royalist leaders for carrying on the struggle. Simultaneously, Egypt would begin withdrawing its troops from Yemen. A demilitarized zone would be established up to 20 kilometers on each side of the Saudi Arabia-Yemen border, where that border was marked, and observers would be stationed there to check on the observance of the terms of disengagement. They would also certify the suspension of activities in support of the Royalists and of the outward movement of Egyptian forces and equipment.

This task was carried out by a Yugoslav reconnaissance unit 114 strong and a Canadian air unit of 50 officers and men. The task was not as easy as it sounded. Much of the border between Yemen and Saudi Arabia was not marked, the functions and authority of UNYOM were limited strictly to observing, certifying, and reporting on the compliance of Saudi Arabia and Egypt with the disengagement agreement, and the governments concerned seemed reluctant to carry out those terms. After a year of frustrating experience it was decided that UNYOM's function should be more as an intermediary than as a peacekeeping mission, and a special representative was appointed in November 1963 to hold extensive discussions with the three concerned governments. By spring 1964, Secretary-General U Thant felt obliged to acknowledge the failure of the parties to implement the disengagement agreement and the difficulties that UNYOM faced in observing and reporting on these matters. The withdrawal of Egyptian forces was slow if not nonexistent, and there were indications that the Yemeni Royalists continued to receive military supplies from external sources. On the other hand, there was no question that the United Nations presence had exercised an important restraining influence on hostile actions in the area. The mission was withdrawn in September 1964, and shortly thereafter relations between the parties improved and the disengagement agreement became a reality.

THE UNITED NATIONS INDIA-PAKISTAN OBSERVATION MISSION (UNIPOM)

The India-Pakistan war of September 1965 was serious not only because of the active hostilities between two large states that could ill afford a full-scale war, but also because of the potential for involvement of other powers including the Soviet Union, China, and the United States. This was a full-scale international crisis in which the Security Council was unusually active. The Secretary-General himself went to the subcontinent from 7 to 16 September in an effort to secure a cessation of hostilities. On his return, U Thant suggested that the Council should order a cease-fire, consider what assistance it could provide in ensuring observance of the cease-fire and the withdrawal of forces by both sides, and request the two heads of government to meet in order to discuss their situation with a view to resolving their outstanding differences. On the 20th of September, after the hostilities had spread from Kashmir to the international border between India and West Pakistan, the Council demanded a cease-fire and withdrawal of all armed personnel to the positions held before 5 August 1965, when the hostilities had begun.

The Council also requested the Secretary-General to provide the necessary asssistance for supervising the cease-fire and ensuring the withdrawal of forces.

This decision called for the establishment of a new observer mission, the United Nations India-Pakistan Observer Mission (UNIPOM). This was to be a temporary organization to exist until such time as the Security Council's resolution was complied with, and was for the sole purpose of supervising the cease-fire along the international border outside the State of Jammu and Kashmir. Ninety observers from ten countries were recruited and assigned to this duty by Ralph Bunche. Their work had to be closely coordinated, both administratively and operationally, with the standing observer mission of the United Nations Military Observer Group in India and Pakistan (UNMOGIP), which had been supervising the cease-fire line in Kashmir since 1948.

Violations of the cease-fire continued to occur and there was no prospect of the withdrawal of troops in October and November, nor were diplomatic efforts to get the governments to agree on a schedule of withdrawals successful. On 10 January 1966, the Prime Minister of India and the President of Pakistan, after meeting in Tashkent at the invitation of Chairman Kosygin, announced their agreement for full withdrawal to the positions of 5 August 1965 by the end of February 1966. The modalities and procedures of this withdrawal were supervised by UNMOGIP and UNIPOM and by a representative of the Secretary-General, General Marambio, who was to make binding decisions in the event of disagreement between the parties. The withdrawals were completed on schedule, and UNIPOM was terminated by the end of March, UNMOGIP continuing to function as it had done since 1948.

Ralph Bunche was the director of these operations that entailed, especially in their early phases, a great deal of argument with India and Pakistan about the nature of the new mission and its relationship to the cease-fire in Kashmir. There was also much discussion about methods and principles with the Chief Military Observer of UNIPOM, General B. F. MacDonald of Canada. The operation, however, did not pose major political problems, and the positive intervention of the Soviet Union achieved the decision by India and Pakistan that made the successful conclusion of this work possible.

THE UNITED NATIONS OPERATION IN THE CONGO (ONUC)

The crisis in the former Belgian Congo that erupted within a week of that country's accession to independence on 30 June 1960 gave rise to the largest, most complex and difficult peacekeeping operation in the history of the United Nations. The UN operation in the Congo has traditionally been regarded as a failure. In fact, at great cost, it achieved all of the objectives set for it by the Security Council, including the removal of foreign forces, assistance to the government in establishing its authority, and the preservation of the territorial integrity of the Congo within its original boundaries.

In this critical operation Bunche found himself in the unusual position of being on the spot before the operation started. Anticipating great difficulties after the Congo's independence, due to the almost total lack of preparation for this event, Hammarskjöld had sent Bunche to Leopoldville in late May 1960, not only to represent him at the independence ceremonies, but also to be on hand to give whatever assistance and advice he could to the new rulers of the Congo. Bunche therefore had nearly three weeks to observe the chaotic scence and the extraordinary difficulties—political, administrative, personal, and practical—which it presented. The new peacekeeping mission, ONUC (Organisation des Nations Unies au Congo) was voted by the Security Council in the early hours of 14 July 1960.

Bunche's advice was a vital element in Hammarskjöld's decision to bring the situation in the Congo to the Security Council under Article 99 of the Charter, and of crucial importance to Hammarskjöld in setting up this most difficult of all peacekeeping operations. The fact that he was already on the scene to direct the incoming mission also gave Bunche the freedom to build up both the political organization of the mission and its *modus operandi* in the full knowledge of the extraordinary difficulties and complications of the Congo.

It is now sometimes forgotten that for the first two months the United Nations Operation in the Congo was widely regarded not only as a great success, but also as an extraordinary step forward in the capacity of the world organization to assist member governments in circumstances of great danger and difficulty. The United Nations had filled a vacuum of order and authority in one of the largest, richest, and most strategically sensitive countries of Africa at a time when the pressures on both East and West to fill that vacuum would have otherwise been almost irresistible. This accounted for the fact that both the United States and the USSR supported the opposition at the outset. It was when the Congo government itself split up on East-West lines, President Kasavubu and Prime Minister Lumumba denouncing each other in violent terms, that the security and technical assistance program that had been planned by Hammarskjöld and carried out with extraordinary success by Bunche ran into the violent international controversy. This imbroglio dominated Hammarskjöld's last years and threatened at the time to split the United Nations itself down the middle.

With Bunche's advice, Hammarskjöld had tried at the outset to put before the Security Council the principles that would govern the organization and activities of ONUC, as well as its composition and method of operation. What he proposed was a temporary security force to be deployed in the Congo with the consent of the Congolese government until the national security forces were able to meet fully their tasks. Although the force was dispatched at the request of the Congolese government, it was under the exclusive command of the United Nations, vested in the Security Council under the control of the Secretary-General. It was very specifically beyond the orders of the Congolese government and could not become a party to any internal conflict. The United Nations force was to have free access to all areas and full freedom of movement. The United Nations military units were not authorized to use force except in self-defense, nor were they ever to take the initiative in the use of force.

As regards the composition of the force, there would be no units from the permanent members of the Security Council. Units from the African states would be the core of the force, which would also include suitable units from other regions. The initial troops came from Ethiopia, Ghana, Guinea, Morocco, and Tunisia.

As soon as the Security Council resolution 143 (1960) had been adopted, Hammarskjöld appointed Ralph Bunche as his special representative in the Congo to head the new operation. He also appointed Lt. General Carl C. Von Horn of Sweden as commander of the actual military force. Bunche was very much the senior of these two appointments, and until his departure from the Congo at the end of August was the unquestioned leader and organizer of the enterprise.

Bunche's task in the Congo was a daunting one. He had to set up and direct, day and night, the military force as well as the large civilian component of ONUC. The military force, which had an air component, eventually reached a strength of over 20,000, while the civilian component was expected to run all of the installations—airport control towers, hospitals, police stations, telecommunications and transport installations, central banks, and so forth—that had been precipitately abandoned by their Belgian staffs. The military force had to be deployed as rapidly as possible all over the Congo to restore law and order and to protect those parts of the population—white and black—who were threatened in one way or another by the mutiny of the Congolese National Army or the violent civil disturbances that were taking place. There was also an emergency food program. All of this in itself, in the emergency conditions of the Congo at that time, was a round-the-clock job requiring great powers of improvisation, management, authority, and political skill.

Bunche also had to deal with the Congolese government and to try to advise them on all of the matters with which they were totally unaccustomed to deal. President Kasavubu and Prime Minister Lumumba were already on bad terms, and the Cabinet consisted of no less than twenty-seven Members representing tribal and political groupings. Dealing with Lumumba alone was immensely time-consuming since he was changeable in the extreme and normally took rumor for fact. He could go, in the course of one conversation, from civility to violent threats to pleas for assistance, and he was chronically unpredictable and volatile. In this strange environment, violence was always only just below the surface and erupted frequently.

Bunche also had to deal with the Belgian authorities—military and diplomatic—since the most urgent task was to achieve as soon as possible the withdrawal of the Belgian military forces that had returned to the Congo after independence and were the center of most of the uproar in the provinces.

The embassies in Leopoldville were another main preoccupation. Being nervous in the first place and having little reliable information as to what was going on, they besieged Bunche and his staff at all hours with requests for help, unsubstantiated reports, criticism, and unsolicited suggestions. The Soviet and American Embassies were particularly active.

The Katanga problem (Katanga had seceded from the Congo in early July) was already showing signs of becoming a decisive issue for the future of the government as well as in the Security Council, and much time and thought had to be given to contacts with the Belgians, with Moise Tshombe, the secessionist "President," and with the Congo government in discussing how this problem was to be brought under control.

Bunche was also responsible for hour-to-hour reporting to Hammarskjöld in New York on the situation, for only on this basis could Hammarskjöld deal with the Security Council or make the kind of decisions that he alone could make. Bunche always insisted on writing all cables himself in longhand, and he would sit for long hours into the night at this task that had to be fitted into other claims on his time. Among these claims were the endless human emergencies that occurred in the anarchy and violence of this vast country. Appeals for assistance, protection, or other forms of help came in night and day from all sources, Congolese and foreign. Bunche had to rule on most of them since many required novel uses of United Nations soldiers or civilians; but we were proud that very few calls went unanswered.

On top of these duties, Bunche was engaged in a crucial process of evolving the rules and methods of operation of both the military and civilian side of ONUC. On the civilian side, this was relatively easy to do, although it was often necessary to include a military component for the protection of civilian activities. On the military side, however, things ran less smoothly. Quite apart from the United Nations Military Command, very senior officers had been sent with some of the contingents and tended to have their own ideas as to what should be done. Often the military had a limited conception of the political difficulties of a peace-keeping force in a newly independent country, and a firm hand was required from the top. For example, Bunche and the rest of us spent much time arguing the problem of what to do with the rebellious and sometimes mutinous Congolese National Army. Until independence, this force had been led by Belgian officers, all of whom had vanished in the mutiny. Lumumba had compounded the problem, in response to wage claims, by promoting every soldier in the Congolese army one rank. The soldiers were heavily armed, completely undisciplined, and leaderless. General Henry Alexander, the British Chief of Staff of the Ghana Army who had come with the Ghana contingent, was firmly of the opinion that ONUC should disarm the Congolese army. Bunche was equally firmly of the opinion that to do so would be a disastrous political and military mistake, and totally out of line with UNOC's principles. This particular controversy was typical of many involving the military at that time, particularly in relation to the use of force in difficult situations. Constant vigilance and the exertion of authority were therefore required from Bunche and his staff in order to avoid military mistakes that could have violent political consequences.

Bunche also had to deal with the press, who were present in great force in the early months of ONUC. This was important and time-consuming, since Bunche's headquarters was virtually the only source of reliable information on what was happening not only in Leopoldville but in the Congo as a whole.

Bunche's method of discharging this superhuman labor was very simple. He assumed personal control of and responsibility for virtually everything that could have political consequences—and in the Congo even the most minor decisions—for example, a suggestion that we should lay in a stock of tear gas, or whether food could be obtained from the nearest source, South Africa—were likely to have major political repercussions.

Bunche was always available to anyone who had a *bona fide* problem. He lived and worked in the salon of a requisitioned apartment, his staff working around the table with him, and he was available virtually 24 hours a day, both to troubled outsiders or to members of the United Nations team. Bunche had already shown his incredible stamina and powers of concentration during the negotiation of the armistice agreements between Israel and the Arab states on the island of Rhodes in 1949, but Rhodes was a picnic in comparison with Leopoldville. Bunche's stamina and his capacity to respond endlessly to the bizarre developments that characterized the Congo situation were truly astonishing. To the frightened or oppressed he invariably showed patience and compassion, however much time it took. He rarely lost his temper, only occasionally and briefly with one of the more preposterous demands of the military. He had an unquenchable sense of humor and greatly enjoyed the more bizarre aspects of our mission.

Bunche had a very tough, analytic mind, and he was not to be taken in by facile formulations or smooth proposals. He analyzed situations and proposals with tremendous care and total honesty, always referring to the principles underlying the operation and making his decision on the basis of principle, not popularity. In this extraordinary period he showed a mixture of integrity, compassion, humor, and toughness that I have never seen equaled.

When Bunche went to the Congo in June 1960, he was supposed to be in the Congo for only three weeks, but he finally handed over his position at the end of August 1960. He left just before the constitutional crisis and breakdown of the Congolese government, which was the beginning of a year of anarchy, tragedy, and bloodshed. Back in New York he was the anchorman of Hammarskjöld's team running the Congo operation, and he worked as long, or longer, hours for the next two years, although under slightly less dramatic conditions. He dealt not only with the maintenance and complications of the military side of ONUC but also with the proliferating political problems that beset this mission. He traveled to the Congo again at the end of 1961 on a mission to bring together Moise Tshombe of Katanga and the government of Prime Minister Cyrille Adoula and again in February 1963 in connection with the ending of the Katanga secession. When U Thant became Secretary-General after Hammarskjöld's death in September 1961, Bunche continued in his capacity as anchorman and was the main director of efforts to achieve the conciliation of the various factions in the Congo, a task which was more or less achieved by 1964 when the military contingent of ONUC was finally phased out.

THE UNITED NATIONS FORCE IN CYPRUS (UNFICYP)

Only one more major peacekeeping force was to be set up during Ralph Bunche's life, the United Nations Force in Cyprus. The Congo operation had created a very serious constitutional and political crisis in the United Nations, revolving mostly around the relative authority of the Secretary-General and the Security Council in controlling peacekeeping operations and the financing of those operations. The financing problem brought the General Assembly to a standstill in 1964 over the question of the application of Article 19 of the Charter. It was surprising, therefore, that in spite of the fundamental division among the membership caused by peacekeeping, the Security Council was able, on the 4th of March 1964 (resolution 186 [1964]) unanimously to recommend the creation of a peacekeeping force in Cyprus. The Congo experience had one disastrous effect on this Security Council decision, namely that the Soviet Union had agreed to vote for it only on the condition that the financing of the force would be on a voluntary basis.

As usual, Ralph Bunche was the main organizer of this new peace-keeping effort. Although it was possible immediately to appoint a com-mander of the force, securing the initial contingents proved to be far more difficult. The outbreak of intercommunal strife in Cyprus and the disastrous experiences of the British peacekeeping force in trying to deal with the situation, the voluntary nature of the financing, and the ex-treme complexity of any likely solution to the intercommunal problem of the island all combined to make governments hesitant to be the first to join the force. The first contingent, from Canada, arrived on the 13th of March, but the force did not become established operationally until the 27th of March when sufficient troops were at last available to enable it to function effectively. The initial components of the force were a British contingent, joined by Canadian, Swedish, Irish, and Finnish contingents, and an Austrian field hospital.

The Cyprus operation had a number of novel features. It contained, from the outset, civilian police units to function in the vacuum caused by the fact that the two communities had separate police forces. The task of seeking a settlement in Cyprus in parallel with the peacekeeping func-tion was entrusted to a United Nations Mediator. This meant that Bunche had less to do in the early years of the Cyprus force with the search for a political settlement. This situation changed when the Medi-ator, Galo Plaza Lasso of Ecuador, had the temerity, in 1967, to submit a report. His report was strongly denounced by the Turkish side and the office of Mediator lapsed, political negotiations being taken on by the special representative of the Secretary-General in Cyprus, who was also head of the United Nations operation.

The peacekeeping function in Cyprus was by no means easy. Both the Greek and Turkish Cypriot communities were acutely suspicious, not only of each other but of the activity and sympathies of the United Nations force. The contingents were deployed as far as possible to match their areas of responsibility with the island's administrative boundaries. In some places, as in the capital, Nicosia, for example, there was a direct military confrontation to be dealt with. In other areas, there were mixed towns and villages that presented unusual problems of their own. This was an endless job of observation and patrolling, both to prevent con-frontation and to protect those in danger, the overall objective being to prevent a recurrence of fighting.

The Congo operation had made all of us acutely sensitive to the difficulties faced by a peacekeeping force functioning within the bound-aries of a sovereign state and in a context of violent disagreement between different groups within that state. Bunche therefore took particular care in maintaining the guiding principles for the operation of the force in Cyprus. The exclusive control of the force by the United Nations at all times was especially emphasized as well as strict adherence to the provisions of the Security Council's original resolution. That resolution had given the force's function as, in the interests of preserving international peace and security, using its best efforts to prevent a recurrence of fighting and as necessary to contribute to the maintenance of law and order and a return to normal conditions. This mandate was more significant in its ambiguity than in its precision. It was difficult, for example, to define "law and order" in the chaotic conditions of Cyprus and the phrase "normal conditions" begged the question as to what an agreed settlement could possibly be.

The objective of the guiding principles was to try to spell out this deliberately vague mandate. The concept of the use of force only in self-defense was spelled out at greater length than previously with our considerable experience in the Congo in mind. The idea was to establish a basis for effective action in the particular circumstances of Cyprus. The principles on this matter read as follows:

> As regards the principle of self-defence, it is explained that the expression "self-defence" includes the defence of United Nations posts, premises and vehicles under armed attack, as well as the support of other personnel of UNFICYP under armed attack. When acting in self-defence, the principle of minimum force shall always be applied and armed force will be used only when all peaceful means of persuasion have failed. The decision as to when force may be used in these circumstances rests with the Commander on the spot. Examples in which troops may be authorized to use force include attempts by force to compel them to withdraw from a position which they occupy under orders from their commanders, attempts by force to disarm them, and attempts by force to prevent them from carrying out their responsibilities as ordered by their commanders.

In deference to the extreme suspiciousness and sensitivity of both communities, the personnel of the force were enjoined to act with restraint and with complete impartiality. In September 1964, after five months of experience on the ground in Cyprus, the Secretary-General in a report written by Bunche and his colleagues described the function of UNICYP as follows:

> Deployed in sensitive areas throughout the country, the Force attempted to interpose itself between the Greek and Turkish Cypriot military positions, or if that was not possible, to set up its own posts nearby so that its mere presence constituted an effective deterrent to a recurrence of fighting. If, despite its precautionary measures, shooting incidents occurred, the Force was to inter-vene immediately and endeavour to end the fighting by persuasion and negotiation. In each case it also carried out a thorough investigation of the

incident. Frequent patrolling was organized whenever necessary to ensure safety on roads and in towns and villages in sensitive areas.[3]

It was by no means easy to maintain a level of calm and restraint in dealing with the Cyprus question. The soldiers on the ground and their governments at home were often deeply disturbed both by the attitude of the Greek and Turkish Cypriots toward them and by some of the allegations and accusations that were made. The very objectivity and impartiality of UNFICYP became matters for suspicion and criticism. As always in peacekeeping operations, the United Nations, with its insistence on nonviolence, was accused in many quarters, particularly in Britain, of being weak and pusillanimous. In a statement written by Bunche, the Secretary-General emphasized that "the United Nations Force was dispatched to Cyprus to try to save lives by preventing a recurrence of fighting. It would be incautious, even a little insane, for that Force to set about killing Cypriots, whether Greek or Turkish, to prevent them from killing each other." In its early months UNFICYP was faced with a dilemma because the fighting, although at a reduced level, continued for some weeks, and the force could not stand by while innocent civilians were struck down in an undeclared war.

Those who spoke of weakness and pusillanimity were, however, soon faced by an obvious comparison. The British peacekeeping force had at one time consisted of nearly 40,000 troops who were all too often a party to the fighting and became closely involved, suffering considerable casualties and provoking violent resentment. The United Nations force, in the summer of 1964 about 6,500 strong, succeeded after the first weeks in bringing about an unaccustomed lack of physical violence in Cyprus, although there were still outbreaks in specific locations from time to time, and the verbal battle raged on undiminished either in extravagance or volume. By the end of the summer, a general cease-fire was in force.

Although the force had only been put in place initially for three months, all those directly concerned wished it to continue; and it was clear that although a civil war was the worst possible situation in which a United Nations peacekeeping force could find itself, to withdraw UNFICYP would lead to new disasters and a considerable threat to international peace as well. In September 1964, the Council extended UNFICYP for another three months, and further three-month extensions followed. Later the Council began to extend the force for six-month periods, and it has continued in existence to this date in the absence of an agreed permanent settlement.

The force has become, for better or for worse, an extremely important part of the life of the island, carrying out a large array of activities affecting almost every aspect of life in Cyprus. It has produced a situation almost completely without violence and prevented Cyprus, except for the disastrous events of 1974, from constituting a threat to international peace. It also provides the conditions for the pursuit—a most frustrating one—of a permanent settlement.

Conclusion

I have tried to give a summary of the development of United Nations peacekeeping up to 1971 and of Ralph Bunche's dominating role in that development. I have, for reasons of space, had to omit an account of most of his parallel efforts on strictly political problems.

Bunche was a highly pragmatic man with an ingrained and unshakable integrity and sense of principle. His attention to detail was awe-inspiring and sometimes irritating until one realized how often lack of attention to an ostensibly small matter could result in a large problem. He had the most highly developed sense of personal responsibility I have ever encountered and was not prepared, however tired he might be, however dismaying the circumstances, or however late the hour, to give up until he was convinced that he had done everything that he could possibly do. He was determined, often obstinately so, calm, and prepared to take personal risks if he believed them to be necessary. His efforts in Palestine, in the Congo, and in Yemen entailed considerable physical risks, which he always minimized. He insisted on being awakened at night if an important message came in from the field and on taking personal responsibility for dealing with it.

Bunche's authority, and the immense confidence he inspired, derived from these qualities, but also from his personality. He was very direct and straightforward in his professional dealings, although discreet to the point of taciturnity in public and with the press. Everyone knew that he would never take personal advantage or try to take credit, and that he would never deceive or betray anyone. He could be very tough, in a kindly way, in his dealings with subordinates whom he thought were getting out of line. This was necessary sometimes with military commanders who believed they knew best and could not appreciate the political complexity and repercussions of actions or attitudes taken by peacekeeping operations in the field.

Over and above all, Bunche was a man of extraordinary kindness and compassion. He never turned his back on those in trouble. He believed strongly in the potential goodness of human beings, provided they were given the right conditions to behave properly and to make decisions. He devoted his life to create those conditions and to setting an unmatched example of international service.

Notes

1. *The Blue Helmets: A Review of United Nations Peace-Keeping* (New York: United Nations, Department of Public Information, Sales No. E.85.I.18), pp. v–vi.
2. Informal lecture by Ralph Bunche on Palestine delivered to the UN Secretariat, 16 June 1949.
3. *The Blue Helmets,* pp. 269–70.

POSTSCRIPT:
Ralph Bunche, the Human Being and the International Statesman

Kenneth B. Clark

One of the main purposes of the important conference on "Ralph Bunche: The Man and His Times," was "to help acquaint the generation that has grown up since his death with the significance of Bunche's career, its notable achievements, and enduring legacy." As I reflected upon this stated aim of the conference, and later was informed of the distinguished group of scholars and statesmen who had agreed to participate, it became clear to me that I could not contribute anything new or different to our understanding and appreciation of Ralph Bunche as an extraordinary national and international statesman. As one who is not a political scientist nor a student or practitioner of diplomacy, I would have to content myself with sharing my observations and experiences with Ralph Bunche as the human being whom I first met when I was an undergraduate student at Howard University in the 1930s.

Howard University at that time was a part of the dynamic struggle for a positive transition from the injustices inherent in and indicated by the Great Depression. As I recall, the university environment as a whole was caught up in the ferment of concern for social, economic, and racial justice. As a student of social science, philosophy, and social psychology, I could not escape the awareness that my education was not being restricted to the assignments and discussions in the classroom, but that I was being influenced by the permeating concerns and struggles for social justice that dominated the campus. In spite of the fact that the social and economic issues reflected in the dynamic politics of the Roosevelt New Deal were the more overt, it is clear, looking back on those times, that the seeds of a legal and constitutional attack on racial segregation were being sown in the intellectual soil of Howard University. The embryo of the civil rights movement of the 1950s and 1960s was being formed at that time.

It was during this period that I came to know and admire and respect Ralph Bunche, the scholar, but above all the model of a human being who by his total personality demonstrated that disciplined human intelligence and courage were most effective instruments in the struggle for social justice. Bunche was a part of a loose cadre of professors at Howard who, by the nature and depth of their social sensitivity, influenced the future role of a number of their students. Among these examples of mentors, advisors, and, in my case, confidants, were such men as Francis Cecil Sumner, Alaine Locke, E. Franklin Frazier, Abraham Harris, Sterling Brown, and in the Law School, Charles Houston and William Hastie. These men, and others, contributed a mobile and flexible seminar of concern for social justice. They probed at the present, they analyzed the determinants of injustice, and they planned for a just future. Ironically, these men of outstanding intellect were concentrated at Howard University at that time because American higher education was contaminated by a racism that precluded them from being members of the faculty at Harvard, Yale, Princeton, Columbia, or Chicago. They were themselves the symbols of the irrationality of racial and social injustices that, individually and collectively, they sought to fight from within the racially confined academic compound of Howard University. In mounting their struggle, they not only demonstrated the depth of their humanity, their intellectual courage, but also the extent of their influence on the many students who later became frontline combatants in the civil rights struggle.

Ralph Bunche's influence on my social growth, insight, and incorrigible struggle for racial justice was both general and specific. An outstanding example of Bunche as a sensitive human being, who affected me personally and probably determined my destiny, was the fact that he, almost singlehandedly, saved me from being expelled or suspended from Howard University in my senior year. As editor of the student newspaper, I was one of the leaders of a group of students who picketed the restaurant in the Capitol building, which at that time (1935) did not serve Negroes. As would be expected, we were arrested, and our confrontation with that racial injustice was well publicized. Mordecai Johnson, president of the university, believed that by our brash act we had jeopardized the congressional appropriation upon which the university depended. He demanded that we be brought before the faculty disciplinary committee. Bunche was a member of that committee, and he argued persuasively that we should be rewarded, instead of punished, for our act. He convinced the majority of the committee, and we were permitted to remain in school. My personal reward was the beginning of a close personal relationship with a man whom I had respected as a student respects an admired professor. From that time he became my friend, adviser, and confidant. This relationship persisted until the time of his death.

As a research assistant in the Carnegie/Myrdal study, I often discussed some problems related to my assignments with Bunche; and I had the opportunity to listen to him, Myrdal, and other senior associates discuss their findings and interpretations. Here again I was constantly impressed by Bunche's clarity of mind, his courage, his intensity, and his humanity. During this period of the Myrdal study, another dimension of Bunche emerged with greater clarity for me. He seemed incapable of pretense. He did not permit status distinctions to interfere with his communication with members of the staff. He would listen to the ideas of research assistants with as much interest as he would listen to the opinions of Myrdal. And he would evaluate these ideas with objectivity, and without condescension. This, too, was an example and a reinforcement of the unwavering humanity of Ralph Bunche.

Let me share one more example of Ralph Bunche, the human being, as it directly affected my life and my human potential. Soon after receiving my Ph.D. from Columbia University, I accepted the invitation to organize a department of psychology at Hampton Institute. Despite the fact that I was advised by many of my professors at Howard University not to return to a traditionally black college, including Howard, after receiving my doctorate, I accepted the Hampton invitation. Within my first year at Hampton, I was invited to the home of the president and told, quite directly, that he was displeased by my role, that he was informed I was "frustrating the students." He was honest in stating that the purpose of an education at Hampton was to help the students adjust constructively to the racial status quo and not to be defiant. If I could accept this purpose, he would help to make me an outstanding Negro psychologist. If I could not, he saw no place for me at Hampton. Although I was somewhat surprised at the directness of his statement, I answered that I agreed with him, that there was in fact no place for me at Hampton.

I did not know quite what to do after that confrontation except to make an appointment with some of my former professors at Howard University. I spoke with Sumner, Locke, and Bunche. They agreed that I had no alternative except to resign from Hampton. Bunche, however, added that the sooner I left Hampton, the better. At that time he was an official at OSS. Within a matter of weeks he arranged for me to have an interview with a top official in the Office of War Information (OWI). With Bunche's help, I was appointed as a social science analyst studying the problem of the morale of Negroes on the home front. This appointment made it possible for me to leave Hampton promptly without acrimony, since I was taking my talents to the war effort. Throughout this period, I was in frequent communication with Ralph Bunche and saw more and more of the blend of his talents as a statesman and as a humanist.

In my personal contact with and observation of Ralph Bunche over the many years, I never did see any difference between Ralph Bunche, the person, the human being, and Ralph Bunche, the public figure, the statesman, the Nobel Laureate. Bunche was one of the greatest Americans and an extraordinary statesman because he was a profoundly empathic humanitarian. He was incapable of flamboyance, even temporary egoism and posturing. He was concerned with the task at hand and his possible contribution to the attainment of the desired objectives. In seeking to understand Bunche beyond my own observations and contacts, I came across one of the notes he wrote, and which I tried to fit into my view of him:

> I have come in contact with a good many celebrated and occasionally great people. But as one comes to know them, they all have surprisingly apparent frailties and quite frequently serious flaws of character and personality. Greatness, more often than not, is the product of a combination of ability and the accident of time and circumstances.

As I tried to understand Bunche's view of his fellow human beings who achieved a reputation of greatness, I saw that Bunche did not see himself as perfect. He saw himself as a human being with frailties and flaws of character, but he did not permit them to dominate; they did not determine his relationship with and his concern for the welfare of his fellow human beings. In defining greatness as "a combination of ability and accidents of time and circumstances," he placed his own greatness in a perspective beyond the shadow of his ego.

This breadth of perspective may be a key to understanding the ability of Ralph Bunche to face with quiet calm and dignity the anticommunist attacks against him during the McCarthy period. Because of his wise and balanced respect for himself and fellow human beings, Bunche could not retreat from his pursuit of the goals of peace, justice, and equality. He had the courage and the clarity to see that these goals were inextricable and could not be reserved for some and denied to others. This combination of humanitarianism and statesmanship requires for Bunche a continuing recognition beyond the Nobel Prize.

APPENDIXES

SELECTED SPEECHES AND WRITINGS OF RALPH BUNCHE

A P P E N D I X   A

Letter to Dr. William E. B. Du Bois
11 May 1927

This is a letter written by Bunche, as he was about to graduate from college, to the foremost Negro intellectual-activist of his time. Dr. Du Bois had received his Ph.D. in sociology from Harvard University before Bunche was born. In this letter, Bunche reveals his early interest in America's "race problem" and his identification with his people in soliciting help from Du Bois for an opportunity to be of "service" to his "group."

Los Angeles, Cal.
May 11, 1927

Dear Dr. DuBois:

I am sure that you do not remember me though we did meet on more than one occasion when you have visited Los Angeles. However, I

Letter made available by Mrs. Ralph Bunche and reprinted with her permission.

happened to be just another college student, which certainly is no cause for distinction. Nevertheless, I am taking the liberty of corresponding and trust that some consideration may be accorded my mission.

It happens that I am about to receive the A.B. degree in political science at the University of California this spring. I have made a rather creditable record during my college and high school days and have been accorded some recognition for it, including the pages of the Crisis. But I do not wish to dwell upon that. I may only say that my plans for the future are rather definitely formed. In recognition of my work Harvard University has granted me a scholarship, good for next year and I intend to take advantage of this opportunity. Which brings me to the reason for this letter. Since I have been sufficiently old to think rationally and to appreciate that there was a "race problem" in America, in which I was necessarily involved, I have set as the goal of my ambition service to my group. To some extent I am even now fulfilling that ambition. I have been very active in Cosmopolitan clubs, inter-racial discussion groups, and have often been sent from this University to other nearby colleges to speak on the question or to lead discussion groups, and I feel that a great deal of good has been done thereby.

But I have long felt the need of coming in closer contact with the leaders of our Race, so that I may better learn their methods of approach, their psychology and benefit in my own development by their influence. That is why I am anxious to come east and anticipate enjoying the opportunity extremely. Now specifically, I would like to inquire if there is any way that I can be of service to my group this coming summer, either in the east or in the south? Admittedly my resources are limited, but I am willing to tackle any problem or proposition which will give sufficient return for bare living expenses. I feel that there must be some opportunity for me, either connected with the N.A.A.C.P. or as a teacher. I have had a liberal education, extensive experience in journalism, forensics and dramatics, as well as athletics, and am young and healthy. I can furnish the best of recommendations, both from the faculty of the University and from the Race leaders of the Pacific Coast.

I hope that you will not think me presumptuous in taking this liberty. I assure you that it is inspired by a sincere desire to serve my group.

Our local commencement exercises (at which I am to be valedictorian) will be over June 9, and I will be ready to depart on any mission the day following.

I might add that I can refer to Rev. Bradby of Detroit, my birthplace, for further recommendation.

Trusting that I may hear some word of encouragement from you in the near future, I am

Sincerely yours,

Ralph J. Bunche

APPENDIX B

The Fourth Dimension of Personality

UCLA Commencement Address, June 1927

> In this graduation address, the principles that guided Bunche through much of his life begin to take shape, that is, the need to combine action with knowledge and feeling with intellect while manifesting concern for one's fellow creatures by being "socially valuable."

Humanity's problem today is how to be saved from itself. One need not be indicted for pessimism in declaring that "all is not well" with the world. Throughout history man has indulged in self adulation and preached the gospel of human progress. Great advancement has been made, but in spite of successes, there can be no doubt that human relationships are still far from complete adjustment. There are, in short, vital conditions in human associations which bode only ill for man's future.

Address made available by Mrs. Ralph Bunche and reprinted with her permission.

It did not require the Great War to convince us of this sobering fact, although that supreme catastrophe seared deeply into the heart of humanity the burning realization that the world is in distress. Nor did the greatest of human conflicts prove an antidote for humanity's poisoning. Among the nations there are yet wars and rumors of wars. Prejudices—antipathies—hatreds still disrupt with their sinister influences the equilibrium of the world. It has, however, contributed its "jot of good"—it set mankind in universal quest of a panacea for its suffering. Wherein lies the cause of this prolonged distemper with which humanity is afflicted? Some men argue economic causes; others political; still others, racial, religious or geographical. There is, perhaps, a measure of validity in each—but behind each the ultimate cause is to be found in human nature itself. It would seem that there must be some defect—some "structural weakness" in the very nature of men.

The diagnosis? Man professes strict moral codes; promulgates them through great educational systems; and solidifies them in his law. But invariably his subsequent deeds belie and pervert his original intent. He conjures up bitter prejudices, petty jealousies and hatreds against his fellow-men. The world is periodically scourged and scarred by fiendish wars. Man *learns* and *knows* but he does not *do* as well as he *knows*. This is his weakness. The future peace and harmony of the world are contingent upon the ability—yours and mine—to effect a remedy.

Indisputably, society is essential to civilization. Each of us must be trained as a social being. This is not so much an individual concern as it is that of the educational systems of the world, the "training grounds" of society. If these institutions are to fulfill their proper obligations to society, they must develop and give to the world socially valuable men, not alone intellectuals, but men purged of those fictitious, foolish animosities which have caused the world such misery through the ages.

The socially valuable individual is he whose personality is *fully grown.* Ordinarily, personality is considered individuality, whose component elements are reason, self-consciousness, and self-activity. Yet these elements of themselves suffice only to make a man, not the *socially valuable man.*

The good ship "Humanity" often lists badly from an over ballast of cold intellectuality. Mere intellectuality, *per se,* is barren, without feeling or conscience. Rabelais has said that science without conscience—*conscience*—is the depravation of the soul. Since the beginning, the world has boasted sons who have attained the loftiest pinnacles of intellectual development. But with all its mental genius humanity has ever been and is still plagued by hatreds which lead inevitably to war.

We of this day may be indicted on other counts. Our acquisitive instincts are over-emphasized. We, though not inherently so, too soon become materialists in a hyper-materialistic world. Monetary reward becomes an obsession. We learn to get, perhaps to do, but seldom to *be*. We become highly imitative, stereotyped, standardized. Our conceptions of moral values assume an increasing vagueness. We are rational, but we live too much in our own immediacy. Our personalities are developed, but, as has been so well written, too many of us "build as cathedrals were built, the part nearest the ground finished, but that part which soars toward heaven, the turrets and the spires, forever incomplete."

If we are to develop our personalities to their fullest, we must add a fourth dimension to this ordinary self—that we may expand up and out from our narrow, immediate world. This fourth dimension—call it "bigness," soulfulness, spirituality, imagination, altruism, vision, or what you will—it is that quality which gives full meaning and true reality to others. It is that which is the spark of self-development; this which enables man to grow outwardly as well as inwardly; with Hale to

> Look *up*, not down,
> Look *out*, not in,
> And lend a hand.

Vision: It is the quality which *all* men may have in common. It is that "bigness" of soul and heart which enables man to understand—to understand and to love his fellows.

There are scoffers who make light of reference to this visional quality. They deem it airy, mythical. For such as these there is an ancient tale. Many centuries ago there was a dreamer named Joseph, who became so hated by his brethren that they sold him into slavery thinking thus to be rid of the dreamer, and *he* had the corn. It is well said that "The dreamer dies, but *never* dies the dream."

Here this morning, after four arduous years of "higher" education, we confront a new world. If the mission of this education be filled, there is planted in each of us those seeds from which fourth-dimensional personality will spring. We shall have become more altruistic and less selfish. We shall *love* more, and hate less. We shall have become more *internationally-minded*—less insular-minded. We shall have succeeded in "slipping into the skins of others." We need not be less intellectual, we need be more spiritual. We need not think less, we need only *feel* more. We shall not only have developed the intellect, we shall have educated the *heart*.

There is some indication in our modern world that human sympathies, imaginings, visions, are becoming mouldy with neglect, or perverted with abuse. The incalculable value of vision—the human element in human relations—is being lost to sight in the mad scuffle for material supremacy. We forget that "man is just as much a man as his sympathies are wide," that imagination is the "social periscope" through which we see round the rough corners of our fellows; that the great man—the leader, the *socially valuable* man—is he whose personality includes the *visional dimension.*

With the growing world organization of trade and means of communication, wider and wider avenues open for increasing visualization and action. If one can visualize Central America, the Orient, Russia—yet not neglect in imagination and fact his neighbor—he is just so much more the large-hearted citizen of the Universe, member of the universal society.

We have not come to recognize the truth, both psychologically and sociologically, that only in proportion as our world grows does our self grow. We know ourselves only as we know other selves. It follows that our one object in an institution of higher learning should be the development of a *fully-grown personality*—a socially valuable individuality. Without such development we can have no broad and abiding sympathy; without it we are mere clansmen or tribesmen, or narrow members of a guild, trades union or profession. We become self-contained recluses. As we develop a vigorous, responsive imagination, we attain that Olympian sympathy which overleaps the boundaries of craft or class or country, and creates new worlds from old. Each of us may stimulate this process consciously by the development of a dominant idea of self as devoted to the building up of a rich and efficient personality in terms of other equally rich and efficient personalities. It becomes primarily a problem of capturing the imagination—of injecting a new idea into the mores. It is a problem of making good will "good form."

In identifying myself with my fellows and seeking to cooperate in hearty good will and understanding with them, I find my life in deed and in truth. And this is simply formulating into a conscious policy what humanity and the animal and vegetable world, as well, have been doing unconsciously for eons as the price of salvation. The principle of mutual aid and sympathy runs through all nature. In the plant and animal life of the desert there is an unconscious but real cooperation between plant and animal. Plant shades and feeds animal, animal digs and fertilizes for plant. The harsh conditions of desert life originate and enforce a solidarity between flora and fauna which serves the two-fold purpose of alleviating their misery and saving them from extinction. The world may learn a great lesson from this simple natural phenomenon, and by applying it, make the theory of human brotherhood a *living, social* fact. Humanity, in its own interest, must number among its members more who can say with Ben Adhem, "Then write me down as one who loves his fellow-men."

I think that human nature is already biased toward fellowship and service. Psychologists tell us that there is a genuine instinct, insofar as there are instincts, in all normal people for seeing others happy. Men are beginning but faintly to glimpse their real social nature, and human groups are still stumbling about in the twilight like "blind men among tombs," trying to know themselves, seeking release from their toils, struggling to formulate some purposive goal, and to lay out a highway thither. If Goethe be right, and we must win self-knowledge through eating our bread with bitter tears and through living nights in sorrow, human society has surely paid the full price and ought now to be in a fair way to receive its promised guerdon.

My fellow graduates: we are youth, and have the world yet to face. The dawn of each individual career is even now breaking grey and uncertain. Our success, our happiness in the future will be determined by what we *will*. We are told that we have daring, vigor and resourcefulness. Then let us *dare* to live as *men* live! Let us dedicate our vigor and our resourcefulness to the cause of human fellowship! Let us not confine ourselves each to his own little sphere, but *expand* in heart and soul, and become true friends of man! So much we have in common with the youth of all lands—as *we* go, so goes the world. . . .

APPENDIX C

Some Reflections on Peace in Our Time

Nobel Peace Prize Lecture,
Oslo, Norway, 11 December 1950

In this most anxious period of human history, the subject of peace, above every other, commands the solemn attention of all men of reason and good will. Moreover, on this particular occasion, marking the fiftieth anniversay of the Nobel Foundation, it is eminently fitting to speak of peace. No subject could be closer to my own heart, since I have the honour to speak as a member of the International Secretariat of the United Nations.

In these critical times—times which test to the utmost the good sense, the forbearance and the morality of every peace-loving people—it is not easy to speak of peace with either conviction or reassurance. True it is that statesmen the world over, exalting lofty concepts and noble ideals, pay homage to peace and freedom in a perpetual torrent of eloquent phrases. But the statesmen also speak darkly of the lurking threat of war; and the preparations for war ever intensify, while strife flares or threatens in many localities.

The words used by statesmen in our day no longer have a common meaning. Perhaps they never had. Freedom, democracy, human rights, international morality, peace itself, mean different things to different men. Words, in a constant flow of propaganda—itself an instrument of war—are employed to confuse, mislead and debase the common man. Democracy is prostituted to dignify enslavement; freedom and equality are held good for some men but withheld from others by and in allegedly "democratic" societies; in "free" societies, so-called, individual human rights are severely denied; aggressive adventures are launched under the guise of "liberation." Truth and morality are subverted by propaganda, on the cynical assumption that truth is whatever propaganda can induce people to believe. Truth and morality, therefore, become gravely weakened as defences against injustice and war. With what great insight did Voltaire, hating war enormously, declare: "War is the greatest of all crimes; and yet there is no aggressor who does not colour his crime with the pretext of justice."

To the common man, the state of world affairs is baffling. All nations and peoples claim to be for peace. But never has peace been more continuously in jeopardy. There are no nations today as in the recent past, insistently clamouring for *lebensraum* under the duress of readiness to resort to war. Still the specter of war looms ominously. Never in human history have so many peoples experienced freedom. Yet human freedom itself is a crucial issue and is widely endangered. Indeed, by some people, it has already been gained and lost.

People everywhere wish and long for peace and freedom, in their simplest and clearest connotations: an end to armed conflict and to the suppression of the inalienable rights of man. In a single generation, the people of the world have suffered the profound anguish of the catastrophic wars; they have had enough of war. Who could doubt that the people of Norway—ever peaceful, still deeply wounded from an unprovoked, savage Nazi aggression—wish peace? Who could doubt that all of the people of Europe—whose towns and cities, whose peaceful countrysides, have been mercilessly ravaged; whose fathers and sons, mothers and daughters have been slaughtered and maimed in tragic numbers— wish peace? Who could sincerely doubt that the peoples of the western hemisphere—who, in the common effort to save the world from barbaric tyranny, came into the two world wars only reluctantly and at great sacrifice of human and material resources—wish peace? Who could doubt that the long-suffering masses of Asia and Africa wish peace? Who, indeed, could be so unseeing as not to realize that in modern war victory is illusory; that the harvest of war can be only misery, destruction and degradation?

If war should come, the people of the world would again be called upon to fight it, but they would not have willed it.

Statesmen and philosophers repeatedly have warned that some values—freedom, honor, self-respect—are higher than peace, or life itself. This may be true. Certainly, very many would hold that the loss of human dignity and self-respect, the chains of enslavement, are too high a price even for peace. But the horrible realities of modern warfare scarcely afford even this fatal choice. There is only suicidal escape, not freedom, in the death and destruction of atomic war. This is mankind's great dilemma. The well-being and the hope of the peoples of the world can never be served until peace—as well as freedom, honor and self-respect—is secure.

The ideals of peace on earth and the brotherhood of man have been expounded by philosophers from earliest time. If human relations were governed by the sagacity of the great philosophers, there would be little danger of war, for in their collective wisdom over the centuries they have clearly charted the course to free and peaceful living among men.

Throughout the ages, however, man has but little heeded the advice of the wise men. He has been—fatefully, if not willfully—less virtuous, less constant, less rational, less peaceful than he knows how to be; than he is fully capable of being. He has been led astray from the ways of peace and brotherhood by his addiction to concepts and attitudes of narrow nationalism, racial and religious bigotry, greed and lust for power. Despite this, despite the almost continuous state of war to which bad human relations have condemned him, he has made steady progress. In his scientific genius, man has wrought material miracles and has transformed his world. He has harnessed nature and has developed great civilizations. But he has never learned very well how to live with himself. The values he has created have been predominantly materialistic; his spiritual values have lagged far behind. He has demonstrated little spiritual genius and has made little progress toward the realization of human brotherhood. In the contemporary atomic age, this could prove man's fatal weakness.

Alfred Nobel, a half-century ago, foresaw with prophetic vision that if the complacent mankind of his day could, with equanimity, contemplate war, the day would soon inevitably come when man would be confronted with this fateful alternative of peace or reversion to the Dark Ages. Man may well ponder whether he has not now reached that stage. Man's inventive genius has so far out-reached his reason—not his capacity to reason but his willingness to apply reason—that the peoples of the world find themselves precariously on the brink of total disaster.

If today we speak of peace, we also speak of the United Nations, for in this era, peace and the United Nations have become inseparable. If the United Nations cannot ensure peace, there will be none. If war should come, it will be only because the United Nations has failed. But the United Nations need not fail. Surely, every man of reason must work and pray to the end that it will not fail.

In these critical days, it is a high privilege and a most rewarding experience to be associated with the United Nations—the greatest peace effort in human history. Those who work in and with the organization, perhaps inevitably, tend to develop a professional optimism with regard to the prospects for the United Nations, and therefore, to the prospects for peace. But there is also a sense of deep frustration, which flows from the knowledge that mankind could readily live in peace and freedom and good neighborliness if there were but a minimum of will to do so. There is the ever-present, simple but stark truth that though the peoples long primarily for peace, they may be prodded by their leaders and governments into needless war, which may at worst destroy them, at best lead them once again to barbarism.

The United Nations strives to be realistic. It understands well the frailties of man. It is realized that if there is to be peace in the world, it must be attained through men and with man, in his nature and mores, just about as he now is. Intensive effort is exerted to reach the hearts and minds of men with the vital pleas for peace and human understanding, to the end that human attitudes and relations may be steadily improved. But this is a process of international education, or better, education for international living, and it is at best gradual. Men change their attitudes and habits slowly, and but grudgingly divorce their minds from fears, suspicions and prejudices.

The United Nations itself is but a cross-section of the world's peoples. It reflects, therefore, the typical fears, suspicions and prejudices which bedevil human relations throughout the world. In the delegations from the 60 member states, and in the international Secretariat in which most of them are represented, may be found individual qualities of goodness and badness, honesty and subterfuge, courage and timorousness, internationalism and chauvinism. It could not be otherwise. Still, the activities of all are within the framework of a great international organization dedicated to the imperative causes of peace, freedom and justice in the world.

The United Nations, inescapably, is an organization at once of great weakness and great strength.

Its powers of action are sharply limited by the exigencies of national sovereignties. With nationalism *per se* there may be no quarrel. But narrow, exclusively self-centered nationalism persists as the outstanding dynamic of world politics and is the prime obstacle to enduring peace. The international well-being on the one hand, and national egocentrism on the other, are inevitably at cross-purposes. The procedures and processes of the United Nations as a circumscribed international parliament, are unavoidably complex and tedious.

The United Nations was established in the hope, if not on the assumption, that the five great powers would work harmoniously toward an increasingly better world order. The existing impasse between West and

East and the resultant "cold war" were not foreseen by those who formulated the United Nations Charter in the spring of 1945 in the misleading,
but understandably jubilant, atmosphere of war's triumphant end.
Nevertheless, the United Nations has exhibited a fortunate flexibility
which has enabled it to adjust to the regrettable circumstances of the
discord among the great powers and to continue to function effectively.

Reflecting the hopes and aspirations of all peoples for peace, security,
freedom and justice, the foundations of the United Nations are firmly
anchored and its moral sanctions are strong. It is served by a fully
competent international Secretariat which is devoted to the high principles and purposes of this Organization. At the head of this Secretariat is
the Secretary-General of the United Nations, Trygve Lie, a great son of
Norway, and a man whose name will be writ large in the annals of world
statesmanship and peace-making. No living man has worked more persistently or courageously to save the world from the scourge of war than
Trygve Lie.

In its short but turbulent five years, the United Nations, until the past
few weeks, at least, has demonstrated a comforting ability to cope with
every dangerous crisis that has erupted into violence or threatened to do
so. It has never been easily done nor as well as might be hoped for, but
the fact remains that it has been done. In these post-war years, the
United Nations, in the interest of peace, has been called upon to eliminate the threat of local wars, to stop local wars already underway, and
now in Korea, itself to undertake an international police action which
amounts to full-scale war. Its record has been impressive. Its interven-
tions have been directly responsible for checking and containing dangerous armed conflicts in Indonesia, Kashmir, and Palestine, and to only
a lesser extent in Greece.

That the United Nations has been able to serve the cause of peace in
this way has been due in large measure to the determination of its
members to reject the use of armed force as an instrument of national
policy, and to the new techniques of international intervention which it
has employed. In each instance of a threat to the peace, the United
Nations projects itself directly into the area of conflict by sending United
Nations representatives to the area for the purpose of mediation and
conciliation.

It was as the head of a United Nations mission of this kind that Count
Folke Bernadotte went to Palestine in the spring of 1948. On his arrival
in the Near East, he found the Arabs and Jews locked in a bitter, bloody
and highly emotional war in Palestine. He was armed only with the
strong demand of the United Nations that in the interest of world peace
the Palestine problem must be settled by peaceful means.

In one of the most brilliant individual feats of diplomatic history.
Count Bernadotte, within two weeks of his arrival on the scene of

conflict, had negotiated a four weeks' truce and the guns had ceased firing. In order to supervise that truce, he requested of the Secretary-General and promptly received, an international team of civilian and military personnel, numbering some 700 men and women. The members of this compact and devoted United Nations "peace army" in Palestine, many of whom were from the Scandinavian countries, and all of whom were unarmed, under the early leadership of Count Bernadotte wrote a heroic chapter in the cause of peace-making. Their leader, Bernadotte himself, and ten others, gave their lives in this effort. The United Nations and the peace-loving world must ever be grateful to them.

We who had the privilege to serve under the leadership of Count Bernadotte revere his name. He was a great internationalist, a warm-hearted humanitarian, a warrior of unflinching courage in the cause of peace, and a truly noble man. We who carried on after him were inspired by his self-sacrifice, and were determined to pay him the one tribute which he would have appreciated above all others—the successful completion of the task which he had begun, the restoration of peace to Palestine.

In Korea, for the first, and it may be fervently hoped, the last time, the United Nations processes of peaceful intervention to settle disputes failed. They failed only because the North Korean regime stubbornly refused to afford them the chance to work, and resorted to aggressive force as the means of attaining its ends. Confronted with this, the gravest challenge to its mandate to preserve the peace of the world, the United Nations had no reasonable alternative but to check aggressive national force with decisive international force. This it has attempted to do and it was enabled to do so only by the firm resolve of the overwhelming majority of its members that the peace must be preserved, and that aggression shall be struck down wherever undertaken, or by whom.

By virtue of recent set-backs to United Nations forces in Korea, as a result of the injection of vast numbers of Chinese troops into the conflict, it becomes clear that this resolve of its members has not been backed by sufficient armed strength to ensure that the right shall prevail. In the future, it must be the forces of peace that are overwhelming.

But whatever the outcome of the present military struggle in Korea in which the United Nations and Chinese troops are not locked, Korea provides the lesson which can save peace and freedom in the world if nations and peoples will but learn that lesson, and learn it quickly. To make peace in the world secure, the United Nations must have readily at its disposal, as a result of firm commitments undertaken by all of its members, military strength of sufficient dimensions to make it certain that it can meet aggressive military force with international military force, speedily and conclusively.

If that kind of strength is made available to the United Nations—and under action taken by the General Assembly this fall it can be made available—in my view that strength will never again be challenged in war, and therefore need never be employed.

But military strength will not be enough. The moral position of the United Nations must ever be strong and unassailable; it must stand steadfastly, always, for the right.

The international problems with which the United Nations is concerned are the problems of the interrelations of the peoples of the world. They are human problems. The United Nations is entitled to believe, and it does believe, that there are no insoluble problems of human relations, and that there is none which cannot be solved by peaceful means. The United Nations—in Indonesia, Palestine and Kashmir—has demonstrated convincingly that parties to the most severe conflict may be induced to abandon war as the method of settlement in favor of mediation and conciliation, at a merciful saving of untold lives and acute suffering.

Unfortunately, there may yet be some in the world who have not learned that today war can settle nothing, that aggressive force can never be enough, nor will it be tolerated. If this should be so, the pitiless wrath of the organized world must fall upon those who would endanger the peace for selfish ends. For in this advanced day, there is no excuse, no justification for nations resorting to force except to repel armed attack.

The world and its peoples being as they are, there is no easy or quick or infallible approach to a secure peace. It is only by patient, persistent, undismayed effort, by trial and error, that peace can be won. Nor can it be won cheaply, as the taxpayer is learning. In the existing world tension, there will be rebuffs and set-backs, dangerous crises and episodes of violence. But the United Nations, with unshakeable resolution, in the future as in the past, will continue to man the dykes of peace. In this common purpose, all states, irrespective of size, are vital.

The small nations, which constitute the overwhelming majority in its membership, are a great source of strength for the United Nations. Their desire for peace is deep-seated and constant. The fear, suspicion and conflict which characterize the relations among the great powers, and the resultant uncertainty, keep them and their peoples in a state of anxious tension and suspense. For the relations among the great powers will largely determine their future. A third World War would quickly engulf the smaller states, and many of them would again provide the battlefields. On many of them, now as before, the impact of war would be even more severe than upon the great powers. They, in particular, therefore, support and often initiate measures designed to ensure that the United Nations shall be increasingly effective as a practical instrumentality for peace. In this regard, the Scandinavian countries contribute signally to the constructive effort of the United Nations.

One legacy of the recent past greatly handicaps the work of the United Nations. It can never realize its maximum potential for peace until the Second World War is fully liquidated. The impasse between West and East has prevented the great powers from concluding the peace treaties which would finally terminate that last war. It can be little doubted that the United Nations, if called upon, could afford valuable aid toward this end. At present, the United Nations must work for future peace in the unhappy atmosphere of an unconcluded great war, while precluded from rendering any assistance toward the liquidation of that war. These, obviously, are matters of direct and vital concern to all peace-loving nations, whatever their size.

At the moment, in view of the disturbing events in Korea and Indo-China, the attention of a fearful world is focused on Asia, seeking an answer to the fateful question "peace or war?" But the intrinsic importance of Europe in the world peace equation cannot be ignored. The peace of Europe, and therefore of the world, can never be secure so long as the problem of Germany remains unsolved.

In this regard, those who at the end of the last war were inclined to dismiss Europe as a vital factor in reckoning the future security and prosperity of the world, have had to revise their calculations. For Europe, grievously wounded though it was, has displayed a remarkable resiliency, and has quickly regained its place in the orbit of world affairs.

But Europe, and the western world generally, must become fully aware that the massive and restive millions of Asia and Africa are henceforth a new and highly significant factor in all peace calculations. These hitherto suppressed masses are rapidly awakening and are demanding, and are entitled to enjoy, a full share in the future fruits of peace, freedom and security.

Very many of these millions are experiencing a new-found freedom. Many other millions are still in subject status, as colonials. The aspirations and demands of those who have achieved freedom and those who seek it are the same: security, treatment as equals, and their rightful place in the brotherhood of nations.

It is truer today than when Alfred Nobel realized it a half-century ago, that peace cannot be achieved in a vacuum. Peace must be paced by human progress. Peace is no mere matter of men fighting or not fighting. Peace, to have meaning for many who have known only suffering in both peace and war, must be translated into bread or rice, shelter, health and education, as well as freedom and human dignity—a steadily better life. If peace is to be secure, long-suffering and long-starved forgotten peoples of the world, the under-privileged and the under-nourished, must begin to realize without delay the promise of a new day and a new life.

In the world of today, Europe, like the rest of the West, is confronted with the urgent necessity of a new orientation—a global orientation. The pre-war outlook is as obsolete as the pre-war world. There must be an awakening to the incontestable fact that the far away, little known and little understood peoples of Asia and Africa, who constitute the majority of the world's population, are no longer passive and no longer to be ignored. The fury of the world ideological struggle swirls about them. Their vast numbers will prove a dominant factor in the future world pattern of life. They provide virgin soil for the growth of democracy, but the West must first learn how to approach them understandingly and how to win their trust and friendship. There is a long and unsavory history of western imperialism, suppression and exploitation to be overcome, despite the undenied benefits which the West also brought to them. There must be an acceleration in the liquidation of colonialism. A friendly hand must be extended to the peoples who are laboring under the heavy burden of newly-won independence, as well as to those who aspire to it. And in that hand must be tangible aid in generous quantity—funds, goods, foodstuffs, equipment, and technical assistance.

There are great issues demanding resolution in the world: the clash of the rather loosely defined concepts and systems of capitalism and communism; the radically contrasting conceptions of democracy, posing extreme views of individualism against extreme views of statism; the widespread denials of human rights; the understandable impatience of many among some two hundred million colonial peoples for the early realization of their aspirations toward emancipation; and others.

But these are issues which in no sense may be considered as defying solution. The issue of capitalism versus communism is one of ideology which in the world of today cannot, in fact, be clearly defined. It cannot be clearly defined because there are not two worlds, one "capitalist" and one "communist." There is but one world—a world of sharp clashes, to be sure—with these two doctrines at the opposite ideological poles. In between these extremes are found many gradations of the two systems and ideologies.

There is room in the world for both capitalism and communism and all gradations of them, providing only that neither system is set upon pursuing an expressively imperialistic course.

The United Nations is opposed to imperialism of any kind, ideological or otherwise. The United Nations stands for the freedom and equality of all peoples, irrespective of race, religion or ideology. It is for the peoples of every society to make their own choices with regard to ideologies, economic systems and the relationship which is to prevail between the state and the individual. The United Nations is engaged in an historic effort to underwrite the rights of man. It is also attempting to give reassurance to the colonial peoples that their aspirations for freedom can be realized, if only gradually, by peaceful processes.

There can be peace and a better life for all men. Given adequate authority and support, the United Nations can ensure this. The decision really rests with the peoples of the world. The United Nations belongs to the people, but it is not yet as close to them, as much a part of their conscious interest, as it must come to be. The United Nations must always be on the people's side. Where their fundamental rights and interests are involved, it must never act from mere expediency. At times, perhaps, it has done so, but never to its own advantage, nor to that of the sacred causes of peace and freedom. If the peoples of the world are strong in their resolve, and if they speak through the United Nations, they need never be confronted with the tragic alternatives of war or dishonorable appeasement, death or enslavement.

Amidst the frenzy and irrationality of a topsy-turvy world, some simple truths would appear to be self-evident.

As Alfred Nobel finally discerned, people are never deterred from the folly of war by the stark terror of it. But it is nonetheless true that if in atomic war there would be survivors there could be no victors. What then, could war achieve which could not be better gained by peaceful means? There are, to be sure, vital differences and wide areas of conflict among the nations, but there is utterly none which could not be settled peacefully—by negotiation and mediation—given a genuine will for peace and even a modicum of natural good faith.

But there would appear to be little hope that efforts to break the great power impasse could be very fruitful in the current atmosphere of fear, suspicion and recrimination. Fear, suspicion and recrimination in the relations among nations tend to be dangerously self-compounding. They induce that national hysteria which, in its rejection of poise and rationality, can itself be the fatal prelude to war. A favorable climate for peaceful negotiation must be created and can only be created by painstaking, unremitting effort. Conflicting parties must be led to realize that the road to peace can never be traversed by threatening to fight at every bend, by merely being armed to the teeth, or by flushing every bush to find an enemy. An essential first step in a civilized approach to peace in these times would call for a moratorium on recrimination and reproach.

There are some in the world who are prematurely resigned to the inevitability of war. Among them are the advocates of the so-called "preventive war," who, in their resignation to war, wish merely to select their own time for initiating it. To suggest that war can prevent war is a base play on words and a despicable form of war-mongering. The objective of any who sincerely believe in peace clearly must be to exhaust every honorable recourse in the effort to save the peace. The world has had ample evidence that war begets only conditions which beget further war.

In the final analysis, the acid test of a genuine will to peace is the willingness of disputing parties to expose their differences to the peaceful processes of the United Nations and to the bar of international public opinion which the United Nations reflects. It is only in this way that truth, reason, and justice may come to prevail over the shrill and blatant voice of propaganda; that a wholesome international morality can be cultivated.

It is worthy of emphasis that the United Nations exists not merely to preserve the peace but also to make change—even radical change—possible without violent upheaval. The United Nations has no vested interest in the status quo. It seeks a more secure world, a better world, a world of progress for all peoples. In the dynamic world society which is the objective of the United Nations, all peoples must have equality and equal rights. The rights of those who at any given time may be in the minority—whether for reasons of race, religion or ideology—are as important as those of the majority, and the minorities must enjoy the same respect and protection. The United Nations does not seek a world cut after a single pattern, nor does it consider this desirable. The United Nations seeks only unity, not uniformity, out of the world's diversity.

There will be no security in our world, no release from agonizing tension, no genuine progress, no enduring peace, until, in Shelley's fine words, "reason's voice, loud as the voice of nature, shall have waked the nations."

APPENDIX D

The International Significance of Human Relations

Lincoln's Day Address, Springfield, Illinois
12 February 1951

As an international civil servant, Bunche had to be circumspect in pronouncements about the internal affairs of any member state of the United Nations including his own country, the United States. But he found a way of expressing himself about the condition of America's Negro minority, tying it to the United Nations concern for human rights, freedom, and justice throughout the world. In this Lincoln's Day address, Bunche masterfully weaves the two themes together as he examines his convictions as a UN official and as an American.

I am delighted at this first opportunity to visit Springfield. It is particularly gratifying to be here—in a community in which he lived and worked—at this observation of the birthday of a man of rare greatness—the most stalwart figure of our nation's history.

It is not within my feeble capacity, or indeed, within the puny power of words, to do fair honor to Abraham Lincoln. It is not, perhaps, within the power of any of us among the living to do so, except as we may individually dedicate ourselves to the fulfillment of the imperative human objectives which he sought.

Lincoln was a man of great good will. The debt owed to him by our nation is incalculable. The legacy of human values which he bequeathed to us is priceless. Yet, like all of us, Lincoln was mortal, and being mortal, was fallible.

The problems which confronted him challenged to the utmost human wisdom and patience. The decisions he was called upon to make were momentous. A nation was at stake. It is no discredit to him that history records his moments of indecision, his groping, even his bows to political expediency. But in the crucial hours of decision, he found a boundless strength which flowed from his unwavering faith in the "plain people," from the equalitarianism of this great West in which he was reared, from his undecorated belief in the equality and dignity of man.

I have chosen to devote some attention today to the problem of human relations in the precarious world in which we live out our anxious existence. For this would seem to be peculiarly appropriate on this auspicious occasion.

Lincoln, himself, was called upon to save this nation from as great a crisis and conflict in human relations as has ever confronted any nation. And though he met the challenge and saved the nation, even Lincoln could not avert a cruel, tragic, devastating internecine war. Indeed, eighty-six years later, that war is still not fully liquidated, and at times it may seem not entirely clear who actually won it.

Moreover, it must be clear that the greatest danger to mankind today is still to be found in the deplorable human relations which everywhere prevail.

Were Lincoln alive today, I imagine that he could scarcely avoid taking a dark view of the relations among peoples the world over, not, by any means, excluding his own country. It would be understandable if even a quick survey of the current state of world and domestic affairs should induce in him one of those occasional moods of melancholia which some historians have attributed to him.

For what is the situation? The relations among peoples are broadly characterized by dangerous animosities, hatreds, mutual recriminations, suspicions, bigotries, and intolerances. Man has made spectacular progress in science, in transportation and communication, in the arts, in all things material. Yet, it is a matter of colossal and tragic irony that man, in all his genius, having learned to harness nature, to control the relations among the elements and to mold them to his will—even to the point where he now has the means readily at hand for his own virtual self-destruction—has never yet learned how to *live* with himself; he has not mastered the art of human relations. In the realm of human understanding the peoples of the world remain shockingly illiterate. This has always been and today remains man's greatest challenge: how to teach the peoples of the world the elemental lesson of the essential kinship of mankind and man's identity of interest.

We live in a most dangerous age—an age of supersonic airspeeds, of biological warfare, of atomic and hydrogen bombs, and who knows what next. In no exaggerated sense, we all today exist on borrowed time. If we of this generation deserve no better fate, surely our children do. They, certainly, can never understand why we could not do at least as well as the animal kingdom.

We need peace desperately. But the world has always needed peace. Today, however, the question is not the simple one of peace or war, as it has been in the past. The question now is sheer survival—survival of civilization, survival of mankind. And the time is short, frighteningly short.

How is the question to be answered? We may improvise, we may build diplomatic dams, we may pile international pact upon international pact. We may arm to the teeth and to the last ounce of our physical resources. But all this will never be enough so long as deep fears, suspicions, prejudices, and hatreds characterize the relations among the peoples of a now small world.

It is mankind, it is ourselves that we must fear more than the atomic or hydrogen bomb. It is in man's perversities, in his brooding suspicions, in his arrogances and intolerances, in his false self-righteousness and in his apathy that the real danger is to be found. In the final analysis, there is but one road to peace and that is the road of human understanding and fellow feeling, of inflexible determination to achieve peaceful relations among men. That, clearly, is a long, hard road, and today it is too little traveled.

If the relations among men were everywhere, or let us even say *most* everywhere, internationally and domestically, good, there would be little to fear. For then the free peoples of the world would have unassailable strength, and more than that, unwavering confidence in their ability to protect themselves collectively and fully against any maverick who might go on the loose. On the other side of the coin, bad human relations are, indeed, an encouragement and stimulus to the adventures of mavericks. It is on the disunity of peoples that dictators prey.

I am optimistic enough about my fellow beings to believe that it is human *attitudes*, not human nature, that must be feared—and changed. On the international scene, it is these attitudes which have brought the world to the menacing state of affairs of today—the ominous "localized" wars, the "cold war," the maneuverings for power and dominance, the dangerous rivalries, the propaganda battles—cannibalistic struggles in which ethical principles, and moral law are often callously jettisoned. If peoples could not be induced to suspect, to fear, and finally to hate one another, there could be no wars, for governments, from whatever motivations, can only lead peoples into wars—the peoples must fight them. And in these wars, countless numbers of human beings—by nature essentially good, whatever their immediate attitudes—must be sacrificed solely because the peoples of one society or another embark, or permit themselves to be embarked, upon fatal adventures of conquest or domination. On the domestic scene, it is human attitudes, not human nature, which nurture the racial and religious hatreds and bigotries which today permeate many societies, and even in democracies thrive in the fertile soil of complacency.

The picture is foreboding and the immediate future looms ominously. But perhaps there lies the hope. Can man, a thinking animal, capable of both emotion and cool calculation with regard to his self-interest, be brought to his senses in time? Can he see the black doom which awaits him at the end of the path he now follows? I have enough faith in the potentiality of mankind for good to believe that he can save himself. May it be fervently hoped that he will muster the determined will to do so.

Certainly, there is nothing in human nature which renders it impossible for men to live peacefully and harmoniously with one another. Hatred, intolerance, bigotry, chauvinism are never innate—they are the bad lessons taught in society. Despite the fact that in recorded history, mankind has been as much at war as at peace, it cannot be concluded that war is inevitable—a natural state of mankind. Nor do I believe that because hatreds, bigotries, intolerances, and prejudices loom large in the pages of history, these are the natural conditions of man's societal existence on earth.

I think it no exaggeration to say that unfortunately, throughout the ages, organized religion and education have failed miserably in their efforts to save man from himself. Perhaps they have failed because so often they have merely reflected the mean and narrow attitudes of the very peoples they were striving to save.

Human understanding, human brotherhood and solidarity, will be achieved, if at all, only when the peoples of many lands find a common bond through a compelling sense of urgency in achieving common goals. The purposes and principles of the United Nations—with peace and justice and equality as the universal common denominators—afford that bond and the common goals. The implements of modern warfare afford the urgency, if people once understand the frightful implications and elect to survive.

Lincoln, instinctively a true democrat, believed deeply in the essential justice of the plain people, whose better impulses and good will he trusted ultimately to prevail. Given half a chance, I believe that the free peoples of the world today, in their collectivity, will justify Lincoln's faith.

It is not necessary to seek to transform people into saints in order that impending disaster may be averted.

Throughout the world today, thinking and psychology have not kept pace with the times. That people inevitably think in terms of their self-interest is something very little can be done about. But is it not equally tenable that a great deal can be done about influencing people to think and act in terms of their *true* self-interest? In this dangerous international age, notions of exalted and exaggerated nationalism, national egocentrism and isolationism, of chauvinism, of group superiority and master race, of group exclusiveness, of national self-righteousness, of special privilege, are in the interest of neither the world nor of any particular group in it. They are false views of self-interest and carry us all toward the disaster of war. And in the war of tomorrow there can be no true victor; at best there will be only survivors. Our old concepts and values are no longer valid or realistic. The future may well belong to those who first realign their international sights.

I sincerely believe that the generality of peoples throughout the world really long for peace and freedom. There can be no doubt that this is true of the generality of the American people, despite some impatient and ultra-jingoistic hotheads in our midst. If this is true, it is the one great hope for the future. The problem is how to crystallize this longing, how to fashion it into an overpowering instrument for good. The United Nations recognizes acutely the desperate need, but has not yet found the ways and means of mobilizing the peace-loving attitudes of the peoples of the world over the stubborn walls of national egoisms.

Every peace- and freedom-loving nation, every government, every individual, has a most solemn obligation to mankind and the future of mankind in the fateful effort to rescue the world from the morass in which it is now entrapped and to underwrite a future of peace and freedom for all. This is a time of gravest crisis. Constructive, concerted actions and policies—not negativism and recrimination—are called for. There are many motes in many eyes. There is in the world no nation which can stand before the ultimate bar of human history and say: "We have done our utmost to induce peoples to live in peace with one another as brothers."

It must be very clear that what the world needs most desperately today is a crusade for peace and understanding of unparalleled dimension; a universal mobilization of the strong but diffused forces of peace and justice. The collective voice of the free peoples of the world, could be so irresistible as to dwarf into insignificance both A- and H-bombs and to disperse and discourage the warlike and war-minded.

In the existing state of affairs, societies admittedly owe it to themselves to be prepared and protected against any eventuality; they must build up their national defenses. They must do so, incidentally, only because they have not, for reasons of national sovereignty, been willing to give the United Nations the decisive power and means to cope with a powerful act of military aggression. With vigorous measures to ensure national defense, given the present international circumstances, reason and reality could perceive no quarrel. But it would also appear that reason and reality would dictate that since armament can never be an end in itself and must expand itself, if at all, only in war, the only way peace-loving societies might cover their ever-mounting losses from the tremendous expenditures on armaments would be to exert an effort of at least equal magnitude for peace—to the end that the armaments would never have to be used. This, it seems to me, would be at once good economics, good humanitarianism, and good self-interest.

In the final analysis it is peoples who must be won and who alone can win the world-wide struggle for freedom and justice. People can be rallied to ideas. They must be given more than guns and an enemy to shoot at.

And now, if I may take advantage of my nationality and speak for a moment simply as an American citizen rather than an international official, I may ask where do we, as Americans, stand with regard to the challenge of human relations? It is a question, surely, in which Abraham Lincoln would be deeply interested were he with us today.

The United States is in the forefront of international affairs today. The eyes of the world are focused upon us as never before in our history. A great part of the world looks to us for a convincing demonstration of the validity and the virility of the democratic way of life as America exalts it. It would be catastrophic if we should fail to give that demonstration. We cannot afford to fail.

But it is only too apparent that our democratic house is not yet in shipshape order. There are yawning crevices in our human relations; the gap between our democratic profession on the one hand, and our daily practices of racial and religious intolerance on the other, while less wide than formerly, is still very wide.

Race relations is our number one social problem, perhaps our number one problem. It is no mere sectional problem; it is a national—indeed an international—problem. For any problem today which challenges the ability of democracy to function convincingly, which undermines the very foundations of democracy and the faith of people in it, is of concern to the entire peace- and freedom-loving world. Surely, it must be abundantly clear that it is only through the triumph of democracy and the determined support of peoples for it as an imperative way of life that secure foundations for world peace can be laid.

That race relations are gradually improving both in the South and elsewhere in the nation, cannot be doubted. But neither can it be doubted that these relations remain in a dangerous state, that they are a heavy liability to the nation, and constitute a grave weakness in our national democratic armor.

Certainly the costs of anti-racial and anti-religious practices are enormously high. Attitudes of bigotry, when widely prevalent in a society, involve staggering costs in terms of prestige and confidence throughout the rest of the world, not to mention the contamination and degradation resulting from the presence of such psychological disease in the body of the society.

Throughout the nation, in varying degree, the Negro minority— almost a tenth of the population—suffers severe political, economic, and social disabilities, solely because of race. In Washington, the capital of the greatest democracy in human history, Lincoln, the Great Emancipator, sits majestically in his massive armchair behind the marble pillars, and overlooks a city which stubbornly refuses to admit his moral dictum that the Negro is a man; a city in which no Negro can live and work with dignity; a city which, administered by Congress itself, subjects one-fourth of its citizens to segregation, discrimination, and daily humiliation. Washington is our nation's greatest shame precisely because it is governed by Congress and is our capital. Of all American cities, it should symbolize and vitalize our democracy.

In his time, Lincoln saw that slavery had to be abolished not only because as an institution it was contrary to human morality, but also because it was inimical to the interests of the "plain people" of America. By the same token, present-day practices of racial segregation and discrimination should be outlawed as inimical to the interests of all who believe in and derive benefit from democracy, whatever their race or religion.

The vitality of this great country derives from the unity of purpose and the devotion to its democratic ideals of the diversified peoples—by race, religion, and national origin—who make up its population. Disunity and group conflict constantly sap that vitality.

As a nation we have also found great strength in the fact that we have always been able and willing to face our shortcomings frankly and attack them realistically. It is in this spirit and in this knowledge that I, as an American, take occasion to point to our shortcomings. I do not imply, in any sense, that the rest of the world is free of such imperfections, or in given instances, far greater ones.

To enjoying our maximum strength, we need more *applied* democracy. We need to live up to the principles which we believe in and for which we are hailed by the world. We too need a mobilization—a mobilization through the country of men and women of good will, of men and women who are determined to see American democracy fulfill its richest promise, and who will ceaselessly exert their efforts toward that end.

Our nation, by its traditional philosophy, by its religious precepts, by its Constitution, stands for freedom and equality, for the brotherhood of man, and for full respect for the rights and dignity of the individual. By giving unqualified expression to these ideals in our daily life we can and will achieve a democratic society here so strong in the hearts and minds of its citizens, so sacred to the individual, that it will be forever invulnerable to any kind of attack.

We cannot eradicate prejudices and bigotries overnight, of course, I seek no miracles. But neither is there anything sacrosanct about the present rate of advance. The pace of progress can be greatly accelerated if a great many of our organizations and institutions—schools, churches, labor unions, industries, and civic organizations—would put a stronger shoulder to the wheel.

I am certain that the majority and more of the American people believe firmly in our democratic way of life and are willing that all our citizens, of whatever color or creed, enjoy it. But on the Negro problem our thinking has become obfuscated by illusions, myths, and shibboleths, and we have been, by and large, complacent about it.

Many of us seek to divorce ourselves from responsibility for this embarrassing contradiction in our democracy by personally deploring race prejudice and practices of discrimination and segregation, and dismissing them as not being representative of the country.

But this is false. So long as such practices widely persist in the society, so long as they are tolerated anywhere in the land, they represent America; they represent you and me. They are part and parcel of the American way. They affect the life and the future of every American, irrespective of color. They betray the faith of the noble man we here honor today.

This may be said of attitudes and practices directed against all American minorities—Negroes, Indians, Spanish-Americans, Orientals—and as well of religious bigotries—anti-Semitism and anti-Catholicism.

The time is past when we may find refuge in rationalizations. The very principles upon which our way of life is based are being dangerously challenged in the world-wide ideological struggle. To the realistic, even cynical, world of today, democratic profession has meaning only in democratic deeds. We cannot, for example, convert the vast masses of Asia and Africa to a democracy qualified by color. But it is vital to the future of human freedom in the world that these peoples, constituting the preponderance of the world's population, be attracted to the democratic way.

We must face the facts honestly. Those who may seek to find comfort in the concept of gradualism on the assumption that time, seen as an inexorable solvent, will eliminate the problem, now find that time has caught up with us. Today, our country needs desperately its maximum strength—its maximum manpower, unity, and moral leadership. But in this very hour, our resources of manpower are squandered in racial strife and racial barriers to employment, our unity is disrupted by racial and religious animosities, and our prestige and moral leadership in the world suffer from the contradictions between the democratic ideals we proudly profess and the domestic practices of which we cannot boast. These contradictions have already cost us prestige, good will and more lives than we have needed to lose on far-off battlefields. In the future these costs in the lives of fine American boys—white, black, brown, yellow, and red—could be far greater, for the same reason.

In this critical period, it appears to me, we have two vital tasks to perform, even while, imperatively, we prepare and man our defenses. We must exert an extraordinary effort to put our interracial house in order. We must strive by our deeds to convince watchful peoples everywhere that we not only profess democracy, but that we deeply believe in it and live it, and that it is applicable to and good for all peoples, whatever their color or creed.

To me, it seems that this is no superhuman or impossible task for my country. It does not require that people of different colors or creeds must begin to clasp each other to their bosoms. It requires no revolution, beyond a psychological one. It does require a substantial change in the attitudes of many of our citizens and our legislators. This is nothing new for America. Within the past century we have seen radical changes in the attitudes of Americans toward many groups in the country—toward the Irish, the Scandinavians, the Polish, the Italians, the Germans, the Chinese, the Latin-Americans, the English, and the American Indians. We have even seen Baptists and Methodists begin to speak to each other.

If I may speak for my own group, all that the American Negro asks is that he be treated like every other citizen—that he be accepted or rejected, not collectively, on the basis of his color, but individually, on the basis of whatever merit he may command. In other words, he asks only the most elemental and fundamental prerogative of citizenship in a democracy—equality of treatment.

What true American can there be, whether from South or North, who would allege that this is too much for any citizen in a democracy to demand; or, indeed, that there could be a democratic society on any other basis?

What kind of a patriot would he be, whether from North or South, who would insist that the nation, in its greatest hour of need, must be denied its full strength solely to ensure that one group of its loyal citizens shall be deprived of equal opportunity, as individuals and on their merits, to rise or fall in the society?

I have great faith in my fellow American citizens. I know that, preponderantly, their consciences are sensitive, their sense of fair play is deep seated, their belief in democracy is genuine and fervent, and that, once they cast off complacency and apathy, once aroused and resolved, their ability to solve problems, to do whatever must be done, is unlimited.

If I may be pardoned for a purely personal reference, I am proud to be an American and I am proud of my origin. I believe in the American way of life, and believing in it, deplore its imperfections. I wish to see my country strong in every way—strong in the nature and practice of its democratic way of life; strong in its world leadership; strong in both its material and spiritual values; strong in the hearts and minds of all of its people, whatever their race, color or religion, and in their unshakable devotion to it. I wish to see an America in which both the fruits and the obligations of democracy are shared by *all* of its citizens on a basis of full equality and without qualification of race or creed.

The United Nations ideal is a world in which peoples would "practice tolerance and live together in peace with one another as good neighbors." If this ideal is far from realization it is only because of the state of mind of mankind. Man's reason and calculated self-interest can be powerful forces for changes in that state of mind. No ideal could be more rewarding. Every individual today has it in his power—in his daily living, in his attitudes and practices—to contribute greatly to the realization of that ideal. We must be strong in our adherence to ideals. We must never lose faith in man's potential power for good.

In this regard, we in America have a historic mission. We are the architects of the greatest design for living yet conceived. We are demonstrating that men of all backgrounds and cultures can be solidly welded together in brotherhood by the powerful force of a noble ideal—individual liberty. To perfect our design for living we need only to demonstrate that democracy is color blind. This we can, and with the support of all men and women of good will, we shall do. Surely, the Great Emancipator had deep faith that we would do so.

APPENDIX E

The Attack on the UN

The Progressive, June 1953

When Bunche wrote this article in 1953, the United Nations organization and its ideals were being severely denigrated in the United States because of the unpopularity of the Korean "Police Action" and the atmosphere poisoned by McCarthyism. Although both Korea and McCarthy have receded from our collective memory, other issues have created an even deeper mistrust of and animosity for the United Nations among the American people in recent years. Bunche's analysis of the problem, except for references to particulars of the time, is as timely today as when he wrote this article.

The world today is deeply in crisis, has been so throughout the postwar period, and may very well continue to be into the indefinite future. In simple terms, mankind is confronted with the constant threat of a third World War—the atomic war—with all of the forbidding implications which this must have for the future of humanity, civilization, and the ideals of human rights and freedom we in this country hold even more dear than life itself.

The nub of this crisis is the worldwide conflict with aggressive communism, expressed broadly in the "Cold War" between West and East, and more particularly and tragically in the protracted but thus far limited shooting war in Korea between United Nations forces on the one hand, and communist North Korean and Chinese forces on the other.

Viewed in world terms, this struggle for freedom and morality, and for preserving peace, is more ideological than military in its present phase. The stakes of this momentous struggle are no less than the peoples of the world. This, indeed, is what the "Cold War" is all about. Both sides in that struggle are seeking to reach and win the minds and hearts of people everywhere. We are the protagonists of the cause of human freedom; of liberty and justice and dignity for the individual; of government as the servant and not the master of the people. We believe that the relations among men must be governed by moral law; that there must be a moral order; that civilized men must have a conscience and be responsive to it. We believe in respecting the rights of others, whether these be states or individuals. We believe that every people must be free of the fear of aggression from any source.

These things we are for. They are fundamental in our thinking and our approach to world affairs. We are, therefore, firmly against totalitarianism and aggression.

But we may easily ignore the fact that our sort of freedom, just as our standard of living, has never been widely enjoyed in the world. The preponderance of the world's people still know of our way of life largely as a concept only; they have never experienced it. I think, for example, of the impoverished and long-suffering hundreds of millions in Asia and Africa, and in other parts of the world as well. These are peoples who have only recently awakened, and have emerged or are aspiring to emerge from suppression. It is at least understandable if they do not readily become alarmed about threats to freedoms and liberties and an abundant life which they have known mainly by hearsay.

It is imperative that we reach and hold them, for they are indispensable to our cause. But the appeal cannot be effective if it is largely negative and against something which they cannot fear as intensely as we do since they have so much less to lose; if it merely exhorts them to join us in a struggle which cannot be as clearly and sharply defined for them as it is for us.

That is why, it seems to me, that neither guns, indispensable as they are, nor words, however noble, can be enough in this struggle. We delude ourselves if we assume, as some are inclined to do, that it is might alone which impresses the Asians and to which they respond. In the new Asia and Africa which are developing, the leaders and peoples alike are today speaking the same social language we do. They share our aspirations for a better life and are determined to have it, as they should and must. We can, therefore, best strengthen the cause and the forces of freedom by doing all that we can to increase the numbers of those who enjoy its blessings; by extending a strong and helping hand to those who aspire and strive in order that they may build free institutions and traditions as we have built them. In other words, we fortify freedom by extending it.

We must convince the peoples of Asia, Africa, and the Middle East that our concern for them is sincere and enduring; that we are not merely seeking temporary allies in times of stress to meet the dire threat to our own freedom and way of life.

Clearly, arms for defense are imperative under present world conditions. But they are but one, not the only means to the peaceful ends sought. Indeed, in direct proportion as recruits and friends are won to the causes we espouse, and our position is thus strengthened, the necessity of ever having to rely exclusively upon our own military resources becomes less probable and less decisive. That is why it seems to me that those who embrace isolationism today are so short-sighted and wrong; why those who deride the idea of collective security and who condemn the United Nations are not at all realistic about the national interest.

The international ideals and objectives of the United Nations are the same as our own. The United Nations seeks peace and freedom for all people, equality among peoples, security of people everywhere against aggression, and an international order governed by principles of morality and justice. Toward these ends, its primary concentration is on the resolution of differences among nations by peaceful means. To such differences it applies its processes of mediation, conciliation, and negotiation. And in doing so it has had some notable successes in bringing a stop to wars and inducing disputing parties to resort to mediation and negotiation, as in Indonesia, Kashmir, and Palestine. It has had failures too, the most tragic in Korea, where the UN itself has resorted to force in order to resist an action of aggression.

In the United States today, the UN has become a favorite target of criticism, and there can be little doubt that the international peace organization is held by many Americans in less high esteem than formerly. There are some who damn it with faint praise and others who just damn it. Some of the latter are professionals, who earn their living by damning, who regularly make insincere and dishonest attacks against some real or imaginary fault or weakness, not with the purpose of strengthening the UN but because they are fundamentally opposed to it and wish to destroy it by undermining public confidence.

I do not for a moment suggest that the UN should be spared criticism. There are sound grounds for criticism, for the UN has many faults and weaknesses. All of us would be happier if the UN functioned better and were able to afford us greater assurance and security against the threat of war. Indeed, the UN welcomes criticism, when it is earnest and honest and not born of prejudice and blind emotion, and especially when it is constructive.

But as I listen to the hue and cry of the critics of the UN these days, I listen in vain for a constructive word and the alternative they may have to offer. They are zealous wreckers but seldom builders.

I think, for example, of the orgy of criticism about the tragedy of Korea. But I believe that most of us know that, costly, painful, and frustrating as it continues to be, it was right for the UN to oppose aggression in Korea, as it has been right for the United States to support that intervention; that it would have been a shameful, fateful, and quite possibly fatal weakness to abandon the courageous Republic of Korea to the aggression from the North. Had the United Nations lacked the moral courage to do so, it might well have come to pass by now that American boys, alongside their allies, would be fighting on other battle-fields, in far greater numbers, and in a far greater war. For nothing encourages aggression like success.

And now, finding ourselves involved in this intervention for the sole purpose of protecting South Korea, could the solemn obligation to humanity to do everything honorably possible to avert the catastrophe of atomic world war, permit the UN deliberately to expand the Korean war into world war?

II

This is the dilemma in which the UN finds itself in Korea. Many critics have been goring the UN with the horns of that dilemma, but they have proffered no helpful advice on how the UN might get out of it, so long as the communist forces reject all reasonable proposals for bringing the fighting to a halt.

There are many other criticisms of the UN, of course. Many people are disappointed and disillusioned because it has not done more to relieve us of the terrible anxiety and insecurity about the future. Undoubtedly, in the early postwar years, the UN was over-sold to Americans, and we have expected far too much from it, much more than we could reasonably and realistically expect, given postwar conditions.

The United Nations, for example, was not able to prevent the cold war and cannot stop it. Indeed, the UN itself has been caught in the cross-fire of that propaganda war. But the UN has always been a restraining influence and has kept open the door of hope, for in the UN both sides in the cold war have been constantly brought together to exchange views even though agreement has been at a minimum.

In the UN we go by the axiom that so long as we can keep disputants talking it out, even if angrily and insultingly, there is a chance to keep them from shooting it out. There are no crosses on the battlefields of debate.

III

Some people, of course, get impatient with talk and debate and disagreement, and advocate a surgical operation on the UN with the Soviet bloc removed. This is much more emotional than rational. The United Nations is designed to achieve peace out of differences, not to hold peaceful meetings. Precisely because it is dealing with differences and disputes among nations, it is never likely to approach the cordial atmosphere of a sewing circle. If the relations among nations and peoples ever become that good there should be much less need for the UN. But the sharper the conflicts among nations the more indispensable the UN becomes. And especially is it desirable to include within its ranks exactly those nations whose differences are most acute and menacing to world peace.

We frequently hear that the UN poses a threat to our national sovereignty. This is sheer humbug, for the UN has no executive or legislative authority; it is not a world government or even an approach to one, and can impose nothing upon us—nor has it ever attempted to do so. We are subject to international pressure, to be sure, but this is moral, not legal—the pressure of international public opinion, and to that we would be subject even if there were no UN. Some of those who cry that the UN is trying to be a world government condemn it in the same breath for its ineffectuality in such crises as Korea and its inability to make other nations toe the line.

Economy-minded critics complain about the "high cost" of the UN. This has been greatly overdone. The total budget of the UN for this year is $44,200,000, collected from its 60 member nations throughout the world. The U.S. share of this total, based upon a carefully worked out and agreed formula, is $15,523,000. *That means that the UN costs each American per year almost exactly one dime.* Moreover, more than two-thirds of the UN budget is spent in this country, since the headquarters is here, and thus a sum well over $30,000,000, twice the amount we pay in, finds its way to our pockets. That, to my layman's mind, would appear to be a pretty fair return.

I have a suspicion that some of our fellow citizens do not base their hostility to the UN on any of these grounds. They dislike it, simply because it requires us to have too much to do with "foreigners," and there are just too many "foreigners" in the organization. I am afraid that there isn't much we can do about this. For the world is full of "foreigners" and in this new international age with its miracles of transport and communication through which all peoples have been brought much closer together, we will have to learn how to live with and understand all of them, unless atomic war should eliminate all of us. But we should not rush to the conclusion that other peoples are against us merely because they do not jump through a hoop every time we bat an eye.

There are other international organizations, serving political and defense needs of regional groupings. But it is the UN alone which is equipped to seek peaceful resolution of differences among nations. Within the framework of the UN, consultations and negotiations on most of the vital problems of the international community are constantly underway. In and out of the meetings, the discussions—formal and informal, individual and collective—go on. There is negotiation, mediation, arbitration. Most of us know this kind of procedure has its ups and downs and uncertainties, and has a tendency to generate heat. Negotiation is still the most sensible and productive approach to disputes, and it does produce results.

IV

We do well, I think, to reflect on the fact that the representatives of 60 nations come regularly, at no little expense to their taxpayers, from all over the world, to the frequent meetings of the various organs of the UN. They come, year after year, month after month; the representatives of Western Europe, of the Commonwealth of Nations of Asia, of Latin America, of the Middle East, and of the Soviet bloc too, even though their positions and propositions are voted down almost invariably. Nations not in the organization seek to gain admission.

Why do they come, if the organization is as futile as some of its critics would paint it? There is little they can hope to take back to their countries to indulge selfish national desires. The UN serves *international,* not national, interests.

I think it obvious that these representatives come because their peoples demand that they come, for their peoples cherish hope and can find no nourishment for it elsewhere than in the United Nations. It is significant that no member nation of the United Nations has ever withdrawn from it, even though its actions on occasion have so displeased some members that they have stalked angrily out of its meetings—only to walk back in again (in one notable Soviet bloc instance, seven months later).

The United Nations has achieved an effective international community, a family of nations in embryo, with international public opinion as an increasingly strong sanction. There would be much to lose and little to gain for any nation to leave the United Nations and try to go it alone.

APPENDIX F

On Race: The Alienation of Modern Man

10 July 1969

This is Bunche's last speech delivered on 10 July 1969 at the Fifth East-West Philosophers Conference in Honolulu, Hawaii. Although failing eyesight forced Bunche to read his speech from a hand-printed text in very large letters, the clarity of his thought and its forcefulness are in no way diminished. This speech is in essence a summing up of Bunche's intellectual and public life, preoccupied as it was with the question of race and the improvement of the human condition, particularly for the oppressed people of color throughout the world, not excluding the United States. Here Bunche not only looks back, but he also looks ahead with remarkable precision at the "obstacles" and the "abrasive issues" that he saw emerging and that have come to a head twenty years later. The speech begins and ends with characteristic expressions of his optimistic conviction of humanity's capacity for goodness.

One might wonder a bit as to why the broad theme of alienation chosen for this Fifth East-West Conference should be limited

---

to "modern" man only. It might well have involved man's alienation experience throughout his history. True as this is, however, justification for the concentration onas contesump"orary times is readily found in the stark fact that acute alienation in an era oh f unlimited nuclear destructive tipower direly threatens the continued existence of man on earth.

It wouat alienation in its various manifestations has been a prime trait of man as far back as knowledge about the species goes. In all of his thousands of years here man has lived in a constant state of alienation, in his relations with nature, with his fellow-men, with younger generations, with himself, his gods, his beliefs, ideas and values. Indeed, modern man himself is now responsible for an incredible alienation of his environment by polluting it to such an extent that something akin to global suicide is in prospect if heroic measures are not soon taken.

This, however, is not at all to endorse the Hobbesian view of the natural life of man as poor, nasty, and brutish, or to say that man is innately evil or warlike and that wars are therefore inevitable. I feel sure that man will still be here thousands of years hence. For I believe that despite so much wickedness and evil design in the world, man is essentially good, that his capacity for fellowship, for compassion and for self-sacrifice need have no limits, and that such a conclusion can be amply documented. It is not impossible for man to achieve a life on this planet of harmony and peace rather than discord and war. The United Nations has its being in this belief; it charts the way to peace.

But the road to such a state of human affairs is long and tortuous and the grim and grisly evidences are all around us of a constant and, indeed, increasingly extensive alienation: man's inhumanity to man (so frequently cited as to have become a cliché); his penchant for ruthlessness and disregard for human life; deep-seated prejudices and bigotries, racial and religious; the widespread disenchantment with and alienation from the established order and the establishments. I may repeat that man will survive but he has much to overcome in himself in order to do so. The best answer to dangerous alienation, I think, is change for the good, progress.

Man's propensity for dispute and conflict is a world-wide phenomenon. It has both international and national aspects and implications.

I have chosen tonight to consider race and color as a major, possibly a preponderant factor in alienation.

First off, may I explain that I have made this choice not because of my own racial identity, but primarily because I come from mainland United States, where the growing alienation of the black American is the outstanding domestic problem and becomes ever more severe and dangerous. The implications of this, not only for my country, but for the world, are profound and far-reaching. In my view, the increasing estrangement of one eleventh of the American people—the black citizen—

and the divisiveness and corrosiveness of the American race problem threaten the security of the United States far more than VietNam.

Secondly, I come from the United Nations, where it is apparent that, on the international side, race is all-pervasive and often decisive, and presents a formidable obstacle to that harmony amongst peoples that is essential to a world at peace, which is the main objective of the United Nations. To be accurate, I should say that it is not race as such that I shall talk about, but that perversion in social attitude called "racism," and the strains, hostilities, animus and alienation which it generates.

There is, I fear, a steady tendency toward polarization of the white and non-white peoples of the world which can lead to ultimate catastrophe for all. I should explain that I use "white" and "non-white" entirely in their popular connotations. In my view, in the world today polarization of races and their alienation are virtually synonymous. The factors of race and color, directly or indirectly, figure prominently in almost all of the vital world issues and the dangerous confrontations.

There are, of course, alienations and conflicts among white people and among non-white people. The pages of history are replete with accounts of alienations between white peoples which had their most violent expressions in World Wars I and II. Among non-white peoples, conflict situations such as those in Nigeria, Malaysia and between India and Pakistan over Kashmir, have been inheritances from the colonial past. Mainland China has alienated many peoples, white and non-white alike.

Alienations of peoples, expressed in suspicions, fears and conflicts, have led to the production of the monstrous nuclear devices. In this context, disarmament, the complete elimination of nuclear weapons and severe limitation of conventional arms, is indispensable to a secure future for mankind; "limited" nuclear disarmament is a delusion. Thus, the fateful alternative confronting mankind is to alienate and perish or harmonize and survive.

Racism, certainly, is the foremost obstacle to harmonization of peoples; it is the antithesis of harmony, being alienation at its emotional worst.

The affluent peoples of the world, who are also the giants in development, trade, industry, technology and military power, are mostly white. But the white peoples themselves are only a minority in world population and each year they represent a smaller percentage of the whole. A 1967 United Nations estimate of the population of the world gives a figure of 3,420,000,000 people. Of these, 1,068,000,000 or 31.2 percent were white. A decade earlier, the white percentage had been 33 percent. The non-white percentage in 1967 thus was 68.8 percent.

Since Roman times at least, the leadership of the world, political and economic, has been controlled almost entirely by its white minority. The white nations tended to dominate the world and to have the only effective voices in its councils. But now that picture is changing markedly. The non-white nations, having for the most part only recently emerged from the suppression and subjection of colonialism, now have, numerically at least, the strongest position in world councils, and their voices are ever more demanding. Wealth and military power, however, are still overwhelmingly on the white side. A majority of the member states of the United Nations, including the most populous member, are non-white.

It is reliably estimated that on the basis of present growth rates, by the end of the twentieth century, that is, within thirty years, the total population of the world will approximate 6,365,000,000 people. That explosive increase will be predominantly non-white, and the white minority, relatively, will then have become almost tiny; not to mention how diminutive it will be a century from now, in 2070, when projections foresee a world population total of 23,324,000,000 at current growth rates. One may already envisage with foreboding the prospect before long of a non-white backlash on a global scale.

Only those who have been the victims of racism can know the severity of the wounds it inflicts, and the depth of the resentment of the wounded. Such wounds—indignities, humiliations, insults, and deprivals—never fully heal.

I do not predict, nor do I like even to think about, the prospect of worldwide conflict between white and non-white peoples. But this cannot be excluded. In fact, there are not a few who regard war between the races as inevitable, some of whom, indeed, hold that it has already begun. Among militant black voices in my own country, for example, there are some who talk of a "third force" in the world which would be an alliance of all the non-white peoples, including the American blacks.

The threat of overpopulation is one of mankind's most critical problems. Efforts to control population growth, which is greatest among the developing peoples, mainly non-white, are handicapped to some extent by suspicions that such efforts are motivated and initiated by affluent white societies as one means of maintaining their dominance.

The world, unfortunately, is not yet nearly alert or responsive enough to the population crisis, its complexities and its dangers, nor to the prospect of increasing racial alienation implicit in that crisis.

The population explosion brings in its train a crisis of inadequate food supply. Predictions have been made in responsible quarters that, as early as fifteen or twenty years from now, conditions of severe famine will develop in a number of areas of heavy population. The peoples who will suffer and die from starvation will be mainly non-white. The intolerable plight of great masses of these people, who have known for so long only misery as their way of life, may then reach the desperation stage and become unbearable to the point of violent reaction. This hostility almost inevitably would be directed in the end against the affluent white few.

There is no bigger obstacle to the building of solid foundations for secure peace than the great and dangerously widening gap between the "haves" and "have-nots" of the world. The affluent haves are few; the poverty-ridden have-nots are very many and are rapidly increasing. Here again the race factor looms prominently. The haves are very largely white; the have-nots are predominantly non-white.

Despite heroic international efforts to reverse the trend and narrow the gap by technical assistance to the developing states and by other means, the gap continues to widen ominously due to striking and continuous technological advances in the highly industrialized states.

In other words, a non-white society is a poor society, with a very few exceptions, of which Japan as a developed country is the most notable. The poor or developing countries do show advances in productivity, national and per capita income. But the developed countries enjoy higher rates of growth and income and thus become ever "richer" in relation to the developing lands.

During the period 1960–67, for example, the total product of the developed countries increased by 44 percent, for an average annual rate of growth of the total product of 5.5 percent. Population in the developed countries during this period increased by 9 percent, resulting in a seven-year growth of per capita product of 32 percent for an average annual per capita increase of 5 percent.

In the developing countries, total product during the same period increased by 36 percent, for an average annual rate of growth of the total product of 4.4 percent. However, the population increase during these years in the have-not countries was 17 percent, or almost double that of the have countries. This brought down the per capita product increase for the seven-year period to 17 percent, for an average annual per capita gorwth rate of only 2.2 percent, or less than half the 5 percent figure of the developed group.

Both the percentage increase and the rates of growth are lower for the developing countries than for the developed ones, both in absolute and in per capita terms. Thus the economic gap has continued to widen between the white haves and the non-white have-nots, and the relative position of the latter has continued to deteriorate. It may be noted that there have been several instances of relatively underdeveloped economies which in recent years have achieved high rates of growth, actually reducing the gap as far as they are concerned. Among these have been Romania, Pakistan, Iran, Turkey, and Mexico.

In the fifteen poorest countries of the world, all of which, to be sure, are non-white, the per capita national incomes, in U.S. dollars, for the year 1967, ranged from a low of $42 for the Maldive Islands and Upper

Volta, to $75 for Haiti. In this list, the figure for Ethiopia was $60, for Nigeria $72, and for India $73.

In striking contrast, the per capita national income for 1967 in the United States was $3,303.00; in France $1,738.00; in the United Kingdom $1,5600.00; in the Federal Republic of Germany $1,512.00; and in the Union of Soviet Socialist Republics $1,069.00.

What counts most, naturally, is how this gap between have and have-not peoples affects human needs, how it relates to the conditions of life for the individual in the less developed societies. That is to say, what chance is there for the hundreds of millions of individuals in such lands to aspire to a life that is worthy of a human being—enough to eat, decent housing, adequate education and medical care, a normal life expectancy, and the opportunity to make the most of individual talent and ability.

Some of the basic statistics about conditions of life in the poor lands are sobering.

Over 60 percent of the people in the poor countries are chronically undernourished, with diets containing about one-third of the protein and two-thirds of the calories which are regarded as essential to the maintenance of health and productivity in a developed or industrial society. Children, especially, are victims of the conditions of life in these societies. In many of them, half of the children will die in infancy from malnutrition, while more than half of those who survive infancy will be physically and mentally stunted throughout the rest of their lives.

In a great many developing countries, average life expectancy is forty years or less, due in large measure to malaria, tuberculosis, cholera, bilharziasis, and many other endemic diseases.

About half of the populations of the developing countries are functionally illiterate, that is, unable to read the simplest instructional material. The odds are two to one against a child receiving any education at all, and ten to one against his going to college. A majority of the teachers have themselves had no schooling beyond the elementary level.

Even in the poorest lands, of course, there are some, usually a very few, who manage in one way or another to prosper and live well.

The unhappy but inevitable conclusion from all this is that the "civilization" which characterizes the planet Earth is enjoyed mainly by a white minority of its inhabitants. How long can this endure?

In the international sphere, colonialism in its various manifestations has been the major cause of alienation and of estrangement between white and non-white peoples. The colonial system in its modern version, implicitly arrogant and self-serving, was instituted and perpetuated chiefly by self-righteous and superior-minded Europeans. Its positive achievements notwithstanding, colonialism's evil legacies will bedevil the world for years to come. It has been the cause of many wars since it was instituted and is the direct source of the major conflict situations, all of them having racial aspects, now confronting the world: Vietnam, the Middle East, Nigeria, Southern Rhodesia, and Kashmir.

Division along racial lines and alienation of races is the very essence of the institution of colonialism. I doubt if this ever has been more clearly and forcefully stated than by, surprisingly enough, John Foster Dulles in the course of a speech in October 1947 to the Fourth Committee of the United Nations General Assembly. Mr. Dulles said:

> . . . Now, Mr. Chairman, . . . I want to make my position perfectly clear. I believe, the United States Delegation believes, that the old colonial system should be done away with—it is obsolete, if indeed it ever had justification, but it certainly has no justification for the future. It has borne some very evil fruit primarily in that it has put people of one race to rule over peoples of another race and that has been very bad for both races. . . . I can't find words to express myself sufficiently strongly on my belief that that system must come to an end and it must be liquidated in a prompt and orderly way . . .

There are no more abrasive issues in the United Nations than those involving racial injustice, and among these the colonial issue is foremost. After all, a majority of the 126 members of the United Nations—the members from Africa, Asia, and the Caribbean particularly—have had comparatively recent experience with colonial subjection.

There is a natural tendency among the member states of the United Nations to form regional blocs to represent common interests. Of these, the African and Asian blocs are numerically the largest. On racial and colonial questions, although not on others, they enjoy solidarity and unity and generally vote together. Debates at the United Nations on such issues as Southern Rhodesia, South West Africa, the Portuguese colonies, and apartheid generate much heat and emotion. Very often, the voting on resolutions on such issues is near unanimity, the dissenting members being the Union of South Africa and Portugal.

With abundant reason, non-white peoples tend to be acutely sensitive about matters of race and color. It follows that the suspicions and resentments arising from racial consciousness and experience often complicate, obstruct, and frustrate efforts of the United Nations and other bodies in political, economic, social, and assistance fields.

It bears repeating that in all international affairs today the race factor is omnipresent. For example, the question would seem entirely valid, and now and then I hear it raised, whether the People's Republic of China would not long ago have been admitted to the family of nations and seated in the United Nations if the Chinese were not "yellow" people— and so many of them. It is not in the interest of the peace of the world to refuse membership in the international community to and thus to make a maverick of a nation of more than 700 million people.

All of the other communist states, including Albania, all having white populations, have long since been taken into the community of nations. The essence of the "yellow peril" bogey survives, even if the phrase itself is now unfashionable.

The Vietnam war has very deep racial implications. There, the United States is fighting "yellow" men who are also considered Communists. This makes it rather easy for Americans to rationalize their involvement and to broadcast daily the number of those despised little yellow men that the American and South Vietnamese forces have killed. The derogatory name Americans give to their North Vietnamese opponents is "Viet Cong," which literally means, I understand, "yellow bandits." Would the United States be engaged in that war if the North Vietnamese and the National Liberation Front were white?

In this regard, it has racial significance, no doubt, that there is no disposition on the part of the United States (or the United Kingdom) to envisage the use of force, or even to apply strong measures short of force, to liberate the overwhelming majority black population of Southern Rhodesia from the ruthless, racist tyranny of a small, white minority led by an arrogant and shameless racial bigot, Ian Smith. The United Kingdom in recent years, however, has found it possible to send British troops to Kenya, Tanzania, and Anguilla.

The black Americans who have fought or are asked to fight in Vietnam find themselves in a paradoxical position. They must employ every violent means at hand to maim and kill the enemy—North Vietnamese and the South Vietnamese enrolled in the National Liberation Front. This is to protect the rights and freedom of 17 million South Vietnamese, a considerable number of whom obviously resent and resist American presence in their country. On the other hand, there are 22 million black Americans whose Constitutional rights are being violated flagrantly and persistently. But the black veteran from Vietnam, like all other blacks, is not permitted to do very much about that. He cannot resort to force in his own country, certainly. He cannot "disturb the peace" and must respect "law and order," although white citizens are not compelled to respect the law of the Constitution where its application to black citizens is concerned. The black veteran, along with all others, may in some places even be denied permission to demonstrate or to march peacefully in protestation against racism and racial injustice. The government requires black citizens to fight for the South Vietnamese but will not even empower the issuance of a cease-and-desist order to white employers who flagrantly deny employment to black men and women solely on grounds of race. That, in the eyes of the senator from Abraham Lincoln's state, Everett Dirksen, would be intolerable "harassment" of business.

The estrangement between white and black Americans intensifies and becomes increasingly disruptive and dangerous. It could reach catastrophic proportions.

The core of the problem is the glaring disparity between the theory and the practice of American democracy. The attitudes and actions of white Americans do not, and many begin to feel, cannot correspond to the ideals and promises of the American Constitution and system. This is not merely because some Americans are hard-bitten racists who oppose bitterly and openly the very idea of integration and equality in rights and opportunities for the black American. The harsh fact is that most white Americans, many without realizing it, harbor in themselves, as an inheritance from the society's history of mores, some degree of racism or bigotry. This is reflex and subconscious bigotry, which may become readily recognizable only in the face of some stern personal challenge. One current symptom of this is the inclination of a good many "fair-minded" Americans, including TV and radio media, to show much sympathetic interest in separatism and pro-separatist voices. Many other whites, finding their consciences whipping them, are gullible and susceptible to outlandish black demands such as the claims for "reparations."

Thus, there has been all along in the American society a built-in and comfortable complacency about the unequal status of and the injustice to the black, second-class fellow citizens. It has been enough to be able to say that equality and integration will one day be achieved here and that progress is being made. That, until recently, could always be counted upon to avert acute trouble. That is no more the case. That is no longer enough for most black Americans. These black men, however involuntarily at first, have been on the mainland shores since the beginning of the country. With far less reward than has gone to their white fellow countrymen, the blacks have given their labor, their talent, their loyalty, blood, and lives in the building and protection of the American nation. They have made also distinct and distinctive cultural contributions to the American society.

In more than three hundred years in the land, nearly 200 years since the adoption of the Constitution, and more than a century after the Emancipation Proclamation, the black American is still deprived of full citizenship, is still excluded from the mainstream of American life, is still the victim of gross social injustice by a white majority in which racism is widely prevalent.

Now, after a long-enduring faith and patience without parallel, I think, in human history, the black citizen has lost his patience—and his fear—and is, I am afraid, also losing his faith in the American establishment and system insofar as their promises to him are concerned. He is demanding, not appealing, nowadays, and his demands begin to take unexpected courses—courses which could only be born out of profound frustration and complete disillusionment.

It is said by some that there is already underway in the United States a black revolution. Others deny it. Certainly, such a development springing from the obvious inadequacy of the civil rights struggle and a feeling of futility and desperation, cannot be excluded. In any case, the insistent demands of the black American today, the growing militancy behind those demands, the increasing involvement of ordinary black men and women in them, and the radical changes in attitudes and practices and even in the structure of the society required by them, are of the nature and dimension of a revolution. Nonviolence has been the traditional tactic of the black American in carrying on his struggle, but an increasing number of black people, especially in the ranks of the young, see violence as an essential weapon in desperate circumstances and scorn the nonviolent, Gandhian counsel of leaders such as the late Martin Luther King. The majority of American blacks, however, still look upon integration and not separation as the desirable goal and believe in a non-violent struggle. However, last week's announcement of the national Government's dismaying new policy of relaxing the deadline on school desegregation compliance by allowing "exceptions," is anything but reassuring to every black American.

Some of the leading voices in the "black revolution" seek to orient the goals and to build the future of black men on what has been the pattern of race in the United States all along—separate racial communities. The American society is, and has always been, a dualistic society—a white segment and a black segment of the population quite rigidly separated.

Ironically, despite the intensified civil rights struggle in the post–World War II years, the white and black communities are more separated—and alienated—than at any time since Emancipation. This is because of the increasing ghettoization of the black people in the urban centers, particularly of the north. Now, the majority of the 22 million Negroes live in the northern cities and most of them dwell in the black ghettoes of those cities. The increasing alienation of whites and blacks is reflected in "black power" on the one hand and "white backlash" on the other.

The black American in the ghetto is, by and large, confined there by the racial mores of the society, by the consequent economic and social forces, and because the ghetto understandably comes to be seen as something of a haven from an unfriendly white world. The ghettoite realizes soon enough that he is where he is because he is unwanted and rejected beyond the ghetto. He resents this as he resents his underprivilege in employment, education, health service, housing and all other human needs. In such a situation, it is no big step to the conclusion that equality and integration are cruel mirages, to bitterness and animosity toward the white man, and to the determination that if the white man rejects the blacks, he cannot expect also to continue to control them. The establishments are seen as white-dominated for white interests. It follows that black men begin to think of having their own establishments and controlling themselves. This readily translates into black separatism.

The depth of the despair experienced by the black American is best measured by the fact that white segregationists and black separatists now find, if for different reasons, some common ground: both reject integration and demand separation of the races; both are racist in their approaches.

Racism, white or black, is a sickness and a society in which it is prevalent is an afflicted society.

The black American can attain no major goals in the American society except by his own determined, united and unrelenting effort. He must believe in himself, he must know and have pride in himself, his background and his culture. In these respects, "black power" serves a necessary purpose.

There are only two solutions: separation or integration (or, as some now prefer to say, an "open society"). Some black nationalists project a "black national community in co-existence with the white community." As I see it, separatism is based on a philosophy of defeat, of surrender to bigotry. It is unrealistic and impractical in the light of the unavoidable facts of a minority group in the world's most powerful society. It offers a false escape and is more emotional than workable.

It seems painfully clear to me that there is no possibility in the affluent, highly industrialized and technological white-majority American society for anyone to be at once black, separate and equal.

It follows that only the goal of integration makes practical sense. Whatever the outlook, integration and equality are worth struggling and fighting for. The black American has a huge investment, a vested interest and a birthright in the American society.

The racial struggle will become increasingly harsh, with more frequent confrontations between whites and blacks. There will be more "hot summers" and likely hotter ones—and winters, as well. There are signs of the direction the society may take which are disturbing, not alone for black Americans.

Racist backlash is widespread. The recent municipal elections in Los Angeles, Minneapolis and New York marked triumphs for racism, reaction and backlash. The order of the day was "law and order." President Nixon has said that the message of these election contests has come through "loud and clear": the American people are "fed up . . . with violence and lawlessness." There have been a good many warning signs that very many black Americans also are "fed up" with their inferior status. But the eruptions in the ghettoes, disruptions on the campuses—unhappily, some of which recently involved clashes between white and black students—and crimes in the streets, though serious breaches of the law, are not the only serious manifestations of lawlessness. The ardent protagonists of law and order rarely refer to "justice" or to that intolerable form of lawlessness which denies social justice and constitutional rights to the black one-eleventh of the nation's citizenry.

As long as racism persists in the American society, alienation will characterize the relations between the white and black sectors of the population.

More ghetto eruptions are inevitable. These outbursts thus far have been confined principally to the ghetto areas. But there is no certainty that this will continue to be the case. Ghettoization of black citizens intensifies polarization of the races and nurtures conflict between them. This, in turn, will lead to more recourse to "law and order." Racial conflict in the United States could intensify to such degree as to approach a chronic state of guerrilla warfare in the jungles of glass, steel and concrete which are the urban centers. If that conflict should ever extend beyond the confines of the ghettoes and threaten the vital communications, transportation and industrial facilities, the reaction of the white community would be severe, the hue and cry for more and more "law and order" could then transform the society into something in the nature of a police state. In fact, over-action by police in some places, the too obvious readiness of some high authorities to oppose dissent with force, the shocking wire-tapping by the Federal Bureau of Investigation of the private telephone of a highly respected citizen and leader, the late Martin Luther King, give cause already for alarm.

White men, whether in the majority as in the United States and the United Kingdom, or in the minority, as in South Africa, Southern Rhodesia and the world at large, must find a way, if such there is, to purge themselves completely of racism or face an ultimate fateful confrontation of the races which will shake the very foundations of civilization and, indeed, threaten its continued existence and that of most of mankind as well.

The picture I have presented has been largely but unavoidably negative and gloomy. The theme of this Conference requires the focus to be on alienation, which is a negative and disheartening subject. But alienation in its racial and many other forms is a bitter fact of life.

There is a brighter side of life, of course. A different topic and speech, however, would be required to elaborate on it. Suffice it now to say, only that the system of colonialism, in its traditional form at least, is in its twilight. Since the United Nations came into existence in 1945, more than 800 million people have emerged from colonial rule to gain independence; 58 of the present member States of the United Nations were in colonial status at that time. The problems of overpopulation and hunger present unprecedented challenge, but they are not insoluble. The ever-widening gap between rich and poor is the most formidable of all problems. Still, astronomical sums are now being wasted in arms, nuclear and conventional, which the great military powers dare not use against each other; and for a war in Vietnam that no one can win, which makes it senseless and incomprehensible. A diversion of a substantial part of such sums and their intelligent use for and by the developing peoples to strengthen their economies and raise their living standards could at least reverse the present trend and narrow the gap. Racism is a matter of men's attitudes and these can be changed and, I believe, they will be changed when men come fully to realize the fatal alternative. Mankind is well-practiced at pulling back from the brink of self-extinction.

Mankind should be able to eliminate the causes of alienation, to work out reasonable and equitable solutions to all problems of human relations. The crucial question is, has man the will—the will to do what must be done to rescue the world. Can the will of man be summoned and mobilized in time, or shall the world continue to indulge in its tragically outmoded habit of futile warfare to the insane point of self-extermination.

The United Nations, I am confident, will persevere in its historic efforts to achieve secure and enduring peace in the world. It seeks always to induce the parties to disputes to rely upon reasoned discussion and negotiation rather than armed force in the resolution of differences. The UN, I believe, can succeed in this effort, but only if it receives resolute support from the peoples of the world.

I like to believe, and I do believe, that despite all of his frailties and follies man will not only survive on earth through reason, common sense, and the will to live, but that through the unlimited creative capacity of his genius, he will continue to advance.

BIBLIOGRAPHY

Major Writings by Ralph Bunche

BOOKS AND MONOGRAPHS

French Administration in Togoland and Dahomey. Ph.D. Diss., Harvard University, 1934.

A World View of Race. Bronze Booklet Series. Washington, D.C.: Associates in Negro Folk Education, 1936. Reprint, Port Washington, N.Y.: Kennikat Press, 1968.

A Brief and Tentative Analysis of Negro Leadership. Research memorandum prepared for the Carnegie-Myrdal Study, *The Negro in America,* New York, 1940. [Available in the archives and on microfilm in the Schomburg Library of the New York Public Library.]

Conceptions and Ideologies of the Negro Problem. Research memorandum prepared for the Carnegie-Myrdal Study, *The Negro in America,* New York, 1940. [Available in the archives and on microfilm in the Schomburg Library of the New York Public Library.]

Ideologies, Tactics, and Achievements of Negro Betterment and Interracial Organizations. Research memorandum prepared for the Carnegie-Myrdal Study, *The Negro in America,* New York, 1940. [Available in the archives and on microfilm in the Schomburg Library of the New York Public Library.]

The Political Status of the Negro. Research memorandum prepared for the Carnegie-Myrdal Study, *The Negro in America,* New York, 1940. [Available in the archives and on microfilm in the Schomburg Library of the New York Public Library.]

The Political Status of the Negro in the Age of FDR. A version of the research memorandum prepared for the Carnegie-Myrdal Study. Edited, with an introduction by Dewey W. Grantham. Chicago: University of Chicago Press, 1973.

Report on the Needs of the Negro. For the Republican Program Committee. July 1939.

The Atlantic Charter and Africa from an American Standpoint. Committee on Africa, the War, and Peace Aims. New York: Phelps Stokes Fund, 1942.

The Anglo-American Caribbean Commission: An Experiment in Regional Cooperation. American Council Paper No. 7 presented at 9th Conference of the Institute of Pacific Relations, Hot Springs, Virginia, January 1945.

ARTICLES AND CONTRIBUTED CHAPTERS

"The American City as a Negro Political Laboratory." *Proceedings,* 34th Annual Meeting, National Municipal League, December 1928.

"The Negro in Chicago Politics." *National Municipal Review* 17, no. 5 (May 1928).

"French Educational Policy in Togoland and Dahomey." *Journal of Negro Education* 3, no. 1 (January 1934).

"A Critical Analysis of the Tactics and Programs of Minority Groups." *Journal of Negro Education* 4, no. 3 (July 1935).

"Triumph—Or Fiasco?" *Race* 1, no. 2 (1935–37).

"A Critique of New Deal Social Planning as It Affects Negroes." *Journal of Negro Education* 4, no. 1 (January 1936).

"Education in Black and White." *Journal of Negro Education* 5, no. 3 (July 1936).

"African Survivals in the New World." *Journal of Negro Education* 6, no. 3 (June 1937).

"Culture Conflict in South Africa." *Journal of Negro Education* 6, no. 3 (June 1937).

"The Land Equation in Kenya Colony." *Journal of Negro History* 24, no. 1 (January 1939).

"Programs of Organizations Devoted to Improvement of the Status of the American Negro." *Journal of Negro Education* 8, no. 3 (July 1939).

"The Role of the University in the Political Orientation of Negro Youth." *Journal of Negro Education* 9, vol. no. 4 (October 1940).

"Africa and the Current World Conflict." *The Negro History Bulletin* 4, no. 4 (October 1940).

"The Negro's Stake in the World Crisis." *Proceedings,* Association of Colleges and Secondary Schools for Negroes, 1940.

"Disenfranchisement of the Negro." In *The Negro Caravan,* ed. Sterling A. Brown, Arthur P. Davis, and Ulysses Lee. N.Y.: Dryden Press, 1941.

"The Irua Ceremony among the Kikuyu of Kiambu District, Kenya." *The Journal of Negro History* 26, no. 1 (January 1941).

"French and British Imperialism in West Africa." *Journal of Negro History* 6 (January 1941).

"The Negro in the Political Life of the United States." *Journal of Negro Education* 10, no. 3 (July 1941).

"Legal Status of the Negro." *American Journal of Sociology,* July 1942.

"International Trusteeship and Accountability: the Problem of Colonies." *Rights and Liberties in Our Time* (August 1945).

"Trusteeship and Non-Self-Governing Territories in the Charter of the United Nations." *Department of State Bulletin* 13 (December 1945).

"The Palestine Problem." In *The Near East and the Great Powers,* edited by Richard Frye. Cambridge, Mass: Harvard University Press, 1951.

"Peace Through Freedom." In *Frontiers for Freedom,* edited by R. Gordon Hoxie. Denver: University of Denver Press, 1952.

"Peace and the United Nations." *Tenth Montague Burton Lecture on International Relations.* The University of Leeds, 1952.

"Presidential Address." *American Political Science Review* 47, no. 4 (December 1954).

"Ethics and Morality in International Affairs." Harvard Medical Alumni Bulletin (Summer 1961).

"An International Bill of Rights." In *Build the Future: Addresses Marking the Inauguration of Charles Spurgeon Johnson* (Nashville: Fiske University Press, 1964).

"The United Nations Operation in the Congo." In *The Quest for Peace: The Dag Hammarskjold Memorial Lectures,* edited by Andrew W. Cordier and Wilder Foote. New York: Columbia University Press, 1965.

Books and Studies about Ralph Bunche

Halila, Souad. *The Intellectual Development and Diplomatic Career of Ralph J. Bunche: The Afro-American, Africanist and Internationalist.* Ph.D. diss., University of Southern California, 1988.

Mann, Peggy. *Ralph Bunche: UN Peacemaker.* N.Y.: Coward, McCann and Geoghegan, 1975.

Touval, Saadia. *The Peace Brokers: Mediation in the Arab-Israeli Conflict 1948–1979.* Princeton, N.J.: Princeton University Press, 1982.

Williams, Babatunde. *Makers of Peace: Dr. Ralph Bunche and Chief Albert John Luthuli.* Ibadan: African Education Press, 1965.

CONTRIBUTORS

CHALLENOR, HERSCHELLE S. Director, UNESCO, Program for the World Decade for Cultural Development; former Staff Director, Subcommittee on Africa, Committee on Foreign Affairs, U.S. House of Representatives.

CLARK, KENNETH B. Distinguishd Professor Emeritus of Psychology, City University of New York, the City College and the Graduate School; former student and colleague of Bunche at Howard University; member, New York State Board of Regents (1966–1986); Author of *Prejudice and Your Child* (1955), *Dark Ghetto* (1965), *The Pathos of Power* (1974).

FINKELSTEIN, LAWRENCE S. Professor of Political Science, Northern Illinois University; worked with Bunche in the State Department (Office of Dependent Area Affairs) and in the United Nations Secretariat; author and editor of *Politics in the United Nations System* (1988).

HENRY, CHARLES P. Professor of Afro-American Studies at the University of California, Berkeley; director of Ralph Bunche Internship Program of Amnesty International; author of *Growing Down: Folk Thought and Afro-American Ideology* (1989); co-author, with Lorenzo Morris, of *The Chit'lin Controversy: Race and Public Policy* (1978).

HUGGINS, NATHAN I. Professor of Afro-American History and head of the William E. B. Du Bois Center at Harvard University; author of *Harlem Renaissance*, (1971), *Black Odyssey: The Afro-American Ordeal in Slavery* (1977), and *Slave and Citizen: The Life of Frederick Douglass* (1980): co-editor, with Martin Kilson and Daniel M. Fox, of *Key Issues in the Afro-American Experience* (1971).

HUREWITZ, JACOB C. Professor Emeritus of Political Science and former Director of the Middle East Institute at Columbia Unviersity; author of *The Struggle for Palestine* (1950), *Middle East Dilemmas: The Background of United States Policy* (1953), *Middle East Politics: The Military Dimension* (1969), *The Middle East and North Africa in World Politics* (1979).

KILSON, MARTIN Professor of Government at Harvard University; author of *Political Change in a West African State: A Study of the Modernization Process in Sierra Leone* (1965); co-author with Rupert Emerson, *The Political Awakening of Africa* (1965); editor, *New States in the Modern World* (1975); co-editor (with Nathan I. Huggins and Daniel M. Fox) of *Key Issues in the Afro-American Experience* (1971).

KIRBY, JOHN B. Professor of History at Dennison College; author of *Black Americans in the Roosevelt Era: Liberalism and Race* (1980); editor of *New Deal Agencies and Blacks*, 25-reel microfilm project, University Publications of America (1984); author of "Ralph J. Bunche and Black Radical Thought in the 1930s," *Phylon* (Summer 1974).

McHENRY, DONALD F. University Research Professor of Diplomacy and International Relations at Georgetown University; member of U.S. Mission to the United Nations from 1976 to 1981, serving first as Deputy Permanent Representative, and as Permanent Representative and Head of Mission from September 1979 until 1981.

OFUATEY-KODJOE, WENTWORTH Professor of Political Science, City University of New York, Queens College and the Graduate School; author of *The Principle of Self-Determination in International Law* (1977); author and editor of *Pan-Africanism: New Directions in Strategy* (1985).

RIVLIN, BENJAMIN Professor Emeritus of Political Science and Director of the Ralph Bunche Institute on the United Nations at the City University of New York, Graduate School and University Center; worked with Bunche in the Office of Strategic Services (Research and Analysis Branch, Africa Section) and the United Nations Trusteeship Department; author of *The United Nations and the Italian Colonies* (1950); co-author and co-editor, with Joseph S. Szyliowicz, of *The Contemporary Middle East: Tradition and Innovation* (1965).

ROSENNE, SHABTAI Arthur Goodhart Professor in Legal Science, Magdalene College, Cambridge University; Ambassador-at-Large, Israel Foreign Service (ret.), member of Israel Delegation to 1949 Armistice negotiations; author of *The Law of Treaties: A Guide to the Legislative History of the Vienna Convention* (1970), *The World Court: What It Is and How It Works* (1973), and *Procedures in the International Court* (1983).

URQUHART, SIR BRIAN Former Under Secretary-General for Special Political Affairs and close colleague of Ralph Bunche at the United Nations; currently Scholar in Residence at the Ford Foundation; author of *Hammarskjöld* (1972), *A Life in Peace and War* (1987).

INDEX

Numbers in italic refer to pages with photographs.

Abdullah, King, 181–82
Abernathy, Ralph, at Montgomery march, *153*
Abraham, Willie, 104
Accommodationism, 34
Acheson, Dean, 174
Adoula, Cyrille, 205
AFL Teachers Union, 55
Africa: American understanding of, 4; analysis of development in, 83–95; backwardness of, 102–3; bastardization of indigenous cultures in, 114–15; Bunche's fieldwork in, 79–81; corporateness of versus tribal boundaries, 91–92; costs and benefits of colonialism in, 85–88; decolonization process of, 12–13; educated elite of, 88–90, 104–5; education systems in, 75–77; effects of Western ways in, 113–14; French colonial oligarchy in, 72–78, 90–91;

Industrial Revolution in, 74; influence of Bunche on, 100–106; interest to American blacks, 10–11; judicial process in, 77–78; mandate territories in, 72–73; modernization movement in, 92, 103; movement from trusteeship to decolonization in, 109–31; pattern of imperial domination in, 97–98; self-government of, 102, 104–5; taxation in, 74–75; the War and Peace Aims, Committee on, 101–2; weakening of native institutions in, 77–78
Africanism, 69–82
African National Congress (Bunche's fieldnotes on), 80
Agricultural Adjustment Administration (AAA), 36
Alexander, Henry, 204
Alexander, Will, 31, 41
Alienation, 252–64

Allen, Margaret, 58–59
American Dilemma, An, 6, 9, 29, 40; Bunche's contribution to, 97
Anglo-American Caribbean Commission (AACC), 121
Arab-Israeli relations: armistice, 16, 160–61, 177–85; conflict, 170–71, 173, 174–75; truce, 164–65
Arab-Israeli War: Bunche as Acting Mediator of first, xxix, 3–4, 14–16; cease-fires in, 187
Arab League, 159, 168, 174, 182
Arab Palestine, 159–60; creation of Jewish state and, 163–65
Arab-Zionist controversy, 168–69
Atlantic Charter, 135
Atlantic Charter and Africa from an American Standpoint, The, 105
Atomic bomb, 238

Bahrain crisis, xxx
Barnett, Ross, 62
Basutoland (Bunche's fieldnotes on), 80
Belgian Congo. *See* Congo
Ben-Gurion, David, *150,* 159, 162, 166
Bernadotte, Count Folke, 14, 179, 229–30; assassination of, 3, 14, 15, 158–60, 187–88, 191; in Middle East negotiations, 164–66, 188–90; Progress Report to General Assembly of, 157–58; as UN Mediator, 159
Bernadotte plan, 161, 167, 168, 172
Berry, Abner, 51, 56
Bevel, Rev. James, *153*
Bevin, Ernest, 163–64, 168, 174
Bigotry, 241–45. *See also* Racism
Birmingham, segregation in, 58
Black militants, 23
Black Muslims, 23; 61
Black nationalism, 30, 31, 34, 43, 262
Black Power Movement, 41, 261–62
Black protest, 261; Bunche and, 28–49
Blacks: conditions of in America, 8–9; economic oppression of, 35–36; during the Depression, 30–31; need to enter American mainstream, 34–36; and tradition of scholarship, 96–97

Black separatism. *See* Black nationalism
Blyden, Edward Wylmot, 103–4
Booker, Alma, 59–60
Brown, Sterling, 53, 212
Brown v. the Board of Education of Topeka, Kansas, 41, 60, 62
Bunche, Ralph: academic career, 70–71, 78–81; as Acting Mediator of first Arab-Israeli war, 14–16; activism of, xxvi, 8; addressing UN Security Council, *148;* as Africanist, xxvii, 69–82; African perspective on, 96–108; alleged Communist affiliations of, 50–51, 53–56; analytical perspective on African development, 83–95; anticommunism of, 56, 63; on attack on UN, 346–51; awards and accolades, xiv; on black Americans, 4–5; on black militants, 23; black protest and, 28–49; boarding UN Mediator's plane, *148;* carpet-laying business, 69; chairing signing of Egyptian-Israeli Armistice Agreement, *149;* with Chief Albert J. Lutuli, *151;* as child in Detroit, *146;* chronological biography of, xix–xxiv; in civil rights movement, 4, 7–11, 21–23; consideration of alternative careers, 69–70; contributions to black political and social thought, 28–29; contribution to trusteeship and decolonization, 132–45; with David Ben-Gurion, *150;* dissatisfaction with New Deal, 35–37; dissertation on Togoland-Dahomey, 72–78, 105–6, 111; domestic activities during Depression, 32–33; with Domestic Peace Corps members, *152;* early education, 70–71; examining copy of *An American Dilemma, 147;* experience as American black, xxvii; experience of discrimination, 51; FBI investigations of, 53–57; as first black professional officer at State Department, 6; "Fourth Dimension of Personality" speech, 220–24; on French racial openness, 95*n;* funeral of, xiii; global perspective of, 92–94, 97–

106; government service of, 11–13; greeting Secretary of State Stettinius, *147;* at Harvard University, 7; history of "firsts," 5–6; holding Nobel Peace Prize Medal, *150;* at Howard University, 7, 211–12; as human being, 212–14; impact of work at UN, 25–26; importance of life and career of, xv–xvi; on importance of United Nations, 3; as innovator and pioneer, 24; as international civil servant, 18, 20; on international significance of human relations, 236–45; with leaders of anti-Vietnam War march, *153;* lecturing at University of Pennsylvania, xiv–xv; legacy of, 3–27; letters of, 217–19; Lincoln's Day address, 22; Marxism of, 26; with members of Africa Research Section staff, *146;* at Montgomery civil rights march, *153;* moral authority of, 20; Nobel Peace Prize awarded to, xiv, xxxi, 28, 56, 183; obituary tribute to, 25; as peacekeeper, xxix–xxxi, 16–20, 186–210; in planning UN non-self-governing territories system, 116–29; preparation of for achievements in UN, 24–25; with President Johnson and U Thant, *152;* progressive pragmatism of, 83–85; on race and the alienation of modern man, 252–64; on race relations, 8–9; radicalism of, 51–53; realistic idealism of, 20–21; reflections on peace (Nobel Peace Prize Lecture), 225–35; rejection of Assistant Secretary of State appointment, 22; renown after receiving Nobel Prize, 22–23; at Rhodes armistice talks, 177–85; role in founding NNC, 55; role of in decolonization process, 109–31; in Selma march, 22; scholarly career of, xxv–xxvii; with Secretary-General Hammarskjöld, *151;* shooting "snookers," *148;* social influence of, 212–13, as statesman, xxv, xxix–xxx, 20, 211–14; as UN acting mediator, xxix–xxx, 3–4, 105–6, 157–76; in UN Charter

trusteeship provisions, xxix; at UN Secretariat, 13–16; and UNTSO, 188–91; valedictory address at UCLA, 8; views on colonialism and its remedies, 85–90, 110–16; Virginia Council on Human Relations address, 50; work on Carnegie-Myrdal study, 5–6, 36–39, 97
Burns, E. L. M., 192
Byrnes, James F., 125

Cape Town (Bunche's fieldnotes on), 80–81
Caribbean Commission, 122
Carmichael, Stokeley, 23
Carnegie-Myrdal study, xxvi, 10, 40, 81, 213; Bunche's experience with, 5–6, 21, 36–39, 97
Challenor, Herschelle, xxix
Churchill, Winston, 135
CIO, antipathy of toward black workers, 38–39
Civil rights, 4; movement for, 7–8, 21–23, 41–42, 60–63; national security and, 50–57; worldwide perspective on, 57–60
Civil Rights Act, 42, 61
Class system, 52
Claude, I. L., 128
Cohen, Ben, 12
Cold War, 41, 228–29, 238–39, 247
Colonialism, 10–11; accountability and educated elites in, 88–90; as cause of alienation, 257–58; costs and benefits of, 85–88; effects on African people, 98–99; endgame scenario of, 88–93; need to end, 233–34; peacekeeping activities and, 133; reasons for, 97–98; remedies for, 110–16; strategy of subjugation in, 98; system-remedial dynamics in, 87–88; from trusteeship to decolonization, 109–31; UN Charter on, xxx
Color, people of, emergence of in world, 20–21
Communist party, exploitation of black organizations, 10
Congo: crisis of, xxx, 16, 18; United Nations Operation in, 200–205

Conner, "Bull," 61

Contra-posture, 84

Cordier, Andrew, 173

Cranborne, Viscount, 120

"Critique of New Deal Social Planning as it Affects Negroes," 51–52

Cross, Agnes, 58–59

Cyprus, xxx, 205–209

Dahomey, 72–78

Daily Worker, 56

Davis, John A., 7

Davis, John P., 6, 36–37, 54–55

de Azcarate, Dr. Pablo, 160

Declaration on Granting Independence to Colonial Countries and Peoples, 142–44

Declaration Regarding Non-Self-Governing Territories, xxix

Decolonization, 12–13; American plan for, 119–20, 121; Bunche's contribution to, 101–106, 132–45; race and, 133–34; trusteeship and, 142–43; UN program of, 104–105

Dellinger, David, *153*

Democracy, 242, 243

Democratic pluralism, 44

Depression, 29, 30–31, 32

Deutsch, Karl, 91–92

Diagne, Blaise, 90

Dirksen, Everett, 259

"Don't-Buy-Where-You-Can't-Work" campaigns, 31, 33

Dorsey, Emmet, 53

Douglas, Lewis, 162, 165

Du Bois, W. E. B., xxvi–xxvii, 29, 52, 56, 59, 96, 103; letter to from Bunche, 8, 217–19; racial solidarity and, 32–33

Dulles, John Foster, 118, 141, 258

Dumbarton Oaks Conference, 105–106, 116–18, 123, 136–37

Eban, Aubrey, 169, 170

Economic determinism, 11

Egalitarianism, 100

Egypt, 194–97; conflict with Israel, 167–68, 172–73, 184, 192–97; negotiations with Israel for armistice, 173–75, 177–85; signing of armistice on island of Rhodes, *149*

Eisenhower, Dwight, D., 143, 185

Emerson, Rupert, 71–72

Enlightenment legacy, 83–84

Eritrea, 125

Ethnocentric manipulators, 93

Ethridge, Mark, 174

Evers, Medgar, 61–62

Fair Deal, 41

Fair Labor Standards law, 37

Farouk, King, 180

Fascism, 20, 63

FBI investigations, 53–57

Finkelstein, Lawrence, xxix, 52, 137–39

Foreman, Clark, 31

Forrestal, James, 122, 138

Fortas, Abe, 124

Fosdick, Dorothy, 12

"Fourth Dimension of Personality, The," 133; text of, 220–24

Frank, Dr. Glenn, 9

Franks, Sir Oliver, 162, 172

Frazier, E. Franklin, 33, 53, 87, 212

Freedom House, 57

French colonial system, 72–78, 112–13

French Revolution, 114

Gandhi, Mahatma, 59

Gardner, Richard, 18, 19–20

Gare-Booth, Paul, 12

Garvey, Marcus, 30–31

Gaza Strip, 172, 192, 194–95

General Conference International Atomic Energy Agency, 17

George, Zelma Watson, 143

Gerig, Benjamin, 111, 117–19, 124, 137–38, 141

Ghetto violence, 261, 263

Gideonse, Harry, 57

Goulding, Marrack, 19

Grantham, Dewey W., 40

Great Britain: in Negev, 166–167; Palestine policy of, 174; role of in creation of Jewish state, 158–66, 169–74; system of indirect rule of, 114

Great Society, 43, 44
Green, James Frederick, 118, 137
Gross, Ernest A., 55, 57
Guide to North Africa, 11–12
Guide to West Africa, 11–12

Hammarskjöld, Dag, xxx, 17, 18, *151*
183, 188, 192–96, 201–202, 205
Hampton Institute, 213–14
Harriman, W. Averell, 56–57
Harris, Abram, 33, 53, 212
Harris, Jack S., 56
Harvard University, 7, 71; offerings
on Africa in, 71–72
Hastie, William, 6, 31, 57
Haywood, Harry, 55
Hecht Department Store, 59
Henry, Charles P., xxvii–xxviii, 7–8
Herskovits, Jean, 18
Herskovits, Melville, 11, 79
Heschel, Rabbi Abraham Joshua, at
Montgomery march, *153*
Hill, T. Arnold, 30
Hiss, Alger, 12, 51, 56, 117–18
Hobson, J. A., 110–11
Hoo, Dr. Victor, 14, 139–41
Howard conference, 36
Howard University, 7, 52–53;
Bunche's radical days at, 59; en-
vironment of, 211–12
Huggins, Nathan, xxviii
Hull, Cordell, 112, 117–18, 120, 135–
36
Human relations, international signifi-
cance of, 236–45
Humphrey, Hubert, 42
Huntley, Chet, 58
Hurewitz, J. C., xxix–xxx
Hydrogen bomb, 238

Ickes, Harold, 31–32
Imperialism, 111, 114, 233–34. *See
also* Colonialism
India-Pakistan Observation Mission,
UN, 199–200
Institute of Pacific Relations, 51, 55–
56
Institute of the Black World, statement
on Ralph Bunche, 63

Integration, resistance to, 262
Internal Security-Hatch Act, 53
International Atomic Energy Agency,
19
International Committee on African
Affairs (ICCA), 54
International Labor Organization
(ILO), 121, 131n
International organizations, impor-
tance of, 19
International Organizations Employee
Loyalty Board, 55
International Scientific Conference on
Peaceful Uses of Atomic Energy, 17
Iraq, Hashemite Kingdom of, 197
Isolationism, 248
Israel, 165, 169; claim to Negev, 166–
67; conflict with Egypt, 172–73; De-
fense Force, 167; Provisional Gov-
ernment of, 158–59, 161, 166–68,
170–71; in Rhodes armistice talks,
177–85; UN mediation in, 158–61
*Israel's Armistice Agreements with the Arab
States*, 185
Israeli-Egyptian conflict. *See* Egypt

Jessup, Philip C., 171
Jewish state, creation of, 159–66, 179
Johnson, Lyndon B., 6, 42, 44, *152*
Johnson, Mordecai, 10, 11, 53, 212–13
Jones, Dr. Thomas Jesse, 76–77
Jones, Eugene Kinckle, 31
Jordan, Vernon E., Jr., 5
Jordan River issue, 17
Just, Ernest, 53

Kasavubu, President, 201–2
Katanga problem, 203, 205
Keenan, Joseph, 173–74
Kennedy, John F., 18, 57
Kilpatrick, James J., 50–51
Kilson, Martin, xxviii
King, Martin Luther, Jr., 28, 58, 60–
62, 261; at anti-Vietnam War march,
153; funeral of, 23; at Montgomery
march, *153;* in southern rights
struggle, 41–42
Kirby, John B., xxvii

Korean War, 230, 249
Ku Klux Klan, 21

Labor movement, antipathy of toward black workers, 38–39
Lasso, Galo Plaza, 206
League of Nations: colonialism and, 87–88; Mandate System of, 72–73, 75, 115–16, 138; resolutions on native status in Africa, 78
League of Nations Covenant, 113; mandates article of, 124–25
Lebanon, UN observer group in, 197–98
Lewis, Dr. Hylan, 7
Liberalism, from New Deal through Great Society, 40–45
Libya, 125
Lie, Trygve, xxx, 14, 58, 127, *150*, 173, 184, 229
Lincoln, Abraham, 236–37, 239, 241, 242
Lincoln's Day Address, 236–45
Little Rock, 58
Locke, Alaine, 53, 212
Lovett, Robert A., 174
Lumumba, Patrice, 201–4
Lutuli, Chief Albert J., *151*
Lynching, banning of, 32–33

MacDonald, B. F., 200
MacLeish, Archibald, 54
MacMillan, Harold, 143
Malcolm X, attack on Bunche, 23
Malinowski, Bronislaw, 11
Mandates Commission, 72–73, 75, 115–16, 138
Mandatory Power's regulations, 78
Mann, Peggy, 22
March on Washington Movement (MOWM), 39–40
Marshall, George C., 162, 165–66, 168–69, 174
Martin, Dr. Robert E., 24–25
Marxism, influence on Bunche's thinking, 26, 50–51
"Marxism and the Negro Question," 52
Masaryk, Jan, 12
Mashler, William, 15

Matthews, Charles, 70
McCarthy, Joseph, 41
McCarthy era, xxviii, 54–55, 214
McClintock, Robert M., 166
McIlwain, Charles Howard, 71
Middle East, 17; first peacekeeping force in, 192–96. *See also* Egypt; Israel
Mill, John Stuart, 112
Mohn, Dr. Paul, 160
Montgomery movement, 41, 61
Moral majority, 43
Morrison-Grady project, 163
Murray, A. Victor, 76
Muste, A. J., 61
Myrdal, Gunnar, 29, 36–37, 39; study of, 5–6, 10, 30–40, 81, 97, 213

Nasser, President, 194–97
National Association for the Advancement of Colored People (NAACP), 30–31, 33; Bunche on board of, 8
Nationalism, 34, 93, 228
National Negro Congress (NNC), 36, 37–38, 54; Bunche's criticism of, 38–39; Communist exploitation of, 10; founding of, xxvii, 8, 51, 55
National Recovery Administration, 31, 35–36
National Theater, segregation seating in, 59
National Urban League, 30, 33
Nation within a nation concept, 33
Natural rights, 112
Nazism, 226
Negev, 161–62, 166–67, 180; British presence in, 163–64; Egyptian-Israeli conflict over, 170–71, 172–73, 179; transfer plan, 165–66, 168, 174
Negro Congress movement, criticism of, 38
"Negro Problem," 33–35
New Deal, 29, 31–32, 35–37, 43; benefits to blacks, 32–33, 37–38; Bunche's attack on, 35; liberalism of, 40–41; negative effects on blacks, 35–36
New Frontiers (Wallace), 32
New Negro Alliance, 33

Nixon, Richard M., 42–43
Nobel, Alfred, 227, 232–33
Nobel Peace Prize, 28, 56
Nobel Peace Prize Lecture, 225–35
Non-Self-Governing Territories, 124–26
Nonviolence, 59, 61, 62
Notter, Dr. Harley, 117
Nuclear disarmament, 254

O'Brien, Lawrence, 56
Office of Strategic Services (OSS), 12, 105, 135
Ofuatey-Kodjoe, Dr. W., xxviii–xxix, 26

Palestine: first peacekeeping operation in, 188–91; partition of, 14, 160, 161, 179–80; UN negotiations in, 157–85. *See also* Arab Palestine; Israel
Palestine Arab Higher Committee, 159–60
Palestine Arab state, 161–62
Palestine Conciliation Commission, 161, 181, 183
Palestine Partition Resolution, 14
Pan-African nationalists, 93
Pasha, Nokrashy, 180
Pasvolsky, Dr. Leo, 12, 117–18, 135, 138, 141–42, 178
Peace (Bunche's reflections on), 225–35, 238, 240–41
Peacekeeping forces, development of, 186–210
Pearson, Lester, 192
"People's Movement," 39
Perez de Cuellar, Secretary-General, 186–87
Phelps-Stokes Fund, 143
Plessy v. *Ferguson*, 7
Political Status of the Negro in the Age of FDR, The, 9, 40, 97
Politics of accountability, 88–90
Poor People's Movement, 43
Population explosion, 255–56
Powell, Adam Clayton, 23, 61
"Power, of Non-Violence, The," 59
Powers, Thomas F., 125

Preventive war, 234–35
Progressive pragmatism, 83–85

Race relations: Bunche's remarks on, 231–45, 252–64; decolonization and, 133–45
Racial grove politics, 43
Racial identity, 134
Racial solidarity approach, 32–33
Racial violence, 262–63
Racism, 10–11, 21–22, 24; colonialism and, 99; international, 254, 258–60; need to eliminate, 241–45; search for solution to, 33–34; in U.S., 259–61; as unsettling force in world, 133–34; as violations of UN Charter, 22. *See also* Bigotry
"Ralph Bunche: The Man and His Times" conference, xiv
Randolph, A. Philip, 36, 39, 55
Reagan, Ronald, 43
Regionalism, 122
Republican Party, defection of blacks from, 8–9
Rhodes armistice talks, 177–85, 191
Rieber, Dean, 71
Riley, William E., 160, 180, 182
Robinson, Cleveland, *153*
Rockefeller, David, 57
Rockefeller, John D. III, 57
Roosevelt, Eleanor, 31, 41, 55, 61
Roosevelt, Franklin D., 30, 35–36, 43, 124; Atlantic Charter and, 135; on colonialism and nationalism, 135–36; and Japanese mandated islands, 137–39; New Deal of, 31
Rosenne, Dr. Shabtai, xxx, 15
Rosenwald Foundation, 72
Rusk, Dean, 6
Rustin, Bayard, 43

San Francisco Conference, 120–24, 138; UN charter negotiations at, 139–42
Saudi Arabia (and UNYOM), 198–99
Schapera, Isaac, 11
Science and Society, 51, 55; Bunch on editorial board of, 87
"Second Reconstruction," 29

Segregation, 59, 261–62. *See also* Civil rights
Self-determination, 52, 113, 114, 115, 135
Selma march, 22, 28, 42–43, 62
Serot, Colonel Andre, 14
Shertok, Moshe, 159
Shriver, Sargent, 44
Sinai, Israeli invasion of, xxx, 194–95
Sinai War, 17
Sly, John Freeman, 71–72
Smuts, Jan Christian, 112
Social Darwinism, 112
Socially valuable individual, 220–24
Social Security Act, upholding of, 37
Somaliland, 125–26
South, civil rights struggle in, 41–43
Southern Conference for Human Welfare, 55
Soviet bloc, 250
Soviet Union, Bunche's early views of, 84–85
Spencer, Herbert, 112
Spock, Dr. Benjamin, *153*
Stanley, Oliver, 121
Stassen, Harold, 118, 120, 123
State Department, 6, 56; Bunche at, 12–13; colonial policy of, 136–37
Stavropolous, Constantine, 180–81
Stettinius, Edward R., Jr., 118, 124, 138, *147*
Stimson, Henry, 122, 138
Suez Canal, 167, 184, 188, 192–96
Sumner, Francis Cecil, 212
Surplus manufactures, 111
Syrian agreement, 183

Tchernychev, Ilya S., 17
Tedder, Air Marshal Lord, 172
Tenant Purchase program, 37–38
Thant, U, xxx, 18, 19, *152*, 196, 197, 198, 199, 205; on Bunche's achievements, 25
Third World, 255–64
Thompson, Charles, 53
Togoland (Bunche's study of French administration in), 72–78
Toppan Prize, 7
Transjordan, 162, 164
Tribal boundaries, 91

Troutbeck, John M., 166
Truce Supervision Organization, 159–60, 166–61, 187–88, 189–91
Truman, Harry: civil rights commitment of, 41; offer to appoint Bunche Assistant Secretary of State, 22; trusteeship and, 138–49
Trusteeship, 106, 119; advocates of, 123–24; Bunche's contribution to, 132–45; decolonization and, 142–43; development of, 118–29; drafting UN charter provisions on, 139–42; forming policy on, 137–39; versus mandate system, 141; principle of, 135–37
Trusteeship Council committee, 106, 127
Tshombe, Moise, 203, 205
Tuskegee education model, 76

UCLA, 70–71
UNESCO, 114
United Arab Republic, 198
United Nations, 4, 12–13, 17, 19, Bunche at Secretariat of, 13–16; Bunche on importance of, 3; Bunche's analysis of attack on, 246–51; Bunche's role in peacekeeping function, xxx–xxxi, 16–20, 186–210; Conciliation Commission, 173–74, 181, 183; Conference on International Organization (UNCIO), 105–6, 116, 120, 124, 138; cost of, 250–51; decolonization program of, 104–5, 233–34; development of first Emergency Force (UNEF), 192–97; General Assembly resolutions 181 (II), 179; General Assembly Resolution 1514, 142–43; goals of, 227–35; in Korean conflict, 249; non-self-governing territories system of, 116–29; observer operations—in Congo, 200–205; —in Cyprus, 205-9; —in India-Pakistan, 199–200; —in Lebanon, 197–98; —in Yemen, 198–99; in Palestine negotiations, 157–85; peacekeeping activities of, 16–20, 186–210, 229–35, 240; Truce Supervision Organization (UNTSO), 159–60, 166–67,

187–91; Trusteeship Division of, 106, 127

United Nations Charter: Article 19 of, 205–6; Chapter XI of, 140; —Article 73 of, 126, 142; —and trust-pervision Organization (UNTSO), 159–60, 166–67, 187–91; Trusteeship Division of, 106, 127

United Nations Charter: Article 19 of, 205–6; Chapter XI of, 140

—Article 73 of, 126, 142

—and trusteeships, 124–28

Chapter XII of, 142; Chapter XIII of, 142

United States, racism in, 259–62

UNSCOP, 14

Urquhart, Sir Brian, xv, xxx

Vietnam War, 264; racial implications of, 259

Vigier, Henri, 160, 182–84

Von Horn, Carl C., 202

Voting Rights Act, 42

Wagner Labor Relations Act, 37

Wallace, Henry, 32

War Against Poverty, 44

Washington, Booker T., 76, 96

Washington, March on (1963), 42

Washington Committee for Democratic Action (WCDA), 54

Weaver, George L.-P., 10

Weaver, Robert, 31; on Bunche's success, 6

Weiss, Nancy, xv

Wesley, Charles, 53

White, Walter, 31–33, 38

White backlash, 261, 262

Wieschhoff, Dr. Heinrich, xiv

Wilkerson, Doxy, 55

Wilkins, Roy, 22; on Bunche, 5

Williams, Aubrey, 31

Wilson, Dagmar, *153*

Wilson, Edwin C., 117

Women's rights, 59–60

World View of Race, A, 10–11, 52, 83–86, 90, 93, 97, 105, 111–12, 133

Yalta Conference, 116, 137–38

Yemen, xxx, 198–99

Yergan, Max, 54

"Young Negro" speech, 59